Advance Praise for
DIASPORA STUDIES
IN EDUCATION

"To conceptualize Puerto Ricans within the processes of diasporization constitutes a powerful ground-breaking approach that extends and affirms critical perspectives of both the process of *Boricua* biculturalism and our place as cultural citizens of the world. Grounded in the diverse manifestations of Puerto Rican life in the United States, the book offers powerful insights into cultural readings of the *Boricua* experience, which not only bring greater emancipatory potential to the education of Puerto Rican students, but to other communities that share in the great struggles and triumphs of life in the diaspora. This is a beautifully edited book that deserves close attention in our future reconceptualizations of subordinate populations in the United States and abroad."

—Antonia Darder, Leavey Presidential Chair and Professor,
Loyola Marymount University; Author of *Culture and Power in the Classroom*

"Rosalie Rolón-Dow and Jason G. Irizarry have assembled an admirable collection of case studies and personal testimonies of the educational experiences of Puerto Ricans in the diaspora and on the Island. Their insightful volume fills a substantial gap in the academic literature on how Puerto Ricans and other Latinos have faced the forces of displacement, assimilation, discrimination, and marginalization in U.S. schools."

—Jorge Duany, Professor, Florida International University

"*Diaspora Studies and Education* is a wonderful collection of essays and poems that brings the concept of 'diaspora' back to its original meanings. The authors continuously emphasize the dynamic interplays between different diasporic Puerto Rican communities in the mainland United States, as well as between them and the Island of Puerto Rico. Throughout, the book continuously presents the ever-evolving realities of Puerto Ricans, both as individuals as well as in their communities, as they interact with others within specific environments. Finally, what this important book brings to the table is a real-life account of the cultural dynamics faced by, as well as the creative reactions of, Puerto Rican students in mainland U.S. schools."

—Xavier F. Totti, Lehman College, CUNY;
Editor, *CENTRO: Journal of the Center for Puerto Rican Studies*

DIASPORA STUDIES
IN EDUCATION

Critical
Studies of
LATINOS/AS
in the
Americas

Yolanda Medina and Ángeles Donoso Macaya
General Editors

Vol. 2

The Critical Studies of Latino/as in the Americas series
is part of the Peter Lang Trade Academic and Textbook list.
Every volume is peer reviewed and meets
the highest quality standards for content and production.

PETER LANG
New York • Bern • Frankfurt • Berlin
Brussels • Vienna • Oxford • Warsaw

DIASPORA STUDIES
IN EDUCATION

Toward a Framework for Understanding
the Experiences of Transnational Communities

ROSALIE ROLÓN-DOW & JASON G. IRIZARRY
EDITORS

PETER LANG
New York • Bern • Frankfurt • Berlin
Brussels • Vienna • Oxford • Warsaw

Library of Congress Cataloging-in-Publication Data
Diaspora studies in education: toward a framework
for understanding the experiences of transnational communities /
[edited by] Rosalie Rolón-Dow, Jason G. Irizarry.
pages cm. — (Critical studies of Latino/as in the Americas; 2)
Includes bibliographical references and index.
1. Puerto Ricans—Education—United States—Case studies. 2. Puerto Ricans—
United States—Social conditions—Case studies. I. Rolón-Dow, Rosalie,
editor of compilation. II. Irizarry, Jason G., editor of compilation.
LC2692.D53   371.829'687295073—dc23   2013020001
ISBN 978-1-4331-1839-5 (hardcover)
ISBN 978-1-4331-1838-8 (paperback)
ISBN 978-1-4539-1174-7 (e-book)
ISBN 978-1-4331-1838-8
ISSN 2372-6822

Bibliographic information published by **Die Deutsche Nationalbibliothek.**
Die Deutsche Nationalbibliothek lists this publication in the "Deutsche
Nationalbibliografie"; detailed bibliographic data are available
on the Internet at http://dnb.d-nb.de/.

Front cover image: Created by renowned sculptor, José Buscaglia-Guillermety,
the Monument to the Puerto Rican Family was dedicated in the city of Hartford,
Connecticut in September of 2009. The bronze monument stands 12 feet high and
10 feet wide, visually representing migration from the Island of Puerto Rico to the
continental United States and honoring the contributions of Puerto Rican families
to the development of the country. While not visible on the cover of this book, the
back of the monument displays a Puerto Rican flag and lists the names of all of the
towns on the Island.

The paper in this book meets the guidelines for permanence and durability
of the Committee on Production Guidelines for Book Longevity
of the Council of Library Resources.

© 2014 Peter Lang Publishing, Inc., New York
29 Broadway, 18th floor, New York, NY 10006
www.peterlang.com

Printed in the United States of America

To our children:
Carmela, Marcela and Lorenzo Rolón-Dow
Javier and Alex Irizarry
&
to all the diaspora students and teachers
willing to share the experiences that are told in this book

Contents

Foreword

SONIA NIETO

The story of diaspora is the study of the United States of America. Most of us have been people of some diaspora or other, beginning a couple of hundred thousand years ago with the earliest pilgrimages of our African ancestors to other areas of the globe, and many centuries later moving on to the English pilgrims on the *Mayflower*, and more recently to the latter-day pilgrims arriving by foot, plane, or ship from countries around the world. As a result, historically, all of us, either personally or through our heritage, have confronted what it means to live and learn as immigrants, refugees, or displaced and dispersed people.

Puerto Ricans, or *Boricuas*, are a small subsection of this diaspora, yet they provide a dramatic example of it. There are, for instance, more Puerto Ricans living in the continental United States than on the Island. The reasons for this diaspora are complicated and multifaceted, and they include colonization, imperialism, the displacement of farmers to urban areas in Puerto Rico, the scarcity of jobs on the Island, the direct recruitment of Puerto Ricans to the farms of the Northeast United States, the pull of the promise of "streets paved with gold," and the search for better educational opportunities, among others. Currently numbering over 4,600,000 in the United States—compared with just over 3,700,000 on the Island itself—Puerto Ricans represent a striking modern-day case of immigration, displacement, and diaspora. The implications for education are enormous, as demonstrated by the compelling contents of this book.

In *Diaspora Studies and Education*, various authors consider what it means to be Puerto Rican in the United States, particularly as related to education. Editors Rosalie Rolón-Dow and Jason Irizarry, while focusing on the Puerto Rican diaspora, go beyond this one case to create a conceptual framework for understanding the immigration of peoples of other backgrounds as well. Defining diaspora as a process rather than a fixed entity, they examine what they call *diasporization*, making the case that the Puerto Rican diaspora is both unique and similar to those of other immigrants to the United States. For example, Puerto Ricans represent a distinct case of [im]migration (Márquez, 1995) different from all other groups because we are U.S. citizens, whether we are born in Brooklyn, New York or in Ponce, Puerto Rico. Aside from this significant difference, however, our experiences are quite similar to those of traditional immigrants of color who leave their birthplaces for better opportunities and dreams of success for their children. That is, like other immigrants of color, Puerto Ricans have experienced the consequences of second-class status through a history of discrimination, racism, inferior schooling, poor housing, inadequate health care, limited employment opportunities, and other obstacles.

Given the current trends in globalization—including immigration, the importation and exportation of goods and services, and the increasingly similar educational policies that cross geographic borders—this diasporization is a helpful construct that can illuminate the cases not only of Puerto Ricans but also of other immigrant groups. For example, current immigrants to the United States from many different countries, particularly the youth, reflect a distinctive kind of hybridity unknown to earlier European immigrant groups, who were expected to assimilate to a bounded and singular ideal of "American," and were rewarded for doing so. Today's youths, in contrast, largely reject these essentialized notions of nationality, and instead have insisted on creating hybrid and complex identities that are also "American," albeit quite different from traditional ones.

Although few volumes have been dedicated specifically to the education of Puerto Rican students in U.S. schools, the research in this area is not new. By the early 1960s, the Puerto Rican community in New York City already numbered in the hundreds of thousands. Yet it was not until 1968, the year I started my teaching career in an intermediate school in Brooklyn, that a book of information and research for teachers and other professionals working with the Puerto Rican community appeared, edited by Francesco Cordasco and Eugene Bucchioni, Italian American educators with a deep connection to the Puerto Rican community. This book profoundly affected me, not only because it was the first book I had ever come across that was about *my* experience as a child, but also because it spoke to my passion as a young teacher. Given the negative portrayals I had seen and heard in the media, and even as a child, in the New York City public schools until that time, the sensitive and thorough treatment that Cordasco and Bucchioni gave to the topic was particularly moving for me. In 1971 Father Joseph Fitzpatrick, a priest who had worked closely with the New York Puerto Rican community, edited a volume titled *Puerto Rican Americans: The Meaning of Migration to the Mainland*, a book that explored the Puerto Rican diaspora and described Puerto Rican [im]migration as circular in nature, differentiating it from all previous immigrations (Fitzpatrick, 1971). While not focused specifically on education, this book was nonetheless instrumental in introducing the unique nature of Puerto Rican immigration to a wider audience. However, given the era in which these first texts were published, it is not surprising that very few Puerto Rican scholars were included in their pages. It was not until 1992 that Alba Ambert and María Alvarez, the first Puerto Ricans to do so, edited a volume about the education of Puerto Ricans that included chapters written primarily by Puerto Ricans. This was followed by my own edited text, *Puerto Rican Students in U.S. Schools* (2000), in which Puerto Ricans themselves, ranging from teenagers to teachers and academics, wrote most of the research chapters, poetry, and personal narratives. As a senior scholar dedicated to these issues for many years, I am comforted to know that a newer group of stellar academics is picking up the torch and continuing the struggle for a more equitable education for Puerto Rican and other marginalized youths. Given the work documented in this volume, the future is certainly promising.

Diaspora Studies and Education both builds on these texts and breaks new ground. First, it makes clear that diaspora is a complex process that cannot be described by a single experience, but rather is influenced by contexts of time, place, and identity. As a result, it is "messy and ever-changing," as Rolón-Dow and Irizarry explain in their introduction. Moreover, by theorizing the nature of diaspora, particularly as it relates to education, the editors have made a significant contribution to the research on diaspora studies in general. At the same time, both the editors and authors make it clear that the diaspora experience is not simply a theoretical concept, but also a set of lived experiences that are unique and personal, and at the same time, collective and similar to other diasporas. Often painful, these experiences are also always transformative.

In the end, what is especially noteworthy about this volume is the light it shines on the actual people most affected by diaspora, that is, the young Puerto Ricans and other immigrants who increasingly populate our public schools. It is my hope that teachers, administrators, policymakers, politicians, and the general public will grow in their understanding not only of Puerto Rican youths, but also of the impact that the forces of immigration and diasporization have on all of us. When this happens, perhaps they will also begin to appreciate the enormous talents and skills that these young people can contribute to our multicultural, multilingual, and multinational society. After over a century of the Puerto Rican presence in the United States, it is past time for this to happen.

References

Ambert, A. N., & Alvarez, M. D. (Eds.). (1992). *Puerto Rican children on the mainland: Interdisciplinary perspectives.* New York: Garland.

Cordasco, F., & Bucchioni, E. (Ed.). (1968). *Puerto Rican children in mainland schools.* Metuchen, NJ: Scarecrow Press.

Fitzpatrick, J. P. (1971). *Puerto Rican Americans: The meaning of migration to the mainland.* Englewood Cliffs, NJ: Prentice Hall.

Márquez, R. (1995). Sojourners, settlers, castaways, and creators: A recollection of Puerto Rico past and Puerto Ricans present. *Massachusetts Review, 36*(1), 94–118.

Nieto, S. (2000). *Puerto Rican students in U.S. schools.* Mahwah, NJ: Lawrence Erlbaum.

Introduction: Towards a diaspora framework

ROSALIE ROLÓN-DOW & JASON G. IRIZARRY

The idea of diaspora offers a ready alternative to the stern discipline of primordial kinship and rooted belonging.... [D]iaspora is a concept that problematizes the cultural and historical mechanics of belonging. It disrupts the fundamental power of territory to determine identity by breaking the simple sequence of explanatory links between place, location, and consciousness. (Gilroy, 2000, p. 123)

What does it mean to live in between? / What does it take to realize / that being Boricua / is a state of mind / a state of heart / a state of soul... / No nací en Puerto Rico. / Puerto Rico nació en mi. (Fernández, "Ode to the Diasporican")

Both of the authors writing this introduction identify as *Boricua*, or Puerto Rican. Through vastly different experiences, Puerto Rico was born in each of our hearts and souls. Having lived in Puerto Rico during her first 12 years of life, Rosalie's memories include picking mangos with her *abuelo* from his backyard tree, hearing Spanish songs echoing off the church walls on Sunday mornings, falling in love with the Puerto Rican mountains as she spent countless summer days exploring the natural world around her home with siblings and friends, and writing poems in fourth grade that spoke of Puerto Rico as a tiny island to be cherished and loved. She also remembers the mixed feelings that came along with packing up her home's possessions to ship to the United States, and the subsequent letters that her *abuela* faithfully sent to tell her about life back in Puerto Rico. She remembers hearing negative comments from White classmates in the United States that stereotyped what they called "those other Puerto Ricans," and she recalls frustrations, joys, and triumphs as she learned more about (in)equity in education teaching Puerto Rican students in a bilingual Philadelphia classroom.

Jason has memories of the sights, sounds, and smells of Puerto Rican barrios in New York City, and of playing baseball, first in the East Harlem baseball league, where all of the teams were named after towns in Puerto Rico, and then in a league sponsored by Goya Foods, where teams were named after Latino cultural food items such as *recaito*, *malta*, and *arroz*. While the schools he attended did little to affirm his Puerto Rican identity, each day on his way to school he was greeted by his neighbor, Don Pedro, with his neatly pressed *guayabera* shirt, worn no matter how cold the winter day, and he ate, *pastelillos de carne*, Puerto Rican meat fritters, for lunch, purchased from a food truck parked outside the school playground. On warmer days, he devoured *piraguas de coco y tamarindo*, frozen ice treats flavored with tropical fruit syrups. Although the concrete jungle of New York City was hundreds of miles away from the tropical island paradise he occasionally journeyed to as a child to visit family, he daily navigated distinctly Puerto Rican spaces where DiaspoRicans had claimed space and were making an indelible mark on the city and on the development of his ethnic/cultural identity.

Despite these different experiences, and despite the fact that we can both "pass" as White if we choose, we both identify as Puerto Rican. Within the world of academia, we find kinship with one another as we share similar professional interests, concerns, and experiences that stem from that identification. Both personally and professionally, we have grappled with dilemmas related to what it means to live and work as Puerto Ricans in various "in between" spaces. That is, we have lived in between Puerto Rico and the United States; between middle-class experiences our professions enable and working-class/poor experiences of childhood; between Spanish, English, and Spanglish; between the White world of academia and diverse contexts of our home communities; between colonized and colonizer; between theory, practice, and advocacy. In our "in between" living and working, we find that embracing diaspora as a process and concept is particularly helpful. In this introduction, we provide a brief sketch of the ways we understand diaspora as a conceptual framework. The work of the authors featured in this book address themes underlying this framework as they address the education of Puerto Ricans. Yet, we hope to show the potential of a diaspora framework for better understanding the experiences of other groups that are impacted by experiences of displacement, movement, and resettlement, by life in between and across national boundaries and cultural practices, and by the struggle to belong and be educated in a wide range of communities.

A diaspora within a diaspora: The Latino/a diaspora as context

The growth of the Latino/a population is undoubtedly transforming the United States demographic profile. In the arena of education, the impact of the Latino/a population is evident as more administrators and teachers come face to face with this fast-growing, youthful population and as the community contexts where education takes place are increasingly influenced by the Latinization of U.S. sociocultural and political landscapes (Irizarry, 2011). Currently, one in five public school students are Latino/a, and it is projected that by 2050, the Latino/a school-age population will increase by 166%, surpassing the number of non-Latino/a White children in U.S. schools (Fry & Gonzalez, 2008). Increasing attention is being focused on this population, given its dramatic growth over the last several decades and the increasing settlement of Latinos/as in a range of rural, suburban, and urban areas that have not been traditional destinations for Latinos/as. While the growth and youthfulness of the Latino/a population is noteworthy, its impact on the sociocultural, political, and economic landscapes is also unprecedented because of the ways that globalization and transnationalism have transformed the ways that 21st-century (im)migrants[1] are incorporated into society and the ways they negotiate identity, social inclusion, and citizenship.

Education is a primary site where the dilemmas, tensions, and possibilities of demographic and sociocultural change are confronted and negotiated. Examining the intersections of Latino/a life with education thus calls for frameworks that account for the ways that categories such as migrant, citizen, and Latino/a are culturally produced and deployed in the 21st century. This book further develops diaspora as an analytic framework because of its utility in efforts to articulate and analyze themes that are relevant to the quality and nature of Latino/a individual, family, and community life, and the ways these intersect with education. Diaspora as a concept and process helps focus attention on the ways that (im) migrants shape transnational lives in between and across national borders (Flores, 2009), the ways they negotiate hybrid identity formations across generations and multiple geographic locations (Lukose, 2007; Villenas, 2007), and the ways they struggle for social inclusion, belonging, and expanded citizenship rights. When joined together, the phrase *Latino/a diaspora* is often used to describe a quantifiable group of people that is transforming the demographics of the U.S. population, or to indicate a collection of geographic locations that serve as homes to long-established or more recent groups of Latino/as. In this book, however, we aim to develop a conceptual framework that will articulate a more active use of *diaspora*, focusing on the processes that impact the *diasporization* of the Latino/a population, and more specifically, examining those diasporization processes in the arena of education.

Puerto Ricans as a case study

Media and academic attention focused on the Latino/a population often highlights the experiences of Mexican immigrants and Mexican Americans, the largest subgroup within the Latino/a population. Puerto Ricans, however, are the second largest Latino/a group in the United States. Among Latino/a migrants to the United States, Puerto Ricans hold a unique position because of their long-standing relationship with the United States, the Island's ongoing political status as a U.S. commonwealth, and because they are U.S. citizens. Despite the unique features of the Puerto Rican experience that commonwealth and citizenship status entail, examining the diasporization of the Latino/a population through the Puerto Rican lens is useful and relevant for a number of reasons.

First, examining the educational experiences of Puerto Ricans allows for a focus on the ways that students experience education as an institution with the power to influence social rights and social inclusion, a theme relevant across a range of diasporic groups. The second-class nature of Puerto Rican citizenship has often been evident in U.S. schools, where colonial relations and racialization processes have been extended and reproduced (Walsh, 1998). Historically, Puerto Ricans were not well served by U.S. schools, and Puerto Rican students remain one of the groups most negatively impacted by the unequal nature of schooling achievement and opportunity in our country (Nieto, 2000; Rolón-Dow, 2007). The issues of equity and struggles for full citizenship rights and inclusion that Puerto Ricans experience in education are relevant to numerous populations impacted by diaspora processes.

Another reason why the education of Puerto Ricans provides a relevant case study is that it allows for an examination of the ways diaspora processes take shape across time, in multiple geographic contexts and in relation to other groups. The most dramatic growth of the Puerto Rican population in the United States occurred between the late 1920s and the early 1970s; during this period, the impact of Puerto Rican migration was most prominent in urban centers (Acosta-Belen & Santiago, 2006; Whalen & Vázquez-Hernández, 2005). Yet, Puerto Ricans continue to engage in circular migration patterns between the Island and the United States, and between different Puerto Rican communities within the United States. These continued migration patterns facilitate ongoing interactions between "new" and established migrants; nurture transnational dispositions, identities, and practices; and challenge assimilation models of immigration Furthermore, migration from the Island to the United States has most recently increased and the Puerto Rican population has further dispersed across a wider geographic area, with the most notable growth occurring in the southern states (Silver & Vargas Ramos, 2012), calling for an examination of the ways that diaspora sensibilities take shape in areas that were not traditional destination points for Puerto Ricans, and in relation to other Latino/a groups that may be long-established or new in these places.

While we will focus on Puerto Ricans, we believe that a diaspora framework, developed and theorized through the unique contributions to this edited volume, can be useful not only for those concerned specifically with the education of Puerto Rican youth, but also for the study of other diasporic communities who are impacted by experiences of displacement, movement, and resettlement, by life in between and across national boundaries and cultural practices, and by the struggle to belong and be equitably educated in a wide range of communities.

Diaspora as conceptual framework

Brubaker (2005) argued for conceptualizing diaspora as a category of practice rather than thinking of diaspora as a bounded group to be quantified. Conceptualizing diaspora as a category of practice allows for a focus on understanding particular stances, claims, or projects that are culturally produced (see Levinson & Holland, 1996, for further discussion of cultural production theory) by groups of people or on behalf of groups of people typically characterized as diasporas. Diaspora is thus a process (Flores, 2009) that is continually produced, negotiated, and/or resisted in relation to other groups, across generations and geographic locations and in and through the sociopolitical, historical, and cultural conditions germane to a particular group. While conceptions of diaspora as a culturally produced process might suggest that diaspora experiences of different groups hold little in common, we want to outline some common conditions, concerns, and themes that course through the cultural production of diasporic projects. As the authors in this book explore these conditions in different aspects of the education of Puerto Ricans, we will collectively build a case study that highlights the usefulness of diaspora as a framework relevant for examining the educational experiences of varied groups and communities.

Lukose (2007) writes that "Diaspora studies has disentangled identity formation from assimilationism and produced careful studies of hybridity and creolization that pay attention to creativity and the possibilities of new cultural and national identity formations" (p. 411). An exploration of the concepts of hybridity and difference is an important theme in building and utilizing a diaspora framework. Various scholars have pointed to the importance of exploring the ways that youth forge complex identities in relation to multiple raced, classed, and transnational contexts (Flores, 2009; Hall, 1998; Villenas, 2007). The notion of hybridity provides a way to move away from essentialized notions of identity and towards more flexible notions of what being Puerto Rican might mean given the particular experiences and the communities that are meaningful in the lives of Puerto Ricans in varied contexts.

The impetus for the book bridges personal and professional curiosities, and is rooted in an unwavering commitment to improve the educational experiences of Puerto Rican youth and members of other diasporic communities who have been and continue to be underserved by schools in the United States. We envision culture and the diaspora experiences referenced here not as monolithic or static but rather as fluid, multidimensional phenomena. Likewise, the contributions to this book are far-reaching and speak to multiple dimensions of diaspora. Although we organize the book around three themes that emerged across the diaspora experiences to which the authors speak, we acknowledge that the scholarship included in this volume forwards a broad vision of diaspora, one that is messy and ever-changing and does not fit perfectly into discrete categories. As scholars we have made the conscious choice to make meaning of the "messiness" and live with ambiguity, instead of forcing pieces to fit into a prescribed mold. In this way, we assert that the collection of works featured here contributes to a grounded theory (Glaser & Strauss, 1967) of diaspora. We include what can be read as "traditional" academic chapters, as well as personal narratives and poems, to contribute to a more robust understanding of diaspora, one that is grounded in the lived experiences of the DiaspoRican authors and the communities they represent through their writing.

The first section of the book, *Threads of Diaspora in Relation to Other Communities*, explores the ways that Puerto Ricans confront, negotiate, and culturally produce Puerto Rican, Latino/a, and American identities in relation to other groups and in response to particular local circumstances. How do relationships and experiences with other minoritized groups influence the ways that Puerto Ricans are positioned or position themselves within discourses that consider questions of participation, belonging, and citizenship rights? Nilda Flores-González and Michael Rodríguez-Muñiz focus attention on the participation of Puerto Rican youth in immigrant rights marches, highlighting the ways that Puerto Ricans' interactions with other Latino/a youth build affinities with broader pan-ethnic Latino/a identities and diaspora projects. Jonathan Rosa explores the dynamic intersections between language practices, identities, and diasporization processes. He shows how diasporization is dynamically linked to processes of ethnolinguistic socialization that take place in institutions such as schools, and highlights the ways that people (re)define the ethnolinguistic identities to which they are socialized as they navigate their everyday lives. María Fránquiz engages in auto-ethnographic work to reveal her identity negotiations across time, in a range of contexts. From her experiences as a schoolgirl in Puerto Rico to her experiences as a professor in the southwest United States, she reveals the multiple meanings that she and others ascribe to a Puerto Rican identity, and points to the complex ways that diaspora sensibilities are partially shaped in relation to the history and experiences of varied groups and in the context of particular cultural geographies. The authors in this section show how conceptualizing diaspora as a stance, project, and process can help move educators away from static and essentialized definitions of Puerto Rican cultural values. Instead, it can help focus attention on the ways Puerto Rican youth and their families often produce and negotiate their identities in relation to complex notions of "nation," "American," "Puerto Rican," or "Latino/a" in varied community contexts.

Another central theme in a diaspora analytic framework is the way that diaspora sensibilities are forged in relation to real or imagined home communities (Anderson, 1991; Safran, 1991). These connections may originate because a group has contemporary or historical experiences of dispersal and/ or (re)settlement in relation to a physical homeland (Brubaker, 2005). Alternatively, and particularly for the generations following initial waves of migration, diasporic sensibilities may develop through the process of [re]creating cultural practices along lines of shared historical experiences, affinities, or identifications that may not be easily defined by geographic borders (Clifford, 1994). Home is also important in a diaspora framework because it points attention to the ways individuals and groups feel a sense of belonging and experience inclusionary or exclusionary practices under given circumstances. For Puerto Ricans, processes of dispersal, (re)settlement, and community building are often prompted by the continued colonial relationship between the United States and Puerto Rico. The cultural, political, and economic entanglements with the United States facilitate or demand circular migration between the Island and the United States, and lead to the cultural production of Puerto Rican communities that create homeplaces with networks and allegiances within and across cultural, linguistic, sociopolitical, and geographic borders. Investigating the cultural production of the Puerto Rican diaspora project thus necessitates an exploration of how Puerto Rican individuals and communities negotiate their belonging and forge homeplaces across or in spite of space and over time. A central concern then becomes investigating the ways that particular places (e.g., community centers, classrooms, schools, neighborhoods) facilitate belonging and home-building for Puerto Ricans.

In Section II of the book, *Threads of Diaspora through Circular Migration*, the authors explore the ways that circular migration patterns of Puerto Ricans between the Island and the United States and between multiple communities within the United States shape belonging and produce particular identities and dispositions. How do relational networks and configurations of "home" figure into notions of belonging for Puerto Ricans? How do educators understand and respond to the dynamics of Puerto Rican communities that maintain multilayered conceptions of home and belonging? What sort of relationships and networks exist between educational institutions and the homes and communities of Puerto Rican students, and how do these relationships enhance or detract from the education of Puerto Rican students? Rosalie Rolón-Dow highlights forms of social and cultural capital that are produced in and through collective and individual circular migration patterns of Puerto Ricans. Using Latino/a critical race theory (LatCrit), she shows how diaspora processes and sensibilities intersect with the development of community cultural wealth for Puerto Rican students. Sandra Quiñones explores how diaspora processes intersect with the life histories of Puerto Rican teachers to shape their conceptions and negotiations of what it means to be well educated (*ser bien educado*). She shows how experiences of teachers in relation to their homes and communities were critical in crafting their roles as teachers in ways that nurtured the bilingual and bicultural sensibilities of their students. Shabazz Napier offers a personal account of a cultural reawakening as he was invited to participate on the Puerto Rican National Basketball Team, despite the fact that he had never visited the Island.

A common theme in the experiences of groups and communities engaged in diaspora processes is a struggle with negative experiences of discrimination and exclusion (Clifford, 1994); these struggles lead to questions of citizenship participation and social inclusion. Despite their status as U.S. citizens, Puerto Ricans have a history of struggling against discrimination, racialization, and limited citizenship rights in various arenas of life, including education. What, then, are the ongoing or new experiences of inclusion, exclusion, and discrimination faced by Puerto Rican students across a range of educational settings? How do particular pedagogical and research practices and paradigms take account of diaspora experiences of inclusion/exclusion in ways that lead to further opportunities for equitable educational outcomes? In Section III, *Threads of Diaspora in Established Puerto Rican Communities*, the authors explore this theme by examining struggles and triumphs of DiaspoRicans to develop, preserve, and assert their cultural identities.

Jason Irizarry and Enrique Figueroa critically examine the impact of gentrification on one of the oldest Puerto Rican communities in the United

States, highlighting the nuances of dispersion within diaspora and the impact on community formation and education. Enid Rosario-Ramos traces the ties between Puerto Rican diaspora and colonialism, and provides a case study of an institution that grounds its work in a postcolonial, social justice framework. Eileen Gonzalez documents her experiences (im)migrating to the United States and navigating educational institutions that often ignored, and at times pathologized, her Puerto Rican identity. Grounded in her lived experiences in Hartford, Connecticut, a city with the second largest concentration of Puerto Ricans in any city outside of the Island, Kristen Negron speaks to the challenges she faced in trying to secure quality educational opportunities and shares the meaning she ascribes to that journey.

As Puerto Ricans increasingly settle in towns and cities beyond their traditional community home bases in northeast cities, a diaspora framework can be helpful in investigating the ways that Puerto Ricans gain access to and navigate educational opportunities (Rolón-Dow, 2010). Diaspora studies can provide useful analytic tools for understanding the educational experiences of Latino/a communities as they continually (re)create the cultural landscapes of communities through their new or increasing presence in rural areas, towns and cities across the United States (Villenas, 2007).

The use of a diaspora analytic framework brings a new perspective to the educational literature about Puerto Rican students. Lukose (2007) and Villenas (2007) suggest that insights from diaspora studies may be particularly helpful to educators seeking to build theory and practice that consider the hybrid cultural practices of Latino/a communities across generations and in varied and multiple geographic locations. Given the central role of diasporic processes in shaping the experiences of Puerto Ricans, it is thus important to consider the ways that an analytic diaspora lens may be helpful in revealing themes present in the current educational experiences and conditions of Puerto Ricans. A diaspora framework centers attention on processes of transnational life as they are played out in relation to particular home communities, on hybrid identity formations, on social inclusion, and on citizenship rights—issues that are extremely relevant within the field of education. Furthermore, these issues are germane to multiple groups that tend to occupy an increasing number of seats in U.S. schools, thus making diaspora, and its central tenets, more relevant to those who concern themselves with issues of diversity, equity, and education in the 21st century.

Notes

1. The parentheses in (im)migration are employed to signal the diverse immigration experiences among individuals and communities who journey to the United States,

specifically underscoring potential differences in citizenship status. For example, Puerto Ricans born on the island of Puerto Rico, a colonial possession of the United States for over a century, are U.S. citizens by birth. Therefore, their move from the island to the mainland can be viewed as "migration" rather than "immigration." However, Spanish is the dominant language on the island, and when Puerto Ricans, who are free to travel throughout the United States without restriction, migrate to the U.S., their experiences share many similarities with those of other immigrants from Latin America, especially in their encounters with xenophobia, racism, and linguicism. Nevertheless, there are certain benefits that are conferred upon Puerto Rican (im)migrants that are not extended to immigrants who are not U.S. citizens. Therefore, we use the parentheses to call attention to the complexities of immigration across groups that often are overlooked.

References

Acosta-Belén, E., & Santiago, C.E. (2006) *Puerto Ricans in the United States: A Contemporary portrait.* Boulder, CO: Lynne Rienner Publishing.

Anderson, B. (1991). *Imagined communities: Reflections on the origin and spread of nationalism* (2nd ed.). London: Verso.

Brubaker, R. (2005). The "diaspora" diaspora. *Ethnic and Racial Studies, 28*(1), 1–19.

Clifford, J. (1994). Diasporas. *Cultural Anthropology, 9*(3), 302–338.

Fernández, M. T. (Mariposa). (n.d.). "Ode to the Diasporican." Retrieved from http://www.virtualboricua.org/Docs/poem_mtf01.htm

Flores, J. (2009). *The diaspora strikes back: Caribeño tales of learning and turning.* New York: Routledge.

Fry, R., & Gonzales, F. *One-in-five and growing fast: A profile of Hispanic public school students.* Pew Hispanic Center. August 26, 2008.

Gilroy, P. (2000). *Against race: Imagining political culture beyond the color line.* Cambridge, MA: Harvard University Press.

Glaser, B. G., & Strauss, A. L. (1967). *The discovery of grounded theory: Strategies for qualitative research.* Chicago: Aldine.

Gupta, A., & Ferguson, J. (1992). Beyond "culture": Space, identity, and the politics of difference. *Cultural Anthropology, 7*(1), 6–23.

Hall, S. (1998). Subjects in history: Making diasporic identities. In W. Lubiano (Ed.), *The house that race built: Original essays by Toni Morrison, Angela Y. Davis, Cornel West, and others on Black Americans and politics in America today* (pp. 289–299). New York: Vintage.

Irizarry, J. (2011). *The Latinization of U.S. schools: Successful teaching and learning in shifting cultural contexts.* Boulder, CO: Paradigm Publishers.

Levinson, B. A., & Holland, D. C. (1996). The cultural production of the educated person: An introduction. In B. A. Levinson, D. E. Foley, & D. C. Holland (Eds.) *Critical ethnographies of schooling and local practice* (pp. 1–56). Albany: State University of New York Press.

Lukose, R. (2007). The difference that diaspora makes: Thinking through the anthropology of immigrant education in the United States. *Anthropology and Education Quarterly, 38*(4), 405–418.

Nieto, S. (2000). Puerto Rican students in U.S. schools: A brief history. In S. Nieto (Ed.), *Puerto Rican students in U.S. schools* (pp. 5–37). Mahwah, NJ: Lawrence Erlbaum Associates.

Rolón-Dow, R. (2007). Passing time: An exploration of school engagement among Puerto Rican girls. *The Urban Review, 39*(3), 349–72.

Rolón-Dow, R. (2010). Taking a diasporic stance: Puerto Rican mothers educating children in a racially integrated neighborhood. *Diaspora, Indigenous, and Minority Education, 4*(4), 268–284.

Safran, W. (1991). Diasporas in modern societies: Myths of homeland and return. *Diaspora: A Journal of Transnational Studies, 1*(1), 83–99.

Silver, P., & Vargas-Ramos, C. (2012 November). *Demographic Transitions Research Brief* (RB2012–03). New York: Center for Puerto Rican Studies.

Villenas, S. (2007). Diaspora and the anthropology of Latino education: Challenges, affinities and intersections. *Anthropology and Education Quarterly, 38*(4), 419–425.

Walsh, C.E. (1998). "Staging encounter": The educational decline of U.S. Puerto Ricans in [post]-colonial perspective. *Harvard Educational Review, 68*(2), 218–243.

Whalen, C. T., & Vázquez-Hernández, V. (2005). *The Puerto Rican diaspora: Historical perspectives*. Philadelphia, PA: Temple University Press.

Section I: Threads of diaspora in relation to other communities

Heart of hunger

Martín Espada

Smuggled in boxcars through fields of dark morning,
tied to bundles at railroad crossings,
the brown grain of faces dissolved in bus station dim,
immigrants: mexicano, dominicano,
guatemalteco, puertorriqueño, orphans and travelers,
refused permission to use gas station toilets,
beaten for a beer in unseen towns with white porches,
or evaporated without a tombstone in the peaceful grass,
a centipede of hands moving,
hands clutching infants that grieve,
fingers to the crucifix,
hands that labor.

Long past backroads paved with solitude,
hands in the thousands reach for the crop-ground together,
the countless roots of a tree lightning-torn,
capillaries running to a heart of hunger,
tobaccopicker, grapepicker, lettucepicker.

Obscured in the towering white clouds of cities in winter,
thousands are bowing to assembly lines,
frenzied in kitchens and sweatshops,
mopping the vomit of others' children,
leaning into the iron's steam
and the steel mill glowing.

Yet there is a pilgrimage,
a history straining its arms and legs,
an inexorable striving,
shouting in Spanish
at the police of city jails
and border checkpoints,
mexicano, dominicano,

guatemalteco, puertorriqueño,
fishermen wading into the North American gloom
to pull a fierce gasping life
from the polluted current.

from *The Immigrant Iceboy's Bolero*

Thank you to Martín Espada for the use of his beautiful poems to introduce each section of the book.

Latino/a diaspora, citizenship, and Puerto Rican youth in the immigrant rights movement

NILDA FLORES-GONZÁLEZ & MICHAEL RODRÍGUEZ-MUÑIZ

> Some people would be curious about why Puerto Ricans [marched] because they always think that we have this thing against Mexicans, and we don't like them. I mean it's not that serious. We don't want them to leave the country... I think a lot of Puerto Ricans now are aware that if something is gonna benefit the Mexican community then it will indirectly benefit [us] as well. (Jenna, 21 years old)

> [This] is a responsibility we have as Puerto Ricans to be able to go out and vote in the interest of people who are undocumented, and vote in representation of people who don't have that right. So [citizenship] is really more of a point of unity than a point of tension... (Jessica, 24 years old)

Marching in the face of widespread stereotypes of rivalry and tension, Puerto Rican youths joined their Mexican counterparts on the streets of downtown Chicago to demand an end to attacks on Latino and immigrant families and communities. Catalyzing the national immigrant rights movement, Chicago was the site of the first "mega-march" against the controversial Sensenbrenner Bill, on March 10, 2006 (Pallares & Flores-González, 2010). The participation of Puerto Ricans in this protest and subsequent marches contradicts, or at the very least, complicates, long-standing assumptions about Puerto Rican/Mexican relations and the prospects of building pan-Latino/a political projects and identities (see Rodríguez-Muñiz, 2010). Despite the fact that Puerto Ricans, unlike their Latino/a counterparts, are automatically U.S. citizens by birth, Puerto Rican activists in Chicago and other major cities have demanded the legalization of undocumented people.

This chapter examines why Puerto Rican youths, and particularly those who are U.S. born, participated in the immigrant rights marches. Here, we draw on in-depth interviews with nine Puerto Rican youths, which were part of a larger study of youth participation in the immigrant rights movement (Flores-González, 2010). Between the ages of 16 and 25, these youths were born on the U.S. mainland, but their parents and/or grandparents were born in Puerto Rico. About half of them had previous experiences with activism, gained through involvement in the Puerto Rican Cultural Center, a local grassroots community organization located on the northwest side of the city (see Flores-González, 2001; Ramos-Zayas, 2003; Rinaldo, 2002). For the remainder, the immigrant rights marches were their first political activity. We seek to explain how these youths made sense of their presence in the movement, and following research on identity, politics, and social movements (García-Bedolla, 2005; Polletta & Jasper, 2001; Taylor & Whittier, 1992), we explore the relationship between political solidarity and Latino/a identity formation among Puerto Rican youth in the diaspora.

Studies reveal that Latino/a youth have the lowest levels of political engagement (Lopez, 2003). Hart and Atkins (2002; Atkins & Hart, 2003) argue that in high poverty, urban neighborhoods, where most youth of color live, there are fewer opportunities for civic and political engagement. When they do engage, they are more likely to do so civically rather than politically. Higher civic engagement is mostly due to high school "service learning" requirements that instruct students to volunteer in civic organizations but give little room for political expression and development. As a result, youth have limited opportunities to learn about and exercise their political rights (Camino & Zeldin, 2002). In fact, during the immigrant rights marches in Chicago, the Chicago public schools discouraged students from participating in the marches by threatening them with an "unjustified absence." Oliva (2010a) found that most schools were unable to enforce this mandate because students had their parents call or send a note to school, and in this way the students effectively circumvented the mandate without openly defying school policy.

To understand how Puerto Rican youths make sense of their participation in the immigrant rights movement, we need to understand how they define citizenship, and the means available for them to engage politically. Thus, here we underscore the influence of family, school, and community on political socialization, and more importantly, on the political attitudes and actions of Puerto Rican youth in the diaspora (see Andolina et al., 2003; Atkins & Hart, 2003; Camino & Zeldin, 2002; Ginwright, Cammarota, & Noguera, 2005; Hart & Atkins, 2002; Sherrod, 2003; Youniss et al., 2002; Zukin et al., 2006). We argue that these issues must be considered in light of diasporic encounters and experiences between Mexicans and Puerto Ricans, the city's largest and oldest Latino/a populations.

Our analysis reveals that Puerto Rican youths interpreted and articulated certain commonalities with Mexicans, while at the same time acknowledging specific differences, such as their U.S. citizenship. In contrast with other academic and popular accounts, our research shows that citizenship served not as an impediment to, but rather as a resource for participation. Inhabiting a social milieu marked by the intersection of two diasporic communities, these second-generation Puerto Ricans shared with Mexicans migration narratives, familial and community ties, and experiences of racialization and linguistic, political, and economic exclusion. Viewing themselves as "similar, but not identical" (see Rodríguez-Muñiz, 2010) to other Latinos/as, they mobilized their access to U.S. citizenship to advocate on behalf of the undocumented.

Latinidad and politics of citizenship

In Chicago and other urban settings there exists a widespread assumption that Puerto Rican–Mexican relations are filled with competition and conflict. Along with other social differences (i.e., class, race, gender), scholars consider citizenship one of the major "faultlines" (Itzigsohn, 2004) within and among Latino/a communities. In their recent work *Latino Crossings*, anthropologists De Genova and Ramos-Zayas (2003) find evidence for this position. Drawing on data from their respective ethnographies on Mexican and Puerto Rican Chicago (De Genova, 2005; Ramos-Zayas, 2003), they describe how Puerto Ricans and Mexicans in varied social settings—schools, factories, and neighborhoods—often differentiated each other along the axes of race and citizenship. De Genova and Ramos-Zayas situate these practices within "the unequal politics of citizenship." They argue that the different relationships to the U.S. federal government and society have "engendered significant divisions" between Puerto Ricans and Mexicans (De Genova & Ramos-Zayas, 2003, pp. 2–3). Consequentially, these populations perceive themselves as having "very little in common," and thus they claim that expressions of Latinidad are deeply fractured and tenuous (p. 26). In short, differential legal histories and statuses have instituted a wedge between many Puerto Ricans and Mexicans in everyday life, and in effect, have weakened the potential for shared identification. In addition to identity formation, scholars have found that citizenship impacts the process for Latino/a political unity.

In his seminal work *Latino Ethnic Consciousness*, Felix Padilla (1985) elaborates an early, but influential thesis: pan-Latino/a politics are conditional on situations and conditions where distinct Latinos/as share experiences in common. Based on research on Chicago's post–civil rights Puerto Rican and Mexican political leadership, Padilla conceptualized "Latinismo" as "an emergent expression of shared structural and cultural feelings, excited as a strategic, wide-scale unit by disadvantaged people as a new mode of seeking political redress in American society" (p. 154). Building on the sociological literature on "situational ethnicity" (Okamura, 1981; Yancey, Ericksen, & Juliani, 1976), Padilla viewed Latino/a political collaboration as situationally and contextually contingent. Following this pragmatic logic, differential access to U.S. citizenship represents a serious limitation. As one of Padilla's respondents describes it, Puerto Ricans cannot and should not be expected to participate in immigration-related struggles:

> We cannot get South Chicago [area spatially associated with Mexicans] to get mad at Westtown [Puerto Rican neighborhood] if Westtown doesn't support their immigration situation [issue of undocumented workers]. That is a Mexican problem that cannot be resolved through a Latino effort. But we can get them to come and talk to Westtown about jobs, about things that are hitting everybody. (Padilla, 1985, pp. 62–63)

For this Mexican community leader, Puerto Ricans could not be counted on for support in cases where political issues did not impact them directly. They could, however, be expected to collaborate with Mexicans on shared issues, such as employment or discrimination. Though it is not necessarily a source of conflict, in Padilla's account, U.S. citizenship does mark the limits of co-operation in pan-Latino/a politics.

Taken together, the important writings of Padilla and De Genova and Ramos-Zayas suggest that differences in citizenship decisively hamper the potential for shared Latino/a identities and political collaboration among Puerto Ricans and Mexicans. Though the effects of differences such as citizenship should not be underestimated, these works generally treat citizenship as an *objective* factor. Neither work pays much attention to the meanings of citizenship, or more specifically, how different meanings could shape and influence the effects of objective differences in legal status. By neglecting this dimension, we cannot gain a handle on how Latino/a subgroups negotiate these differences and manage, however temporarily, to construct lines of unity. It further assumes that citizenship is an ever-salient issue in Puerto Rican and Mexican relations.

Recognizing the variable meanings and significance of citizenship among Latino/a sub-groups can help us better appreciate the documented existence of intra-Latino/a families (Pérez, 2003; Rúa, 2001), everyday interactions (e.g., Itzigsohn, 2009; Ricourt & Danta, 2003), experiences in community institutions (e.g., Dávila, 2004; Flores-González, Rodríguez, &

Rodríguez-Muñiz, 2006), and political movements (e.g., Lao-Montes, 2001; Rodríguez, 1999) to the making of Latino subjectivities. Consequently, we argue that the historical relationships and shared experiences of Latino/a subgroups and their contemporary interactions in everyday life, community institutions, and political movements cannot be adequately analyzed when citizenship is treated a priori as an objective division that constantly intervenes to diminish opportunities for building pan-Latino/a "imagined communities" (Anderson, 2006; Flores, 2000). Rather than view citizenship as a "brute fact" in social relations, we treat citizenship as a multivalent feature that variably matters in social contexts.

Latino/a panethnicity: Similar, but not identical

Our empirical case questions the assumed objectivity of citizenship to structure Latino/a relations. Building on Rodríguez-Muñiz's (2010) analysis of Puerto Rican activism in the immigrant rights movement, we argue that Puerto Ricans and Mexicans creatively establish grounds for collaboration and solidarity by imagining Latino/a subgroups as "similar, but not identical." This framework approaches pan-ethnic identity formation as a site of ongoing negotiations between perceived commonalities and differences, which in this case allow Puerto Rican participants to incorporate "Mexican" issues into their political struggle. Situations and contexts matter, but so do the meanings and understandings. This dynamic, of course, is not unique to Latino/a panethnic projects, but rather is an important dimension of identity formation writ large. Writing substantively about the Black Caribbean diaspora, Stuart Hall (1990) reminds that identities are "'framed' by two axes or vectors, simultaneously operative: the vector of similarity and continuity; and the vector of difference and rupture" (p. 226). The dialectical relationship between these vectors, he makes clear, cannot be treated simply as objective realities, but as constituted by social actors "within representation" and meaning (p. 236). Any account of pan-ethnic identity formation and the building of a pan-Latino/a diaspora must attend to the variable meanings that individuals and collectives assign to seemingly objective facts of social existence. Citizenship, as well as other social differences, must be read and interpreted, and as a result, can be leveraged and used by actors in numerous ways.

Puerto Rican youth participation in the immigrant rights movement offers an example of pan-ethnic political collaboration where neither social causes nor legal status are held in common. We found that youths make sense of their involvement by stressing commonalities with Mexicans, while at the same time acknowledging differential access to U.S. citizenship. They express that they experience many of the same issues and conditions, as well as living in close proximity. For example, discrimination results in segregated neighborhoods, schools, and workplaces where Puerto Ricans and Mexicans are grouped together (De Genova & Ramos-Zayas, 2003; Padilla, 1947; Pérez, 2003). In fact, the "Puerto Rican" neighborhood in Chicago has become increasingly panethnic as Mexicans are increasingly moving there (Ramos-Zayas, 2003). In the 1990s, the "Puerto Rican" high school in the city had a student population that was 58% Puerto Rican and 23% Mexican. Since 2005, the number of Puerto Ricans and Mexicans has become roughly equal (Oliva, 2010b).

To conceptualize these shared encounters and experiences, we draw on Ricourt and Danta's (2003) panethnicity framework and Itzigsohn's (2009) amendment. Ricourt and Danta (2003) identify four dimensions involved in the formation of Latino/a panethnicity. First, they discuss "experiential panethnicity," which refers to the sharing of everyday life, or *convivencia diaria*. The second dimension, "categorical panethnicity," describes the individual uptake of pan-Latino/a labels as personal identities. To capture the contribution made by Latino/a-based community organizations, Ricourt and Danta use the concept "institutional panethnicity." Yet, as our analysis reveals, even ethnic-specific organizations can contribute to Latino/a panethnicity. The fourth dimension, which they term "ideological panethnicity," concerns the discourses adopted and articulated by leaders in the name of "Latino/a community." In his recent study on Dominican incorporation, José Itzigsohn (2009) introduces a fifth dimension: "political panethnicity." By political panethnicity, Itzigsohn means the political mobilizations through which "a group acquires a voice in public life and attempts to influence the large social context in which the process of incorporation unfolds" (p. 168). The immigrant rights movement, as Puerto Rican youths describe it, represents an example of political panethnicity.

As narrated by these young actors, intimate social relations resulting from encounters between Puerto Rican and Mexicans in neighborhoods, schools, workplaces, and political acts draw these two groups into a common Latino/a diaspora-in-the-making. These experiences confirm their commonalities with Mexican immigrant youth, but also the differences introduced by their legal status. Despite this "objective" contradiction, Puerto Rican youths deploy their citizenship, which differentiates them from undocumented Mexicans, to demand legalization for immigrants. In practice, they view themselves, like other Latino citizens, as representatives of "those who cannot represent themselves." Our analysis reveals how understandings of citizenship can serve as an opportunity, rather than as a challenge to practices of Latino/a solidarity.

Constructing Latinidad: Shared histories, experiences, and lives

Puerto Rican youths joined thousands of individuals to protest repressive legislation and policies targeting undocumented persons and their families and allies. No single rationale motivated participation, as ideologies and meanings were as diverse as the populations that assembled in Chicago's downtown (Pallares & Flores-González, 2010). Our analysis traces the understandings and meanings that Puerto Rican youths articulate about their involvement in the immigrant rights movements. Their insights reveal the construction of "commonalities," but also the persistent recognition (and mobilization) of "differences." The management of these vectors, as Hall (1990) termed it, helped to make their participation thinkable and possible. To be sure, it was, at least in part, within the highly-visceral context of marching under the Chicago sun, banner and flags in hand, that Puerto Rican youths negotiated and refashioned their social position and identities.

When asked to give accounts of their participation, Puerto Rican youths made sense of their involvement by emphasizing a set of commonalities they perceived themselves to share with Mexicans. They drew lines of similarity through migration narratives, romantic and familial relationships, and diasporic experiences of racialization and linguistic, political, and economic exclusion. In making these assertions, youths consistently acknowledged differences, such as U.S. citizenship and some of its privileges, but also invested their legal status with particular meanings. One of the practical implications of these accounts and their activism is the very formation of a pan-Latino diasporic community.

One of the major themes articulated by youth participants pertained to their own and familial experiences of migration. Despite being U.S. citizens by birth and having the freedom to move between the Island and the U.S., Puerto Rican youths saw themselves as immigrants or the children of immigrants. The collective memory about the Puerto Rican migratory experience was employed to position themselves closer to Mexican immigrants. Often, they stressed challenges to incorporation, arguing that Puerto Rican migrants faced many of the same hardships and challenges as their Mexican counterparts. Twenty-three-year-old Jacquelyn remarked, "The migration for Puerto Ricans wasn't an easy migration…but I feel like those struggles that they went through we cannot forget. Those are similar struggles that the undocumented are going through and we shouldn't forget." Concretely, they described the experiences of their grandparents or parents, who arrived with limited English skills and often faced discrimination, and were confined to low-income, low-status jobs. Twenty-year-old Lissette, for instance, shared the challenges faced by her grandparents, who came to Chicago in the 1950s:

> [My grandfather] had to work whatever they would give him because even though he was a citizen, being Puerto Rican, [they] still discriminated against you and his English wasn't very good. They looked down upon him because he's not from here... My grandmother's experience being a woman she was like the little housewife no matter what. Even if she tried to get a job she could only get gendered jobs. You know, cleaning houses...

Lissette's account highlights the multiple challenges faced by Puerto Rican migrants, such as ethnoracial discrimination, language prejudice, and gender stratification. Youths did not view these dynamics as unique to Puerto Rican migration, but as roughly analogous to those experienced by contemporary Mexican migrants. For some youths, particularly those associated with the Puerto Rican Cultural Center, migratory experiences were placed within a longer political history of U.S. colonization. As De Genova and Ramos-Zayas (2003) discuss, both Mexicans and Puerto Ricans have a colonial history, which began in 1848 and 1898, respectively, by means of military intervention and conquest. It is this history that led journalist Juan González (2000) to characterize Latino/a migration to the U.S. as a "harvest of empire."

In a way, Puerto Rican youths in the diaspora understood Mexican migration through their familial stories and collective narratives. This, however, was not the only source of commonality expressed by these participants. Along with these historical narratives, youths explained their participation in terms of their own lived experience. As Lissette says, "We may not be immigrants and even our grandparents may not have to had to get papers, but it's still an issue [immigration], you know, like...we share a culture with [Mexicans] even if it's not the same [culture] it's still there. And these are people that we know. Like my family, yeah, were Puerto Rican but we've intermarried with Mexicans, Polish. It's there. It's part of our family." Like Lissette, other youths also explained their participation by highlighting their familial and social relationships with Mexicans and other immigrants.

Of course, this comes as little surprise, as Chicago is the only major U.S. metropolitan center in which sizable populations of more than one Latino/a group has cohabitated for generations. Until census 2010, Chicago boasted the second largest populations of Puerto Ricans and Mexicans in the country. Unlike New York and Los Angeles, Chicago has been home to large numbers of Mexicans and Puerto Ricans since the 1940s. For this reason, beginning with Elena Padilla's (1947) pioneering study (see Rúa, 2011), scholars have often turned to Chicago to examine the everyday negotiations of identity and community between Latino/a subgroups (De Genova & Ramos-Zayas, 2003; Garcia & Rua, 2007;

Pallares, 2005; Perez, 2003). Over the past several decades, Puerto Rican youth have lived within a social milieu increasingly populated by Mexicans (De Genova & Ramos-Zayas, 2003), and as a result have vivid experiences of living in some of the same neighborhoods, attending the same schools, and working together. Josué, a 17-year-old, points out that his neighborhood is "a community [where] Puerto Ricans and Mexicans are trying to rebuild a Latino presence."

This spatial and social proximity between Puerto Ricans and Mexicans often translates into close friendships and romantic relationships. Even in analyses that describe instances of conflict or tension (De Genova & Ramos-Zayas, 2003; Pérez, 2003), these relationships at times occur within contexts of intimate familiarity. For instance, Jenna felt motivated to get involved in the immigrant rights movement because it impacts many of her friends: "I have lots of friends who are Mexican and my own boyfriend isn't a citizen, he's a permanent resident, you know, but I have lots of friends who aren't, don't have citizenship yet." Lissette expressed some of the familial motivations for movement participation: "I have family who are married to undocumented immigrants...One of my cousins her husband is *un Mexicano* [a Mexican]. He's documented now *pero* [but] a few times he had to cross the border to go see his mom before she died. And he had to cross illegally."

Even where they lack undocumented friends and relatives, Puerto Rican youths encountered individuals adversely impacted by immigration policies and legal status. For instance, Leticia, a 24-year-old, spoke about her co-worker's vulnerability as the only U.S. citizen in a mixed-status family: "There are certain people who work for me that it may affect, like this one girl she is a citizen because she was born here, but her brother, mother, and father came over when her brother was a couple of months old."

In each of these relations, youths learned about threats and challenges they do not experience directly. In particular, they often knew and spoke about people who had been deported, or who had pending deportation cases. Victoria, a 17-year-old, detailed some of the emotional pain caused by the deportation of family and loved ones.

> I [have] known some people, well, family, who had to go back.... They were good friends of my mother and grandmother and they got deported back to Mexico and they took their kids along with them although they were born here in America. So she took her kids back with her, because if she couldn't stay, she wasn't going to leave her kids here by themselves. So she went back and about 2 to 3 months later, one of her kids got killed in an accident. So emotionally, I've been affected by immigration, but physically I haven't.

Personal cases such as Victoria's forced an awareness of the destabilizing effects of current immigration policy upon families and children. For most of the participants, deportation or the challenges of entering the U.S. were not abstractions, but concrete realities faced by loved ones. Within the movement, they used these experiences and circumstances as "points of unity" around which to organize support for immigration reform among members of the Puerto Rican community. Jessica expressed,

> Definitely, [immigration] crosses all kinds of boundaries because...it runs across the board and is able to affect people from families who have to be torn away from their children or parents who have to be taken away from their children and have to be deported. I think it affects different people in different ways and it definitely crosses those lines. ...we are able to see that immigration does not only affect men or women or these kind of people or these kind of poor or rich people, but it affects people across the board and we are able to find those [experiences] as points of unity which is why also we work with those communities, because there are points of unity that unite us.

Youth participants put their "unity" into action not only by attending marches, but also by participating in other expressions of "solidarity." For example, some of the youths made reference to Elvira Arellano, an undocumented mother of a U.S. citizen child, who for a year defied a deportation order by seeking refuge in a church located in the heart of the Puerto Rican community (see Pallares, 2010; Rodríguez-Muñiz, 2010). These youths were aware of Arellano's story because it was frequently in the local news media. Some had personally met Elvira Arellano, and at least one of the youths had guarded the entrance to the church right after Arellano took refuge there. As Jessica puts it, "Well, [we were] just making sure...standing in front of the church with the Puerto Rican flag. Showing that the Puerto Rican people were there in solidarity. We did that for 24 hours for about a month or two." Through acts like these, they put their belief in political solidarity between Mexicans and Puerto Ricans into practice.

For some, immigration is not just a political issue, but also a profoundly moral one. The politics of the federal government sometimes clashed with their Christian upbringing. Nineteen-year-old Antonio, for example, found himself at odds with his church when he supported the rights of immigrants. As he says, "My church leaders, they found it wrong for me to participate in this march because they believe there is an alternative way into getting into the United States. They can get papers, they can get green cards, work permits, but they shouldn't come here illegally. The Bible says that not only should we respect laws of God, but also man's law." Despite his church's position, Antonio chose to take part in marches. As we explore later on, he viewed participation as a responsibility he assumed as a U.S. citizen.

Though the participants often were shielded from the direct effects of immigration policies and undocumented legal status, they still felt the impacts. They were acutely aware of the threats to the stability and unity of families posed by policies such as the Sensenbrenner Bill. Because they live and go to school with and work alongside Mexicans, they find themselves affected, albeit indirectly, by immigration policies. In this way, the immigration issue crosses intergroup boundaries and connects them in various ways.

Current scholarly assumptions about the divisive role of citizenship have often neglected to explore how close intermingling between Puerto Ricans and Mexicans of different legal statuses might lead to certain sympathies and solidarities. As Rúa (2001) notes, "While political as well as social and cultural arenas are worthwhile sites for the study of latinidad, they overshadow the daily interactions between Latinos of diverse national backgrounds, which serve as the building blocks for political, social, and cultural movements" (pp. 127–128). Daily encounters with undocumented peers and loved ones served here as impetuses for political action.

Latinidad, racialization, and the politics of panethnicity

In addition to their narratives of migration and their intimate knowledge of and connection to undocumented individuals, Puerto Rican youths also drew strong parallels between their position in U.S. society and that of their Mexican peers. Specifically, they asserted shared experiences of racial and linguistic discrimination and the politics of panethnic labels, and critiqued the United States's relationships with Mexico and Puerto Rico. Consistently, such claims were made with differences in full view. Efforts were made to frame Puerto Ricans and Mexicans as similar, but not identical, with respect to social conditions and political relations. Centrally, this involved not simply the objective existence of commonalities of existence, but quite importantly, the subjective construction of commonalities. Their commentary on U.S. society and their place within it offers a critical reading of U.S. citizenship and the relative privileges it affords ethnoracial populations.

As an example of Ricourt and Danta's (2003) "experiential panethnicity," Puerto Rican youth participants routinely emphasized how they shared realities of ethnoracial marginalization and discrimination with other Latinos/as. In their eyes, Puerto Rican and Mexican youth were subjected to the same failing urban schools and policing practices, high rates of poverty, and limited opportunity. Jessica expressed this thus: "For as long as Latinos or as long as Puerto Ricans have been told, brought, and lured into coming to this country, we have gone through absolutely horrible conditions, horrible living conditions, horrible working conditions, the violation of our human rights, the violation of our rights." Also employing the word "horrible," another participant, Josué, stressed not their urban commonalities, but similarities engendered by U.S. policies in Mexico and Puerto Rico: "What the United States is doing to us as Latinos is horrible.... Puerto Rico is piece of...[it] is an object to the United States. We're treated like garbage. And so is Mexico. They just, even [though] it's not a part of, it's not own[ed] by the United States, [but] in some ways it is."

Jessica elaborated on this shared history of U.S. colonialism: "Yeah, we can say Puerto Ricans have citizenship and a lot of Latin Americans and Mexicans don't and you could make that simple line. But...trace back and see that there is history and colonialism." She continued, "The fact is that we've come to this country, or we have been pulled to this country to be able to build it, and it's in the work of our people that this country exists. To me it's harder to think about the differences, I think it would take me a little bit longer to do that than to think about the similarities." For her, these commonalities of colonialism were more significant than differences in citizenship. This argument was prevalent in some Puerto Rican activist organizations such as the Puerto Rican Cultural Center, which some of these youths were involved in. However, even youths without activist backgrounds or ties consistently expressed critical accounts of their realities and similarities with their Mexican peers.

Although these youths were clear about the "differences" between Mexicans and Puerto Ricans, they also recognized that their fate was linked through their racialization and labeling as Latinos/as. Latino/a studies scholars have long derided the homogenizing thrust of categories such as "Hispanic" and "Latino," which obscure the differences and heterogeneities among and within national subgroups (Flores, 2000; Flores-González, 1999; Lugo-Lugo, 2008; Oboler, 1995). These youths were clearly aware of the indiscriminate categorization of all Latinos/as, Puerto Ricans included, as immigrants, and the ensuing discrimination and criminalization as "illegal." To them other groups, do not differentiate between Latino/a groups and/or legal status, and instead label all of them as immigrants and "illegal." In a national political climate marked by racially pejorative representations of undocumented immigrants, being labeled as such is highly stigmatizing. Jessica explains,

> To be an undocumented immigrant is something deemed as inferior, as something that's lower than the lower class, because at least the lower class has the right to vote, at least the lower class has access to all kinds of benefits and things like that. Someone who is undocumented doesn't, so there is this negative association with particularly Mexican immigrants, that the undocumented status has given them. And so for Puerto Ricans it's like, "oh I'm not Mexican" and I feel a lot of Puerto Rican people feel like that.

Jessica recognizes that some Puerto Ricans do in fact distance themselves from Mexicans, and in ways similar to those described by De Genova and Ramos-Zayas (2003). However, dominant ethnoracial stereotypes limit the effectiveness of such distancing strategies. One common stereotype is language. While researchers have documented the existence of a linguistic hierarchy among Latinos/as, subgroups in everyday experiences with other populations these differences are regularly not recognized. Differences between "Puerto Rican" and "Mexican" Spanish are erased in encounters beyond their communities. As intimated by these youths, speaking Spanish, which is fairly common among Puerto Ricans of the first, second, and often the third generation, is often pejoratively assumed to signify an immigrant status. As Lissette put it, "…people discriminate against anyone who's Spanish speaking. It's not just undocumented workers; you could be a well-to-do person with lots of money [but] if you speak Spanish you might be looked down upon." For these youths, such views are offensive to them because, as Samuel, a 28-year-old, remarked, "they [Mexican immigrants] are contributing Americans just like anyone else."

For Lissette and others, these practices of "racial lumping" (Lugo-Lugo, 2008) further show that citizenship is not understood as a straightforward difference. As De Genova and Ramos-Zayas (2003) argue, U.S. citizenship, both historically and contemporaneously, is deeply intertwined with race. Yet, counter to their analysis, this intersection did not function as an automatic or necessary source of division. Instead, their interpretation of the position of Puerto Ricans, within the U.S. ethnoracial order led them to critique and recognize the limitations of their citizenship status. The personal narratives of Puerto Rican youths suggest that they understood themselves to occupy a similar though, again, not identical place within existing social and racial hierarchies. At the same time that they recognized racial lumping, these youths appropriated the term "Latino" as a "racial" category that conveys the position they occupy in the U.S. racial structure. Previous studies have shown that many self-identified Latinos/as give panethnic categories a racial register (Flores-González, 1999; Frank, Redstone Akresh, & Lu, 2010; Golash-Boza, 2006; Itzigsohn & Dore-Cabral, 2000). The category "Latino" was mobilized to compare and assess themselves in relation to other "racial groups." In particular, youths described their experiences as vastly different from those of whites, even those who live "next door." Lissette explains:

> Accessibility to better jobs is given to white people. They have higher paying jobs than the Latinos do. This is again from my personal experiences with my friends knowing white people and Latinos in that community…. A lot of white people that I knew earned more than the Latinos. It was just odd to

see...the disparity between them. It was just polarized almost between the two communities. They might live next door to each other, but they don't know each other. But one of the things that I thought was interesting was that even in the schools Latinos hang out with the Latinos, white people hang out with white people, it's hard to find a mix, that's what I mean. You don't find people who congregate with other races there.

In contrast, as the preceding sections have shown, youths drew many lines of commonality between Mexicans and themselves. Mobilizing the category "Latino" as an expression of shared identity and experience, however, did not require or involve articulations of sameness. Unlike dominant institutions, which have often invested in homogenized and totalizing representations of Latino/a populations, these actors wrestled with their perceived similarities as well as their differences. To participate in the movement, they did not feel compelled to shed their own cultural identities, or even completely downplay their "differences." In many ways, they participated as "Puerto Ricans" and as "citizens," two categories they refashioned to carve out a space for their presence within the immigrant rights movement.

Deploying citizenship

Puerto Rican involvement in the immigrant rights movement involved a rearticulation of the meaning of U.S. citizenship. Citizenship was recognized as a resource and privilege, but one which was not equally distributed, even among "citizens." Their critical analysis of U.S. history and politics, as well as lived experience, demonstrated, in their eyes, the limitations of citizenship. At the same time, citizenship justified their presence within the movement. Jacquelyn explains:

> Indirectly or directly the immigration issue hits home for people. It affects people in different aspects. Some people have immigrants or undocumented immigrants in their family and they may feel like it's unfair to send them back home when they've come here to look for "opportunities." Some people may like myself have [come] to be supportive. To say look I'm a citizen but I still support the immigration issue. I still support immigrants. I think that they shouldn't be sent back to their country. They've come this far, why can't they stay? It varies on the people but I think that in general people don't believe and don't agree with the bill that was trying to be passed.

In very real terms, differential access to citizenship served as neither an impediment nor a source of division among participants. Rather, it provided youths with a call to action, an ethical appeal to advocate for the "voiceless." In short, citizenship, or rather, the meanings of citizenship among Puerto Rican youth and other Puerto Rican supporters, played an important part in movement participation.

On a regular basis, these Puerto Rican youths confronted the popular myth of Puerto Rican–Mexican antagonism. This, of course, is not to say that individual Puerto Ricans and Mexicans at times did not express negative opinions and stereotypes or engage in conflicts over limited resources, urban space, cultural space, or political power. As scholars have noted, these conflicts sometimes occur through the medium of citizenship. However, it is important not to lose sight of the often quite intimate histories and relationships between these populations. Despite innumerable connections and familiarities, youths described being questioned, by both Puerto Ricans and Mexicans, about why they were involved in the immigrant rights movements. Jessica remarked,

> For a lot of people, they can ask "why are Puerto Ricans, who have the right to vote, who have citizenship, involved in a struggle that is really not theirs because they have citizenship, they have the right to vote?" But as Puerto Rican people that are conscious of why we have citizenship, the history behind us, we are able to recognize the need to work in solidarity with Latino/Mexican communities to help them work out the issues of citizenship and immigration in this country.

As Jessica illustrates, Puerto Rican advocacy was often framed as an act of "solidarity." This assertion suggests that these youths did not consider immigration a "Puerto Rican" issue. Though not imagined as "their cause," they did believe, however, that Puerto Ricans had an important role to play. This role was inseparable from their legal status. Though critical of the colonial imposition of U.S. citizenship on Puerto Ricans, they nonetheless argued that as holders of U.S. citizenship, Puerto Ricans had a responsibility to advocate for immigration reform. Thus, while they expressed critical views about the meaning and benefits of citizenship, they recognized that it affords Puerto Ricans, just like other citizens, with certain securities and opportunities denied to noncitizens. To be certain, Puerto Rican youth activists did not view access to citizenship as a panacea—their life experiences, from poverty, discrimination, and displacement, as well as political understandings injected them with an appreciation of the limitations of U.S. citizenship within a racialized and economically stratified society. And yet, as quoted in this chapter's epigraph, Jessica believed that Puerto Ricans had the "responsibility... to go out and vote in the interest of people who are undocumented and vote in representation of people who don't have that right." Despite its historical origins and contemporary deficiencies, they demanded citizenship for their undocumented family members, friends, and colleagues. Rather than a "point of tension," citizenship within the context of an emergent Latino/a diaspora was viewed as a "point of unity." Antonio clearly expressed this emergent sense of responsibility.

> I attended this march because it was a turning point in my life because it's not about me. Who am I? I'm nobody. But, what I have, I'm a U.S. citizen, and I have a responsibility, I have a right that I can do; I can be the voice for the voiceless. I participated because I have family and friends that are Mexican that [have] immigrated to the United States. I have co-workers, I have people in my congregation, I have people that work at cleaning our house or our laundry, and they're not here to do anything wrong. I mean it's painful to see that we have this right, this responsibility, and yet we're not taking action and using what we have, we are taking it for granted.

Empowered by citizenship, they described themselves as the "voice of the voiceless." Victoria elaborated,

> We are the voices for the voiceless, we are voices for the people who are unheard, we are the voices for the people who can't speak English very well, we are the voices for the Latinos. I think by standing up for them, coming to support, even if your documented or undocumented, I think that they change for people to realize, look at it, we are large in numbers, we are unified, we are coming together in issues and struggles such as these and we are here and we are here to stay.

Citizenship, as interpreted by these youths, provided them with a privilege and resource unavailable to undocumented immigrants. For them, citizenship gave them the right to act politically through both conventional and unconventional ways. Although many of these youths had little political experience, and their families, schools, and communities had afforded them few if any opportunities for political engagement, they had developed an understanding of citizenship as a political right, and this understanding derived from their lived experiences as racialized minorities. Drawing on this new understanding, these youths came to assign themselves the role of representing "those who cannot represent themselves." Lissette expressed this:

> It's creating awareness. It's generating support from people who can have a voice, who can vote, who can get out there and not be afraid of being deported because I know that that was an issue with some of the people that I know that were undocumented. They couldn't go because they were scared. That maybe the police would arrest them right then and there or that maybe they would get fired from their jobs. But because so many people went anyway and a lot of them were citizens, you know, it turned on a light bulb in all the politicians' minds and in the mass media. You know, this is an issue not just for immigrants. This is an issue for everyone.

As Lissette puts it, citizens, unlike the undocumented, could advocate without worry or fear, and due to the power of voting they could force politicians to take the cause more seriously. In this respect, some of these youths expressed a more sophisticated view of citizenship that involves political participation. She explained, "You also question what's going on, what your politicians are doing for you. You don't simply go about blindly. You cannot be a good citizen without participating." Such assertions cannot be disassociated from the close relationship between youth activists and local Puerto Rican politicians and community leaders.

In Chicago, Puerto Rican youth witnessed strong support for immigrant rights among the Puerto Rican community leadership (see Rodríguez-Muñiz, 2010). For example, the Puerto Rican Cultural Center (PRCC), an organization several of the respondents were affiliated to, has a long history of supporting immigrant rights and working closely with Mexican immigrant organizations such as Centro Sin Fronteras. The solidarity of the PRCC was part of a broader effort to construct a "Latino agenda". In practice, these relationships have been reciprocal, as Centro Sin Fronteras has actively supported "Puerto Rican" causes. Most recently, Sin Fronteras joined the PRCC and other Puerto Rican organizations to protest the military bombing of the Puerto Rican island of Vieques. These collaborations, which occur at an organizational level, are prime illustrations of how "institutional panethnicity" need not rely on explicitly "Latino" organizations.

Besides the grassroots involvement of groups such as the Puerto Rican Cultural Center, youth were quite aware that Puerto Rican elected officials, most notably Congressman Luis V. Gutiérrez, were deeply involved in immigration rights. Jessica describes this:

> We have someone who comes from our community, a representative of our community who is Puerto Rican. Luis Gutiérrez was able to be practically the spokesperson for the immigration issue that no other congressman or no other congress people want to touch. And here is a Puerto Rican who is sometimes rejected by Puerto Rican people for being able to stand for Mexicans. But this man was able to go to Vieques for the U.S. Navy to get out of there, but he is also this pioneer that no other person has ever done at that level, and challenges the United States on the status of the immigrants in this country, to bring that to the forefront to the capacity that no one else has. I'm proud to say that Luis Gutiérrez comes from this community, he used to be our alderman and he supports us.

In many respects, Gutiérrez best exemplified for them the example of a responsible Puerto Rican advocate. Like Gutiérrez, Puerto Rican youths confronted other Puerto Ricans who were less than supportive of or outright opposed to undocumented immigrants. However, they were convinced that they were correct in taking a stance in favor of immigration reform, and that doing so was essential to the movement. Stressing the electoral efficacy of citizenship, they suggested that citizens and voting power could tip the scales in favor of the immigrant rights movement. (This view, of course, is not unique to Puerto Rican youth activists.) A widespread sentiment after the first wave of mega-marches was best captured by the movement slogan, "Today we march, tomorrow we vote." Though some were not of voting age, these youth participants actively promoted this perspective and the role their community could play in it. As a result, they embraced their legal status, all the while maintaining their social critique of it. They maintained a critique of citizenship (that it does not provide universal protections and benefits— unequal kinds of citizenship). Our argument is that these activists understood and interpreted citizenship as a right that undocumented immigrants should have, but at the same time held a critical view of what citizenship affords racially subordinate groups, such the case of colonized Puerto Ricans.

For these Puerto Rican youths, the undocumented were not being heard, and indeed were silenced by the disregard of the broader U.S. society. Of course, the undocumented were never actually without voice, and throughout the course of mobilizations they began to assert themselves more openly and quite strongly as undocumented persons (see Pallares, 2010). Although perhaps they somewhat overstated their position, these Puerto Rican participants saw themselves as providing a much-needed voice. Though hypercritical of the limits of U.S. citizenship, they felt they were playing an integral role in the movement. They believed that citizens and noncitizens could achieve immigration reform by unifying and demonstrating their numerical size. At the same time, the presence of citizens provided the movement with some level of protection and a constituency that political elites could not easily dismiss.

Conclusion: Finding the points of unity

Chicago's immigrant rights mega-marches set into motion mass demonstrations throughout the country. Within this complicated and multifaceted movement, Puerto Rican youth were a vocal subset of all participants. As the only Latino/a group with automatic access to U.S. citizenship, Puerto Ricans enter the movement as something of an anomaly. Taking to the streets in the thousands, these Puerto Rican youths challenged the belief that Puerto Rican and Mexicans relations are singularly dominated by conflict and tension. In contrast, their actions and deeds reveal efforts to create points of unity.

In this chapter we took the presence of Puerto Ricans in the immigrant rights movement as an opportunity to reflect on the making of pan-Latino/a identities and political projects. Drawing on Rodríguez-Muñiz's (2010) "similar but not identical" framework, we explored how youth understood themselves, their peers, and their participation. Puerto Rican youth viewed themselves as integral to the success of the movement. As U.S. citizens, they assumed "responsibility" to stand in support of the undocumented, especially the Mexican undocumented. Their recognition and mobilization of "differences" in legal status did not stifle, but actually promoted their participation in the movement. At the same time, citizenship was articulated along with commonalities of history and experience. These similarities were expressed with references to experiences of racialization, migration narratives, social, linguistic, political and economic exclusion, and the existence of intimate social relationships and networks. Whereas much of the sociological literature on Latino/a panethnicity has concentrated on the "objective" differences and commonalities, we have explored the subjective construction and deployment of similarities. Puerto Rican youth actions of "solidarity" suggest the need to reformulate our treatment of citizenship. The brute fact of citizenship cannot be assumed to hinder the possibilities for Latino/a subgroups to consolidate shared identities and generate political alliances. Instead, we should direct our attention towards the meanings and investments in citizenship, and how these might serve, in particular contexts, as grounds on which expressions of Latinidad are built and negotiated.

The activism of these young Puerto Rican also signals the nascent development, among the second generation, of a pan-Latino/a diasporic community. As they repeatedly described, Puerto Ricans and Mexican youth coexist within the urban space of Chicago and confront many of the same challenges. While much of the research on diaspora has concentrated on the transnational flows and circulation of peoples and cultural forms, this chapter suggests that the historically conditioned and creatively imagined intersection of diaspora peoples can produce new diasporic realities and identities. As Hall (1990) insists, "Diaspora identities are those which are constantly producing and reproducing themselves anew, through transformation and difference" (p. 235). Negotiating pressures and desires for unity with recognitions and affirmations of difference, Puerto Rican youth were not merely participants in a social movement, but also participants in the forming of Chicago's Latino/a diaspora.

References

Anderson, B. (2006). *Imagined communities: Reflections on the origin and spread of nationalism* (new ed.). London: Verso.

Andolina, M. W., et al. (2003, April). Habits from the home, lessons from school: Influences on youth civic engagement. *PSOnline*, 275–280.

Atkins, R., & Hart, D. (2003). Neighborhoods, adults, and the development of civic identity in urban youth. *Applied Developmental Science, 7*(3), 156–164.

Camino, L., & Zeldin, S. (2002). From periphery to center: Pathways for youth civic engagement in day-to-day life of communities. *Applied Developmental Science, 6*(4), 213–220.

Dávila, A. (2004). *Barrio dreams: Puerto Ricans, Latinos, and the neoliberal city*. Berkeley: University of California Press.

De Genova, N. (2005). *Working the boundaries: Race, space, and "illegality" in Mexican Chicago*. Durham, NC: Duke University Press.

De Genova, N., & Ramos-Zayas, A. Y. (2003). *Latino crossings: Mexicans, Puerto Ricans, and the politics of race and citizenship*. New York: Routledge.

Flores, J. (2000). *From bomba to hip-hop: Puerto Rican culture and Latino identity*. New York: Columbia University Press.

Flores-González, N. (1999). The racialization of Latinos: The meaning of Latino identity for the second generation. *Latino Studies Journal, 10*, 3–31.

Flores-González, N. (2001). Paseo Boricua: Claiming a Puerto Rican space in Chicago. *Centro Journal, 13*, 7–23.

Flores-González, N. (2010). Immigrant, citizens, or both? The second generation in the immigrant rights marches. In A. Pallares & N. Flores-Gonzalez (Eds.), *¡Marcha!: Latino Chicago and the immigrant rights movement* (pp. 198–214). Chicago: University of Illinois Press.

Flores-González, N., Rodríguez, M., & Rodríguez-Muñiz, M. (2006). From hip-hop to humanization: Batey Urbano as a space for Latino youth culture and community action. In S. Ginwright, P. Noguera, & J. Cammarota (Eds.), *Beyond resistance! Youth activism and community change: New democratic possibilities for practice and policy for America's youth* (pp. 175–196). New York: Routledge.

Frank, R., Redstone Akresh, I., & Lu, B. (2010). Latino immigrants and the U.S. racial order: How and where do they fit in? *American Sociological Review, 75*, 378–401.

García, L., & Rúa, M. (2007). Processing Latinidad: Mapping Latino urban landscapes through Chicago ethnic festivals. *Latino Studies, 5*(3), 317–339.

García-Bedolla, L. (2005). *Fluid borders: Latino power, identity, and politics in Los Angeles*. Berkeley: University of California Press.

Ginwright, S., Cammarota, J., & Noguera, P. (2005). Youth, social justice, and communities: Toward a theory of urban youth policy. *Social Justice, 32*(3), 24–40.

Golash-Boza, T. (2006). Dropping the hyphen? Becoming Latino(a)-American through racialized assimilation. *Social Forces, 85*, 27–55.

González, J. (2000). *Harvest of Empire: A history of Latinos in America*. New York: Penguin Putnam.

Hall, S. (1990). Cultural identity and diaspora. In J. Rutherford (Ed.), *Identity: Community, culture, difference* (pp. 222–237). London: Lawrence and Wishart.

Hart, D., & Atkins, R. (2002). Civic competence in urban youth. *Applied Developmental Science, 6*(4), 227–236.

Itzigsohn, J. (2004). The formation of Latino and Latina panethnic identities. In N. Foner & G. M. Fredrickson (Eds.), *Not just Black and White: Historical and contemporary perspectives on immigration, race, and ethnicity in the United States* (pp. 197–216). New York: Russell Sage Foundation.

Itzigsohn, J. (2009). *Encountering American faultlines: Race, class, and the Dominican experience in Providence.* New York: Russell Sage Foundation.

Itzigsohn, J., & Dore-Cabral, C. (2000). Competing identities? Race, ethnicity and panethnicity among Dominicans. *Sociological Forum, 15,* 225–447.

Lao-Montes, A. (2001). Niuyol: Urban regime, Latino social movements, ideologies of Latinidad. In A. Lao-Montes & A. Dávila (Eds.), *Mambo montage: The latinization of New York* (pp. 119–157). New York: Columbia University Press.

Lopez, M. (2003, March). *Electoral engagement among Latino youth.* The Center for Information and Research on Civic Learning & Engagement (CIRLE). Retrieved from http://www.civicyouth.org/PopUps/FactSheets/FS_Electoral_Eng_Latino_Youth.pdf

Lugo-Lugo, C. R. (2008). "So you are a mestiza": Exploring the consequences of ethnic and racial clumping in the US academy. *Ethnic and Racial Studies, 31*(3), 611–638.

Oboler, S. (1995). *Ethnic labels, Latino lives: Identity and the politics of (re)presentation in the United States.* Minneapolis: University of Minnesota Press.

Okamura, J. Y. (1981). Situational ethnicity. *Ethnic and Racial Studies, 4.* 452–465.

Oliva, S. (2010a). Permission to march?: High school youth participation in the immigrant rights movement. In A. Pallares & N. Flores-González (Eds.), *¡Marcha!: Latino Chicago and the immigrant rights movement* (pp. 163–176). Chicago: University of Illinois Press.

Oliva, S. (2010b). *What's race got to do with it? The school politics of Black and Latino racial tensions.* (Unpublished Ph.D. dissertation). University of Illinois at Chicago.

Padilla, E. (1947). *Puerto Rican immigrants in New York and Chicago: A study in comparative assimilation.* (Master's thesis). University of Chicago.

Padilla, F. M. (1985). *Latino ethnic consciousness.* Notre Dame, IN: University of Notre Dame.

Pallares, A. (2005). Ecuadorian immigrants and symbolic nationalism in Chicago. *Latino Studies Journal, 3*(3), 347–371.

Pallares, A. (2010). Representing "La Familia": Family separation and immigrant activism. In A. Pallares & N. Flores-González (Eds.), *¡Marcha!: Latino/a Chicago and the immigrant rights movement* (pp. 215–236). Chicago: University of Illinois Press.

Pallares, A., & Flores-González, N. (2010). *¡Marcha!: Latino Chicago and the immigrant rights movement.* Chicago: University of Illinois Press.

Pérez, G. (2003). "Puertorriqueñas rencorosas y Mejicanas sufridas": Gendered ethnic identity formation in Chicago's Latino communities. *Journal of Latin American Anthropology, 8,* 96–125.

Polletta, F., & Jasper, J. M. (2001). Collective identity and social movements. *Annual Review of Sociology, 27*, 283–305.

Ramos-Zayas, A. Y. (2003). *National performances: The politics of class, race, and space in Puerto Rican Chicago.* Chicago: University of Chicago Press.

Ricourt, M., & Danta, R. (2003). *Hispanas de Queens: Latino panethnicity in a New York City neighborhood.* Ithaca, NY: Cornell University Press.

Rinaldo, R. (2002). Space of resistance: The Puerto Rican Cultural Center and Humboldt Park. *Cultural Critique, 50*, 135–174.

Rodríguez-Muñiz, M. (2010). Grappling with Latinidad: Puerto Rican activism in Chicago's immigrant rights movement. In A. Pallares & N. Flores-González (Eds.), *¡Marcha!: Latino Chicago and the immigrant rights movement* (pp. 237–258). Chicago: University of Illinois Press.

Rodríguez, V. M. (1999). Boricuas, African Americans, and Chicanos in the "Far West": Notes on the Puerto Rican independence movement in California, 1960s–1980s. In R. D. Torres & G. Katsiaficas (Eds.), *Latino social movements: Historical and theoretical perspectives* (pp. 79–109). New York: Routledge.

Rúa, M. (2001). Colao subjectivities: PortoMex and MexiRican perspectives on language and identity. *Centro Journal, 13*, 117–133.

Sherrod, L. (2003, April). Promoting the development of citizenship in diverse youth. *PSOnline*, 287–292.

Taylor, V., & Whittier, N. E. (1992). Collective identity in social movement communities: Lesbian feminist mobilization. In A. D. Morris & C. McClurg Mueller (Eds.), *Frontiers in social movement theory* (pp. 104–129). New Haven, CT: Yale University Press.

Yancey, W. L., Ericksen, E. P., & Juliani, R. N. (1976). Emergent ethnicity: A review and reformulation. *American Sociological Review, 41*, 391–403.

Youniss, J., et al. (2002). Youth civic engagement in the twenty-first century. *Journal of Research on Adolescence, 12*(1), 121–148.

Zukin, C., Keeter, S., Andolina, S., & Jenkins, K. (2006). *A new engagement? Political participation, civic life, and the changing American citizen.* New York: Oxford University Press.

Learning ethnolinguistic borders: Language and diaspora in the socialization of U.S. Latinas/os

JONATHAN ROSA

AmeRícan,   defining myself my own way any way many
            ways, Am e Rícan, with the big R and the
            accent on the í!

...

AmeRícan,   speaking new words in spanglish tenements,
            fast tongue moving street corner "que
            corta" talk being invented at the insistence
            of a smile!

(Tato Laviera, from "AmeRícan")

The rapid rise of the U.S. Latina/o population, now the nation's largest demographic minority group, has heightened concerns about the future of American identity and brought increased attention to the management of ethnolinguistic diversity. As institutions charged with the interrelated tasks of facilitating language socialization and reproducing the nation's identity, schools become central sites in which to track processes of ethnolinguistic identity formation. The educational experiences of U.S. Latinas/os, whose identities are constructed in close relation to ideas about linguistic practices (Zentella, 2009), involve learning the ways that minute features of language are positioned as powerful emblems of national affiliation.

This chapter explores the school-based creation of Latina/o ethnolinguistic identities by drawing on the theoretical lens of *language ideologies*. Defined broadly, language ideologies are "models that link types of linguistic forms with the types of people who stereotypically use them" (Wortham, 2008, p. 43). Latina/o students are often faced with language ideologies that stigmatize their English *and* Spanish linguistic practices, and promote their assimilation to English monolingualism. This stigmatization positions Latinas/ os on the margins of the U.S., regardless of whether they are born and raised within its borders. Thus, language, education, and U.S. Latinas/os become linked as part of an ideological bundle that is articulated in generic models of assimilation. These models define assimilation as a binary process through which (im)migrants and their descendents come to identify as "American" by dis-identifying with some previous national identity. "Americanness" is generally equated with a presumed English-speaking U.S. monoculture, and institutions of public education are understood as primary settings in which assimilation to "Americanness" takes place. Furthermore, assimilation is frequently conceptualized as an individual choice that reflects one's desire to be or not to be American, and language use becomes framed as a clear-cut cultural practice by which to gauge the success of any assimilationist project. Without ever explicitly stating it, these models of assimilation are ultimately anchored in anxieties about a distinct, but related process: *diasporization*.

In this chapter, I reconsider the process of assimilation by locating its directionality vis-à-vis diasporization. I analyze how language ideologies and linguistic practices mediate the creation of diasporic Latina/o identities in New Northwest High School (henceforth NNHS), a highly segregated Chicago public high school whose student body is more than 90% Puerto Rican and Mexican. In this setting, boundaries of Puerto Rican and Mexican difference are alternately emphasized and erased as students engage with ethnolinguistic emblems to negotiate modes of diasporic identification. I show how students' language ideologies and practices unsettle taken-for-granted notions about the nature of ethnolinguistic identities. I argue that the Spanish language is far from a ready-made vehicle for the production of Latina/o diasporic unity *and* that the English language is far from a straightforward symbol of assimilation to Americanness. As one example of the ways that NNHS students reconfigure the symbolic value of English and Spanish forms, I point to a set of linguistic practices that I call *Inverted Spanglish*. By denaturalizing "Spanish" and "English" as distinct and monolithic linguistic categories, we can come to see the ways that specific English and Spanish forms become linked to the creation of diasporic Latina/o identities. This analysis of the negotiation of ethnolinguistic borders demonstrates how the concept of diasporization provides a productive tool for rethinking assimilation.

Language ideologies, assimilation, and diasporization

As powerful institutions of language standardization and socialization, schools are key contexts in which to analyze the ways that language ideologies participate in the creation of Latina/o ethnolinguistic identities. Developed by linguistic anthropologists (Kroskrity, 2000; Schieffelin, Woolard, & Kroskrity, 1998; Silverstein, 1979), the language ideologies framework has frequently been employed and innovated by linguistic anthropologists of education (Wortham & Rymes, 2003). This is because "schools are important sites for establishing associations between 'educated' and 'uneducated,' 'sophisticated' and 'unsophisticated,' 'official' and 'vernacular' language use and types of students" (Wortham, 2008, p. 43).

The language ideologies framework has also been effectively incorporated into language socialization research (Garrett & Baquedano-López, 2002; González, 2005). Language ideologies allow us to understand the hegemony of the English language in the U.S., the educational manifestation of which involves language policies that promote socialization to English monolingualism (García & Torres-Guevara, 2010). This hegemony stems from long-standing ideologies of "one nation–one language," which are tied to the emergence of modern nation-states. By reframing these perspectives as *language ideologies*, we can come to see how the construction of monolingualism as a national norm simultaneously obscures the widespread empirical reality of multilingualism throughout the world, *and* serves to secure positions of power for particular sectors of a given society by requiring the assimilation of ethnolinguistic diversity. Language ideologies also make it possible to identify the profound erasures through which Latina/o students' bilingual linguistic practices are understood as problems to be overcome rather than resources to be developed. Silences around the limitations of normative English monolingualism frame language as a liability for students whose linguistic repertoires could be viewed as more expansive than those of many of the educators, administrators, and policy makers who serve them. The lack of irony in this situation is informed by language ideologies that play a central role in reproducing forms of stigmatization and marginalization that coincide with efforts to assimilate U.S. Latinas/os.

Theories of assimilation can be critically refined when viewed through the lenses of language ideologies and linguistic practices. In his analysis of language and identity among second-generation U.S. Dominican high school students, Bailey (2007) suggests that linguistic practices reveal the shortcomings of both "straight-line" and "segmented" theories of assimilation.[1] Briefly, straight-line theory suggests that assimilation to Americanness and upward socioeconomic mobility occur naturally over time. Segmented theory suggests three possible trajectories: (1) upward socioeconomic mobility and assimilation to Americanness; (2) socioeconomic marginalization similar to other U.S. minority groups; and (3) maintenance of cultural values and some socioeconomic stability within a strong immigrant community. For Bailey, both straight-line and segmented theories "rely on relatively monolithic, idealized identities as reference points for immigrant acculturation" (2007, p. 178). Zentella (2005) argues that this essentializing tendency is a characteristic "pitfall" associated with research on language and identity development. In contrast, Bailey shows how the students in his study engage in linguistic code-switching between English and Spanish, and how they draw on ideologies of language, race, and ethnicity to identify themselves and others in differing ways depending on the context. Bailey provides multiple examples of individuals who alternately identify as "Dominican," "Spanish," "Hispanic," "American," "Black," and "White," among other categories. These shifting identifications reveal the inability of straight-line and segmented theories to capture the nonlinear trajectories of assimilation that are characteristic of (im)migrant experiences.

In popular and scholarly discourse, English language usage is consistently equated with assimilation to Americanness. Despite the fact that Latinas/os "are undergoing [Spanish] language loss similar to, and even exceeding, that of other groups in U.S. history" (Zentella, 2009, pp. 331–332), their purported unwillingness to learn English is often cited as evidence of their "failure" to assimilate (Huntington, 2004). These perspectives depend on the rigid distinction between national identities (i.e., American and non-American), as well as the rigid distinction between linguistic identities (i.e., English-speaker and Spanish-speaker). The language ideologies that inform these views problematically erase widespread bilingualism (i.e., the millions of people in the United States for whom "English-speaker" and "Spanish-speaker" are not mutually exclusive), flatten out infinite linguistic heterogeneity by constructing English and Spanish as monolithic categories, and equate English with Americanness and Spanish with non-Americanness.

Bailey complicates this relationship between language and assimilation by suggesting that an "urban, non-White language style can even serve as a unifying language for Hispanics who speak identical, urban forms of English, but who speak different regional varieties of Spanish, e.g., Guatemalan, Colombian, or Dominican Spanish, based on their families' origins" (Bailey, 2002, p. 12). While Bailey's otherwise deft treatment of code-switching is absent in this formulation, he rightfully points out the possibility for English language practices to mediate shared identification among U.S. Latinas/os across national subgroups. The Spanish language does not play a strictly unifying role for U.S. Latinas/os, because differences among varieties of Spanish (e.g., Mexican Spanish, Puerto Rican Spanish, etc.) are often the clearest ways to distinguish between Latina/o national subgroups. In contrast to prevailing language ideologies, particular kinds of U.S.-based English language use can be constructed as non-American at the same time that particular kinds of U.S.-based Spanish language use can be constructed as American. Thus, Latina/o ethnolinguistic identities take shape as distinctly U.S.-based phenomena *and* as diasporic categories that potentially redefine "Americanness" by linking the U.S. to Latin America in newfound ways.

Approaches to understanding national identities in theories of assimilation often involve the implicit invocation of ideas about diasporization. If assimilation encompasses forms of immigrant acculturation, then diasporization directs attention to the creation and maintenance of linkages (e.g., cultural, ideological, political, economic, etc.) across national divides (Lukose, 2007). While diaspora and diasporization make it possible to consider the multidimensional nature of ethnoracial identities, there is the potential for these concepts to be just as rigid as theories of assimilation. Building from the insights of Appadurai (1996) and Hall (1990), Flores (2009) explains that "[i]n much thinking about diaspora, undue emphasis tends to be placed...either on continuity and tradition or on change and disjuncture" (2009, p. 17). In order to avoid these tendencies, Flores suggests "thinking diaspora from below":

> The grassroots, vernacular, "from below" approach helps to point up the many diaspora experiences that diverge from those of the relatively privileged, entrepreneurial or professional transnational connections that have tended to carry the greatest appeal in scholarly and journalistic coverage. That approach, guided by a concern for subaltern and everyday life struggles of poor and disenfranchised people, also allows for special insights into ongoing issues of racial identity and gender inequalities that are so often ignored or minimized in the grand narratives of transnational hegemony. (2009, p. 25)

The analysis of language ideologies and linguistic practices among urban Latina/o youth serves as a prime opportunity for "thinking diaspora from below." By not taking for granted the existence and/or nature of ethnolinguistic categories such as "Puerto Rican," "Mexican," and "Latina/o," it becomes possible to track the dynamic processes through which diasporic identities are constructed, enacted, and transformed.

New Northwest High School and Latina/o Chicago

NNHS was opened in 2004 to offset overcrowding at a nearby Chicago public high school. As an open-enrollment, "neighborhood" high school, NNHS draws its students from several communities in close proximity to it. Based on the highly segregated demographics of these communities, more than 90% of NNHS's roughly 1,000 students are Latina/o.[2] The majority of these students are Puerto Rican and Mexican. These demographics led me to select NNHS as a field site in which to analyze the relationship between language, race, and ethnicity among Puerto Ricans and Mexicans in Chicago. In preliminary fieldwork that I conducted in schools and communities throughout Chicago, I was struck by the frequency of discourses surrounding the relationships between Puerto Ricans and Mexicans. Based on these discourses, it became clear that Chicago is an important context in which to investigate the everyday construction of Latina/o ethnolinguistic identities.

Chicago is the only U.S. city in which Puerto Ricans and Mexicans, the two largest U.S. Latina/o national subgroups (Bureau of the Census, 2011),[3] have been building their lives alongside one another in large numbers since the mid-20th century. Chicago contains the fourth largest Mexican population of any U.S. city,[4] the fourth largest mainland U.S. Puerto Rican population,[5] and the fifth largest U.S. Latina/o population (Bureau of the Census, 2011).[6] NNHS students make sense of Puerto Ricanness and Mexicanness in relation to long-standing histories of face-to-face, frequently intimate interactions across generations that render their differences all the more tangible and, oftentimes, negligible. They are classmates, boyfriends, girlfriends, teammates, neighbors, and family members. There are many students with one Puerto Rican and one Mexican parent, a situation that has led to the creation of "MexiRican" and "PortoMex" as identifiable categories (Potowski & Matts, 2008; Rúa, 2001).[7] One such student, Victor (Mex[mother], PR[father], Gen. 3, Gr. 11),[8] said that he identifies primarily as Latino because he does not "want to leave anyone out." Rivera-Servera (2012) characterizes these dynamic intra-Latina/o relationships as forms of "frictive intimacy."

I conducted ethnographic and sociolinguistic fieldwork in NNHS and its surrounding communities between 2007 and 2010. This fieldwork consisted of observations and interviews with students in grades 9–12, school employees (including administrators, teachers, and support staff), and community members. During school hours, I worked as a tutor in multiple classrooms. Outside of school, I tutored students in their homes, helped them to complete school projects and apply for jobs, accompanied them to restaurants and barbershops, communicated with them over the phone and via cellular text messages, and brought them to the college classes that I was teaching. I attended various extracurricular events such as soccer games, pep rallies, local school council[9] meetings (I was elected to the local school council as a community representative), and the prom. I also participated in local community organizing efforts at the Puerto Rican Cultural Center, which is located nearby NNHS.

Throughout the fieldwork period, I lived four blocks away from the school. This allowed me to walk to and from the school with students each day, and to accompany them to local restaurants and stores. These interactions with students outside of school played a crucial role in helping me to understand what was going on inside NNHS. I was able to notice the Mexican and Puerto Rican flags juxtaposed in storefronts, apartment windows, and cars; I also encountered the Mexican and Puerto Rican food items stacked side by side on the shelves at the Walgreens and Cermak Produce stores near the school. These experiences clearly demonstrated that Puerto Rican–Mexican displays and interactions are conventional components of everyday life on the Near Northwest side of Chicago.

While my study focused on 1.5-, second-, and third-generation Puerto Ricans and Mexicans with "native" or "near-native" English language skills, I used different varieties (e.g., Puerto Rican and Mexican) and registers (e.g., standard and nonstandard) of English *and* Spanish to navigate a bilingual cultural context in which students and school employees make use of expansive linguistic repertoires consisting of a range of English and Spanish language proficiencies. My Spanish language skills also allowed me to interact with first-generation students classified as English language learners. Students regularly informed me that my Spanish language practices, physical features, and personal style allowed them to rightly identify me as Puerto Rican. As a result, I alternately occupied insider and outsider roles while conducting this fieldwork. The remainder of this chapter explores the politics and practices of ethnolinguistic recognition (Silverstein, 2003).

Language ideologies and competing constructions of Latina/o ethnolinguistic identities

Puerto Rican and Mexican students' language use within NNHS involves socialization to at least three ethnolinguistic categories: "Puerto Rican," "Mexican," and "Latina/o." These ethnolinguistic categories redefine English and Spanish language practices by anchoring them in relation to processes of diasporization. As a public school in a national context in which English language hegemony prevails and monolingualism is framed as the norm, NNHS is charged with the job of teaching students what comes to be viewed as the language that "ideally express[es] the spirit of a nation and the territory it occupies" (Gal, 2006, p. 163). National, state, and municipal educational language policies, as well as various English-only movements, reflect language ideologies that frame the U.S. as a nation in which English is and should be the dominant language (Crawford, 2007; Santa Ana, 2004; Woolard, 1989). Latina/o NNHS students are faced with English-language hegemony that ultimately stigmatizes their English *and* Spanish language practices. These stigmatizations involve "cultures of standard" (Silverstein, 1996) within the school that include students' and school employees' language ideologies about the value associated with varieties of English and Spanish.

While New Northwest High School's Puerto Rican and Mexican students possess varying levels of proficiency in Spanish and English, Spanish is stereo-typed as the primordial Latina/o tongue. This is because one of the primary ways Latinas/os come to be imagined as a coherent ethnolinguistic group is through what linguistic anthropologists describe as a Herderian language ide-ology of one language–one people (Bauman & Briggs, 2003; Irvine, 2006). However, many analysts have noted that the Spanish language, if even spoken at all, oftentimes provides grounds for the recognition of intra-Latina/o dif-ference, not similarity (De Genova & Ramos-Zayas, 2003; Ghosh Johnson, 2005; Mendoza-Denton, 2008; Zentella, 2007). Spanish is by no means an unequivocal unifying force for Latinas/os because many Latinas/os possess limited Spanish language proficiency, some Latinas/os who are "native" and/ or "proficient" Spanish speakers prefer not to speak Spanish due to its stig-matization in the U.S., and varieties of Spanish are frequently the most ready-made signs of intra-Latina/o difference. Importantly, this means that neither Spanish *nor* English is a ready-made vehicle for the construction of Latina/o ethnolinguistic identities. In the sections that follow, I provide evidence for this point by analyzing: (1) non-Latina/o perspectives on Latina/o ethno-linguistic identities within NNHS; (2) Latina/o constructions of "Spanish" within NNHS; (3) Latina/o constructions of "English" within NNHS; and (4) Latina/o constructions of "Spanglish" within NNHS.

Out-group perspectives on Latina/o ethnolinguistic identities

Many non-Latina/o students and employees were unfamiliar with intra-Latina/ o distinctions prior to their exposure to NNHS. From these perspectives, Puerto Rican–Mexican difference is often misinterpreted as strife, or erased altogether. Ms. Ginsberg, a popular young White teacher, said she thinks that the distinction between NNHS's Puerto Rican and Mexican students is one of the most striking things about the school. Ms. Jackson, the school's well-liked librarian and one of the few African American employees, explained that she never would have thought that there is a "big difference" between Mexicans and Puerto Ricans before she started working at NNHS. Sierra, an African American student who graduated from NNHS in 2008 and came back to volunteer in the library with Ms. Jackson, alternated between group-ing Puerto Rican and Mexican students together as "Hispanic," and drawing clear lines of distinction between them:

The best part about this school would be the population because it's a Hispanic school and they're really funny, but it's also lonely because I was the only Black person in a lot of my classes. I felt like sometimes they was being bogus because they would sit in their own little groups and be talking Spanish and don't nobody know what they're talking about...but the main groups of students in this school is the Mexicans and the Puerto Ricans. That's one big divide. Like I used to mistakenly call a Mexican a Puerto Rican and they would get mad like I'm supposed to know the difference. I thought they was just all Hispanic, but they got on me the whole time I was going here about mistaking the two. And they all look the same to me! That's just like an Asian person coming up to you and you call them Chinese, and they Vietnamese and they get mad, like how am I supposed to know what's the difference between ya'll? Ya'll all look alike, but they, they be tripping [getting mad for no reason]...ya'll all do look alike, I'm sorry. I don't know the difference between Mexicans and Puerto Ricans, other than what they told me.

Sierra enjoyed attending a "Hispanic"[10] school because Hispanics—as a group—are "really funny." She also felt alienated at times because she was often the only African American student in her classes. For Sierra, attending NNHS involved learning the distinctions between Mexicans and Puerto Ricans, which she described as a "big divide." In Sierra's view, "Hispanic" is a racialized panethnic category that is similar to "Asian." From her perspective, the difference between Mexicans and Puerto Ricans is analogous to that between Chinese and Vietnamese people; essentially, Hispanics, like Asians, all look alike. Still, Sierra learned that for Mexican and Puerto Rican students, it is crucial to be able to recognize their differences. Importantly, Sierra comfortably alternates between using the umbrella category "Hispanic" and emphasizing differences between Latina/o national subgroups.

Despite her nuanced perspective, Sierra takes "Spanish" for granted as a unifying characteristic among Latinas/os. Puerto Rican and Mexican students alike shared humorous stories about African American students and White teachers who think that everything "Hispanics" do is "just Spanish." These ideas about "Spanishness" became a point of contention at NNHS's 2009 prom. On prom night, there were two problems concerning the music. The first was that Dr. Baez, the school principal, did not appreciate the sexually suggestive manner in which students were dancing with one another to the hip-hop and juke[11] songs. Dr. Baez marched up to the DJ, reminded him that she was writing his check, and told him that if he wanted to get paid at the end of the night he better respond to her requests before those of the students.

The DJ promptly switched genres and began playing merengüe, salsa, bachata, reggaeton, cumbia, and durangüense. This led to the second problem. Tasha, an African American senior who was one of three girls in the

running for prom queen, became visibly upset by the abrupt musical transition. She complained to the DJ and then sat down at a table near the dance
floor with a small group of African American students. Tasha pointed out
that "they" (i.e., the Latina/o students) were dancing just as suggestively to
the "Spanish music" as everyone had been dancing to the hip-hop and juke
music. As the DJ shifted between genres, however, Puerto Rican and Mexican
students went back and forth between their tables and the dance floor after almost every song. From Tasha's perspective, cumbia, reggaeton, salsa,
merengüe, bachata, and durangüense are all part of a single genre: "Spanish
music." Meanwhile, Mexican students complained that the DJ was playing
too much salsa and Puerto Rican students complained that he was playing
too much cumbia.[12]

    Tasha's out-group perspective, which channels broader cultural presump-
tions about Latina/o homogeneity, rests on intuitions about a cultural quality
of "Spanishness" that is associated with music, food, and, most importantly,
language. For Tasha, these genres of music can be lumped together as "Spanish." Tasha views the Spanish language as a homogeneous organizing concept.
NNHS's Latina/o students do not view "Spanishness" in this way. From their
perspectives, there are distinct varieties of "Spanish" music (e.g., cumbia, reggaeton, etc.) and linguistic practices (e.g. "Mexican," "Puerto Rican," etc.).
Despite in-group recognitions of intra-Spanish heterogeneity, the concept of
"Spanishness" is in many ways the most powerful emblem of Latina/o ethnolinguistic identities. This highlights the central role that language ideologies
play in processes of Latina/o diasporization.

Constructing and differentiating "Spanish"

Contrary to their non-Latina/o counterparts, for Latina/o NNHS students
the "Spanish" language is not simply a unified concept. Latina/o students in-
vest great energy in distinguishing between varieties of Spanish. For example,
David (PR, Gen. 3, Gr. 12) stated that Puerto Rican Spanish sounds "cool, like
salsa [music]," whereas Mexican Spanish sounds "lame, like banda [music]."[13]
Similarly, Victor (Mex[mother]/PR[father], Gen. 3, Gr. 11), the "MexiRican"
student described above, claimed that Puerto Rican Spanish is better than
Mexican Spanish because Puerto Rican Spanish is "what's up" (i.e., cool), but
Mexican Spanish is more correct. When I prompted him to provide examples
of Mexican and Puerto Rican Spanish, he told me that whereas Mexicans would
say *"¿Cómo ustedes están?"* (How are you all doing?),[14] Puerto Ricans would
say, *"¿Cómo uhtede ehtán?"* (How are you all doing?).[15] In fact, Victor's place-
ment of the pronoun *ustedes* before the verb *están* characterizes both examples

as Puerto Rican Spanish usages. Moreover, the /s/ aspiration/deletion that Victor sought to highlight in his Puerto Rican impression was also somewhat present in his Mexican impression. He went on to explain:

> Hands on down, man, Puerto Ricans got that shit in the bag.... They can knock out any Spanish thing, bro...like all these other languages, they ain't got nothing on Puerto Ricans. It sounds way better...because like the way it flows.... Like you be hearing some reggaeton music and you hear the way they got flow? Like that.

Victor associates Puerto Rican Spanish with reggaeton, a genre of music with Spanish-language lyrics, Latin American/Caribbean/hip-hop roots, and predominantly Puerto Rican artists. His claims about Puerto Rican Spanish's "flow," a common term used to characterize one's lyrical prowess in hip-hop music (Alim, 2006), are tied to the increasing popularity of reggaeton among U.S. Latinas/os during the first decade of the 21st century (Rivera et al., 2009).[16]

In contrast, Mayra (Mex, Gen. 1.5, Gr. 11), who was born in Mexico City and came to the U.S. with her parents and younger brother at the age of 8, said that one of the main differences between Mexicans and Puerto Ricans is "the language." She provided examples such as the Mexican and Puerto Rican Spanish words for "sidewalk," *banqueta* and *concreto*, respectively.[17] She said that she used to think that the best Spanish is spoken in Spain, but that changed when she heard that the best Spanish is actually spoken in Mexico. She also explained that she definitely would not go to Puerto Rico to hear good Spanish because Puerto Ricans "don't say the words right...they miss some words...like sometimes they lose the 'r,' sometimes they lose the 's,' and it's really weird...and with Mexicans...they know how to talk!" Mayra explicitly articulates the stereotype that Puerto Rican Spanish is nonstandard, especially as compared to Mexican Spanish.

Students continually evaluated one another's speech, tracking the circulation of linguistic forms associated with Puerto Ricanness and Mexicanness. Yesi (PR, Gen. 1.5, Gr. 12) was told by her Puerto Rican friends that her Spanish is slow and that she has a Mexican accent. They questioned whether Yesi, a Puerto Rican, was trying to sound "smart" in Spanish. These students invoked the idea that Mexican Spanish is more proper. Carlos (Mex, Gen. 2, Gr. 9), a self-described bilingual student, explained to me that every Latina/o national subgroup has its own variety of Spanish. He pointed to my stereotypical Puerto Rican pronunciation of /r/ as /l/ in the word *verdad* (really) as an example of how Puerto Rican and Mexican Spanish differ. Carlos went on to say that Mexican Spanish is probably a little bit better than Puerto Rican Spanish because it is more correct. He based this claim about "correctness" on the predominant use of Mexican Spanish in NNHS's Spanish language classes and in Spanish-language television and radio programming. He told me that he mostly listens to Spanish-language Mexican music, such as cumbia and durangüense, but also some reggaeton. On the other hand, he joked with me about the fact that he had only recently learned from friends in NNHS that words such as *chévere* (cool/awesome) and *bochinche* (gossip) are in fact Puerto Rican, *not* Mexican Spanish terms.[18] Thus, Mexican students draw on linguistic forms that are understood to be Puerto Rican and vice versa.

In these examples, students recognize Mexican Spanish as correct (yet "lame") and Puerto Rican Spanish as "cool" (yet incorrect); note that these stereotypes are mirror images of views associated with Standard American English (which is racialized as "White" and seen as uncool, yet correct) and African American English (which is racialized as "Black" and seen as cool, yet incorrect). This mirroring is also evident in the stereotype that Puerto Ricans can effectively produce Puerto Rican *and* Mexican Spanish forms, whereas Mexicans are understood to be incapable of producing Puerto Rican forms; this is similar to the notion that African Americans often switch between African American English and Standard American English, as opposed to Whites who are understood to be incapable of effectively producing African American English forms. These familiar stereotypes structure debates between Puerto Ricans and Mexicans (and members of other Latina/o subgroups) about what practices and characteristics—linguistic and otherwise—constitute an ideal U.S.-based diasporic Latina/o identity. In these debates, it becomes clear that "Spanish" is anything but a singular concept that unifies a Latina/o diaspora in straightforward ways, and that distinctions between varieties of Spanish are continually renegotiated.

Constructing and differentiating "English"

At the same time that Spanish plays a central ideological role in constructing Latina/o ethnolinguistic identities, English language hegemony in the U.S. relies heavily on schools as flagship institutions for language standardization. This positions English both as a public educational norm and as the surest linguistic vehicle for the acquisition of administratively valued cultural capital. While NNHS students and employees speak different varieties of Spanish and English, Standard English is the normative language variety for official business. Most school-wide announcements are made in English, and all staff meetings are conducted in English. Meanwhile, the Spanish-dominant NNHS employees occupy subordinate hierarchical positions as security guards, custodians, and lunchroom workers. In this sense, the Spanish language is the object of indirect stigmatization.

Students clearly receive and report these ideas about English language hegemony. When I asked David (PR, Gen. 3, Gr. 12) whether he has an accent, he responded, "No!...I think I might though." He explained that while playing an Internet-based video game that allows players to hear one another's voices through a microphone, one of his virtual opponents told him to "[S]hut the fuck up, you Mexican!" David went on to describe the confusion that this attack prompted: "Whoa! He came real hard at me. Why you say I'm Mexican? I was just talking English and they come and say I'm Mexican out of nowhere...so yeah, I think I might [have an accent], but I don't know." To be clear, David neither wants to possess an accent nor does he want to be misidentified as Mexican. From his perspective, it does not make sense that one could "sound Mexican" in English; Mexicanness sounds like Spanish.

David's ideas about Spanish and English reflect not only monolingual ideologies that associate "one people" with "one language," but also "monoglot" (Silverstein, 1996) ideologies that erase the infinite heterogeneity within a given language and position a particular variety as the only acceptable norm. David was surprised to learn that he might possess an accent because he understood himself to be speaking unmarked English. Importantly, his ideas demonstrate how monoglot ideologies simultaneously figurate more than one language. The idea that he might "sound like a Mexican" led David to emphasize that he "was just talking English," thus positioning Mexicanness outside of the English language. In this case, monoglot ideologies position Mexican Spanish as "the" Spanish.

However, Mayra (Mex, Gen. 1.5, Gr. 11), who began learning English when she arrived in the U.S. at the age of 8, described feeling self-conscious about having a "Mexican" accent when speaking English. This notion of accent was a common concern among NNHS students. The "accented" English of Mr. Burgos, a popular Dominican math teacher, was a regular topic of discussion and a model for parodic performances. At times students attempted to mimic him directly, like when he told them, "you need your book," pronouncing the /y/ in "you" and "your" similar to the beginning of the English words "June" and "journal," respectively. In other cases, they repeated his speech with exaggerated Spanish pronunciations. For example, when Mr. Burgos told them that they must use the order of operations and work from "left to right always" to solve arithmetic problems, students impersonated him by trilling the /r/ in the word "right" even though he uttered the word using its conventional English pronunciation.

Not surprisingly, this policing of "accented" English creates a divide between NNHS students designated as English language learners and "mainstream" students. While English-dominant students could learn a lot from

English language learners and vice versa, few students move across this divide. In order to do so, English language learners would have to risk bringing attention to their "accented" English (thereby becoming potential fodder for mockery) and English-dominant students would have to risk bringing attention to their limited Spanish proficiency (thereby calling into question their ethnolinguistic authenticity). However, in the context of English language hegemony, English language learners are ultimately at a great disadvantage in these negotiations.

"Unaccented" English is celebrated at the same time that it stigmatizes *all* Latinas/os. David and Mayra, the students described above, have very different experiences learning the English language. Whereas David was born in Chicago and identifies as English-dominant, Mayra was born in Mexico and identifies as Spanish-dominant. Yet, they both face questions about their "accented" English because in the U.S. they are similarly racialized as "Latina/o." Ideas about race inform perceptions of accents; this corroborates the notion that "race has been remapped from biology onto language" (Zentella, 2007, p. 26; see also Urciuoli, 1998, 2001). As opposed to unifying Latinas/os, the English language is differentiated based on shifting, racialized assessments of "accent."

Rethinking Spanglish

The various students discussed throughout this chapter are similar in that they value the ability to speak "unaccented" English at the same time that they are invested in the significance of Mexican and Puerto Rican varieties of Spanish. These sociolinguistic commitments present Puerto Rican and Mexican students with a paradoxical task: they must signal their Latina/o identities by always sounding like they could speak Spanish *in* English, while carefully preventing too much Spanish from seeping into their English. In order to manage these competing attachments, students draw on voicing practices that simultaneously signal their intimate knowledge of Spanish and their ability to speak "unaccented" English. Frequently, this involves the incorporation of Spanish words and phrases into English discourse. When I asked Victor (Mex-[mother]/PR[father], Gen. 3, Gr. 11), one of the students quoted above, to describe his mother's Spanish, he said that she speaks "[r]egular Spanish, like she just learned it from *Inglés sin Barreras*" ("English without barriers"). Here, Victor is referencing an English language learning course, *"Inglés sin Barreras,"* which is widely advertised on Spanish-language television and radio. At first glance, this might appear to be an unremarkable example of code-switching from English to Spanish. However, Victor used his conventional English phonology (i.e., pronunciation) throughout his entire response to this question, even when pronouncing the words *Inglés sin Barreras*. This means that his pronunciation of the word *barreras* ("barriers") sounded like the "bu-" at the beginning of the English word "but," followed by the English words "rare" and "us." But his pronunciation of the word "reggaeton" in the interview quotation above included a "hard" trill of the /r/ at the beginning of the word. Thus, it is clear that Victor could have pronounced *Inglés sin Barreras* with Spanish phonology. Why would he pronounce it using English phonology? What shapes students' alternation in the use of linguistic forms associated with the English and Spanish languages? I refer to these practices as "Inverted Spanglish" because they invert both the pronunciation (from Spanish to English) and ethnic identity (from non-U.S.–based to U.S.-based) conventionally associated with Spanish or so-called "Spanglish" forms (Rosa, 2010). Unlike Jane Hill's notion of Mock Spanish (1998), which she defines as the incorporation of "Spanish-language materials into English in order to create a jocular or pejorative 'key'" (1998, p. 682), Inverted Spanglish focuses on how U.S. Latinas/os simultaneously draw on English and Spanish forms to meet the demand that they speak Spanish *in* English without being heard to possess an accent. An example of a token of Inverted Spanglish is "Latino," which some Latinas/os playfully rhyme with a hyper-anglicized pronunciation of the Spanish word, *platano* (plantain). They do so by pronouncing "Latino" in such a way that "Lat" sounds like the begininning of the English word "latitude," "in" sounds like the English word "in," and "o" sounds like the English word "oh." This contrasts with the "Spanish" pronunciation of "Latino," in which "La-" sounds like the beginning of the English word "lollipop" and "-tino" sounds like the beginning of the English word "denote." As a word that is often pronounced in "English" yet understood as "Spanish," "Latino" is a quintessential token of Inverted Spanglish.

Tokens of Inverted Spanglish mix patterns of word and sound recognizability. In some cases, NNHS Latinas/os apply their normative English pronunciation to in-group Spanish words in interactions with fellow Latinas/os. In other cases, NNHS Latinas/os use exaggerated pronunciations to parody non-Latinas'/os' pronunciation of widely recognized Spanish words in mixed Latina/o and non-Latina/o company. One example of the former is the phrase *con permiso* ("excuse me"), which Ms. Muñiz, a young Puerto Rican teacher, pronounced in such a way that these Spanish words sound like the English words "cone," "per," "miss," and "oh." In this example, Ms. Muñiz juxtaposes an in-group Spanish phrase with her conventional English pronunciation. Conversely, Ms. Muñiz often asks students to do something by following a request with *por favor* ("please") in such a way that it sounds like the English words "pour" and "favor," with the "fa" sounding like the beginning of the English word "fate" and "vor" sounding like the end of the English word "waiver." Here, she produces a hyper-anglicized pronunciation of a widely recognized Spanish phrase. Note that unlike the previous example, she does not pronounce "favor" using her conventional English phonology; this would sound like the "fu" in the English word "fun" and "vor" in the English word "voracious." In each case, these usages signal Latina/o solidarity. Ms. Muñiz said that she talks like this "all the time" and that it is "just something that Latinos do."

Traditional approaches to code-switching and code-mixing cannot grasp the meaningfulness of these linguistic practices, because code-centric accounts often overlook the social significance of voicing (Bakhtin, 1981) and the invocation of models of personhood through language use (Agha, 2009). In Inverted Spanglish, double voicing allows Latinas/os to signal their "native" English and Spanish abilities by combining their English pronunciation with in-group Spanish words, or by combining exaggerated pronunciations with widely recognized Spanish words. The erasure of Puerto Rican–Mexican Spanish difference in these usages introduces a U.S.-based Latina/o diasporic voice. This language use positions 1.5-, second-, and third-generation Latinas/os as prototypical members of this category. Because its characteristic features are knowledge of Spanish words, the ability to speak "unaccented" English, and the presumption of one's Latina/o identity, Inverted Spanglish mediates between the stigmatization that members of these generations face when speaking "English" or "Spanish" as separate codes.

Inverted Spanglish is not a straightforward contributor to the hegemonic position of monolingual English dominance, nor is it a clear-cut critique of this hegemony. In the process of creating an emergent register of language, Inverted Spanglish erases Puerto Rican and Mexican Spanish difference. Whereas Spanish-dominant communication becomes a prime ideological site for the recognition of Mexican and Puerto Rican difference, English is imagined as a linguistic medium in which Puerto Rican and Mexican difference is much more difficult to hear. As one 9th-grade girl (PR, Gen. 1.5, Gr. 9) explained to me:

> You can tell when someone is Puerto Rican or Mexican from their accent in Spanish.... You can hear when someone is Latino from the way they speak English [be]cause they got that something...that spice! I don't know what it is, but you can hear it.

In this example, the student invokes the stereotype that Latinas/os are "spicy." Importantly, she associates this Latina/o panethnic spice with *English*. Thus, ideologies that locate Puerto Rican–Mexican difference within the realm of Spanish and flatten out this difference in English contribute to the fashioning of a diasporic Latina/o subjectivity among U.S.-based Latinas/os. My focus on Inverted Spanglish is not intended to provide a general model of English-Spanish bilingualism among students at NNHS. There are numerous ways in which students move within and across varieties of English and Spanish, many of which mirror existing accounts of monolingual style-shifting and bilingual code-switching. Following García's (2009) Bakhtin-inspired model of "translanguaging" and other recent approaches to "language across difference" (Paris, 2011), I seek to highlight the ways that NNHS students not only navigate, but also transform social and linguistic boundaries. This perspective presents an analytical framework that can be used to understand the translingual practices of students who might otherwise be approached separately as monolingual or bilingual. Inverted Spanglish moves beyond this binary by showing how students simultaneously voice in-group knowledge of Spanish and English. Still, Inverted Spanglish is exclusive to those U.S. Latinas/os for whom "unaccented" English is a part of their linguistic repertoire, so most English language learners are prevented from participating in these particular linguistic practices and social identities. Thus, Latina/o ethnolinguistic diasporization is a complex, power-laden process that is shaped by a range of institutional dynamics and forms of inequality.

Conclusion

The quotation at the beginning of this chapter from famed Puerto Rican poet Tato Laviera points to several characteristic elements of diasporization that I have sought to highlight in this chapter: (1) diasporization involves remappings in which ideas about national identities transform borders between and within languages; (2) diasporization is dynamically linked to processes of ethnolinguistic socialization that take place in institutions such as schools; and (3) diasporization is neither a naturally occurring phenomenon nor merely a matter of personal choice, but a political process in which people (re)define the ethnolinguistic identities to which they are socialized as they navigate their everyday lives. I have introduced the notion of *Inverted Spanglish* in an effort to capture the unique ways that Puerto Rican, Mexican, and Latina/o diasporic identities are constructed in New Northwest High School and its surrounding communities.

Returning to the discussion of assimilation with which this chapter began, it should now be clear that identifying with the U.S. can in fact be a way of engaging in diasporic practices. As a public educational institution with a fraught relationship to social reproduction and transformation, NNHS becomes a context in which students are linked to varying trajectories of diasporization. Constructions of ethnolinguistic identities emerge as key practices by which to track these trajectories. The English language is far from a straightforward sign of "Americanness," and the Spanish language is far from a straightforward unifier across Latina/o national subgroups. Inverted Spanglish positions particular features of the English and Spanish languages as linguistic vehicles through which diasporic Latina/o identities are rendered recognizable. This focus on diasporization allows us to problematize narratives of assimilation that deny the legitimacy of multiple national affiliations. Such narratives obscure the historical and contemporary experiences that inform the embrace of U.S.-based Puerto Rican, Mexican, and Latina/o identities. After all, the forms of inequality that anchor the creation of these diasporic identities in schools and communities are as American as apple pie.

Notes

1. Bailey shows how neither Warner and Srole's (1945) "straight-line" theory nor Portes and Zhou's (1993) "segmented" theory provides a productive model for understanding the ways that U.S. Dominicans experience assimilation. Straight-line theory attempted to generalize from the experiences of late 19th-century and early 20th-century European immigrants, to suggest that assimilation occurs linearly "across time and generations" (Bailey, 2007, p. 159). In order to distinguish between the experiences of these European immigrants and the post-1965 "New Immigration" largely from the Caribbean, Latin America, and Asia, Portes and Zhou developed the theory of segmented assimilation described above.
2. Almost all of the school's non-Latina/o students are African American.
3. In 2010 Mexicans constituted approximately 65% of U.S. Latinas/os, while Puerto Ricans constituted 9.2% of the U.S. Latina/o population.
4. Los Angeles, Houston, and San Antonio have the largest U.S. Mexican populations.
5. New York, Philadelphia, and Orlando have the largest U.S. Puerto Rican populations.
6. New York, Los Angeles, Houston, and San Antonio have the largest U.S. Latina/o populations.
7. Some students claimed that individuals with one Puerto Rican and one Mexican parent would most likely identify as Puerto Rican since it is "cooler." In fact, I found that this happens in both directions, and that it frequently involves identifying in the same way as the parent with whom students understand themselves to share the closest relationship.
8. Latina/o students are coded using abbreviations of self-ascribed categories such as "Mexican" (M) and "Puerto Rican" (PR), as well as generation cohort with respect to (im)migration and grade year in school. For example:
   Pedro (PR, Gen. 3, Gr. 10)
   Name (self-ascribed identity, immigration cohort, grade year)
   Generation 1: born and raised outside of the U.S. mainland until the age of 9 or older

Generation 1.5: born outside of the U.S. mainland, but raised within the U.S. mainland before the age of 9

Generation 2: born and raised within the U.S. mainland by parents who were born and raised outside of the U.S. mainland

Generation 3: born and raised within the U.S. mainland by parents who were born and raised within the U.S. mainland

I use the phrase "U.S. mainland" to distinguish between the continental United States and its territories and possessions. Puerto Rico is a U.S. commonwealth. Thus, someone born in Puerto Rico is born "outside of the U.S. mainland." This allows for a unified designation for people born in Puerto Rico or anywhere else in Latin America.

9. Each Chicago public school has a local school council, which consists of parents, teachers, community residents, a student representative, and the school's principal.

10. "Hispanic" and "Latina/o" are used interchangeably by both Latinas/os and non-Latinas/os in NNHS.

11. "Juke" is a Chicago music style popularly described as "ghetto house"; it is characterized by its grinding rhythms and sexually explicit lyrics. Importantly, the vast majority of hip-hop and juke lyrics consist of English language forms.

12. In a broader Latin American perspective, cumbia is a music genre that is often associated with Colombia and Panama. In this Puerto Rican/Mexican-dominant setting, cumbia is most often associated with Mexico.

13. The music genres of salsa and banda are stereotypically associated with Puerto Ricans and Mexicans, respectively.

14. Most Spanish usages are italicized with English translations in parentheses.

15. This /s/ deletion is characteristic of Caribbean Spanish and takes two forms here. Before a consonant, as is the case with the first /s/ in *ustedes* as well as in *están*, /s/ is realized as a laryngeal fricative /h/. In absolute word final position, such as the second /s/ in *ustedes*, /s/ is realized as an alveolar sibilant.

16. While many NNHS students are reggaeton fans, others such as Jimmy (PR, Gen. 3, Gr. 12) want nothing to do with it. Jimmy, a self-proclaimed hip-hop fanatic, claimed that reggaeton is lame and that it only has one beat. He also said that he could not understand the highly vernacular Puerto Rican Spanish lyrics. Much to Jimmy's dismay, his best friend, Damon, a fellow Puerto Rican senior, listens to reggaeton all the time.

17. She provided other examples such as *pato*, which is Puerto Rican slang for "gay," but simply means "duck" in Mexican Spanish; she also pointed out the counter-example of *puñal*, which means "gay" in Mexican slang, but simply means "knife" in Puerto Rican Spanish.

18. This demonstrates the ideological nature of assessments of the relative "Puerto Ricanness" and "Mexicanness" of different language forms. These qualities are not intrinsic to the forms themselves; they are constructed and potentially reconfigured in context.

References

Agha, A. (2009). What do bilinguals do? A commentary. In A. Reyes & A. Lo (Eds.), *Beyond yellow English: Towards a linguistic anthropology of Asian Pacific America* (pp. 253–260). New York: Oxford University Press.

Alim, H. (2006). *Rock the mic right: The language of hip hop culture.* New York: Routledge.

Appadurai, A. (1996). *Modernity at large: Cultural dimensions of globalization.* Minneapolis: University of Minnesota Press.

Bailey, B. (2002). *Language, race, and negotiation of identity: A study of Dominican Americans.* New York: LFB Scholarly Publishing.

Bailey, B. (2007). Shifting negotiations of identity in a Dominican American community. *Latino Studies, 5,* 157–181.

Bakhtin, M. (1981). *The dialogic imagination: Four essays.* M. Holquist (Ed.), C. Emerson & M. Holquist (Trans.). Austin: University of Texas Press.

Bauman, R., & Briggs, C. (2003). *Voices of modernity: Language ideologies and the politics of inequality.* New York: Cambridge University Press.

Bureau of the Census. (2011). *The Hispanic Population: 2010.* Census Brief C2010BR-04. Retrieved from http://www.census.gov/prod/cen2010/briefs/c2010br-04.pdf

Crawford, J. (2007). Hard sell: Why is bilingual education so unpopular with the American public? In O. García & C. Baker (Eds.), *Bilingual education: An introductory reader* (pp. 145–161). Tonawanda, NY: Multilingual Matters.

De Genova, N., & Ramos-Zayas, A. (2003). *Latino crossings: Mexicans, Puerto Ricans, and the politics of race and citizenship.* New York: Taylor and Francis.

Flores, J. (2009). *The diaspora strikes back: Caribeño tales of learning and turning.* New York: Taylor and Francis.

Gal, S. (2006). Contradictions of standard language in Europe: Implications for the study of practices and publics. *Social Anthropology, 13*(2), 163–181.

García, O. (2009). *Bilingual education in the 21st century: A global perspective.* Malden, MA: Wiley-Blackwell.

García, O., & Torres-Guevara, R. (2010). Monoglossic ideologies and language policies in the education of U.S. Latinas/os. In E. Murillo, Jr., S. Villenas, R. Trinidad Galván, J. Sánchez Muñoz, C. Martínez, & M. Machado-Casas (Eds.), *Handbook of Latinos and education: Theory, research, and practices* (pp. 182–193). New York: Routledge.

Garrett, P., & Baquedano-López, P. (2002). Language socialization: Reproduction and continuity, transformation and change. *Annual Review of Anthropology, 31,* 339–361.

Ghosh Johnson, S. (2005). *Mexiqueño? Issues of identity and ideology in a case study of dialect contact.* (Unpublished doctoral dissertation). University of Pittsburgh.

González, N. (2005). Children in the eye of the storm: Language socialization and language ideologies in a dual-language school. In A. Zentella (Ed.), *Building on strength: Language and literacy in Latino families and communities* (pp. 162–174). New York: Teachers College Press.

Hall, S. (1990). Cultural identity and diaspora. In J. Rutherford (Ed.), *Identity: Community, culture, difference* (pp. 222–237). London: Lawrence and Wishart Press.

Hill, J. (1998). Language, race, and white public space. *American Anthropologist, 100*(3), 680–689.

Huntington, S. (2004). The Hispanic challenge. *Foreign Policy, 141,* 30–45.

Irvine, J. (2006). Speech and language community. In K. Brown (Ed.), *Encyclopedia of language & linguistics* (2nd ed.) (pp. 689–698). Oxford: Elsevier Publishers.

Kroskrity, P. (2000). *Regimes of language: Ideologies, polities, and identities.* Santa Fe, NM: School of American Research Press.

Laviera, T. (1985). *AmeRícan.* Houston, TX: Arte Publico Press.

Lukose, R. (2007). The difference that diaspora makes: Thinking through the anthropology of immigrant education in the United States. *Anthropology & Education Quarterly, 38*(4), 405–418.

Mendoza-Denton, N. (2008). *Homegirls: Language and cultural practice among Latina youth gangs.* Malden, MA: Blackwell.

Paris, D. (2011). *Language across difference: Ethnicity, communication, and youth identities in changing urban schools.* New York: Cambridge University Press.

Portes, A., & Zhou, M. (1993). The new second generation: Segmented assimilation and its variants. *Annals of the American Academy of Political and Social Science, 530,* 74–96.

Potowski, K., & Matts, J. (2008). MexiRicans: Interethnic language and identity. *Journal of Language, Identity, and Education, 7,* 137–160.

Rivera, R., Marshall, W., & Pacini Hernandez, D. (2009). *Reggaeton.* Durham, NC: Duke University Press.

Rivera-Servera, R. (2012). *Performing queer Latinidad: Dance, sexuality, politics.* Ann Arbor: University of Michigan Press.

Rosa, J. (2010). *Looking like a language, sounding like a race: Making Latina/o panethnicity and Managing American anxieties.* (Unpublished doctoral dissertation). University of Chicago.

Rúa, M. (2001). Colao subjectivities: PortoMex and MexiRican perspectives on language and identity. *CENTRO Journal, 13*(2), 117–133.

Santa Ana, O. (2004). Chronology of events, court decisions, and legislation affecting language minority children in American public education. In Santa Ana, O. (Ed.), *Tongue tied: The lives of multilingual children in public education* (pp. 87–110). Lanham, MD: Rowman & Littlefield Publishers.

Schieffelin, B., Woolard, K., & Kroskrity, P. (1998). *Language ideologies: Practice and theory.* New York: Oxford University Press.

Silverstein, M. (1979). Language structure and linguistic ideology. In R. Clyne, W. Hanks, & C. Hofbauer (Eds.), *The elements: A parasession on linguistic units and levels* (pp. 193–247). Chicago: Chicago Linguistic Society.

Silverstein, M. (1996). Monoglot "standard" in America: Standardization and metaphors of linguistic hegemony. In D. Brenneis & R. Macaulay (Eds.), *The matrix of language: Contemporary linguistic anthropology* (pp. 284–306). Boulder, CO: Westview Press.

Silverstein, M. (2003). The whens and wheres – as well as hows – of ethnolinguistic recognition. *Public Culture, 15*(3), 531–558.

Urciuoli, B. (1998). *Exposing prejudice: Puerto Rican experiences of language, race, and class.* Boulder, CO: Westview Press.

Urciuoli, B. (2001). The complex diversity of languages in the U.S. In I. Susser & T. Carl (Eds.), *Cultural diversity in the United States: A critical reader* (pp. 190–204). Malden, MA: Blackwell Press.

Warner, W., & Srole, L. (1945). *The social systems of American ethnic groups*. New Haven, CT: Yale University Press.

Woolard, K. (1989). Sentences in the language prison: The rhetorical structuring of an American language policy debate. *American Ethnologist, 16*, 268–278.

Wortham, S. (2008). Linguistic anthropology of education. *Annual Review of Anthropology, 37*, 37–51.

Wortham, S., & Rymes, B. (2003). *Linguistic anthropology of education*. Westport, CT: Praeger Publishers.

Zentella, A. (2005). Premises, promises, and pitfalls of language socialization research in Latino families and communities. In A. Zentella (Ed.), *Building on strength: Language and literacy in Latino families and communities* (pp. 13–30). New York: Teachers College Press.

Zentella, A. (2007). "Dime con quién hablas, y te dire quién eres": Linguistic (in)security and Latina/o identity. In J. Flores & R. Rosaldo (Eds.), *A companion to Latina/o studies* (pp. 25–38). Malden, MA: Blackwell.

Zentella, A. (2009). Latin@ languages and identities. In M. Suárez-Orozco & M. Páez (Eds.), *Latinos: Remaking America* (pp. 321–338). Berkeley: University of California Press.

Hybrid Latina: Becoming a ChicaRican[1]

MARÍA E. FRÁNQUIZ

My parents married in the 1940s during the time Noel Estrada captured the feeling of the Puerto Rican diaspora experience when he wrote "En mi Viejo San Juan." Estrada was a veteran with the same hope of improving his family's economic conditions that my father had when he signed up as a U.S. Army recruit at the end of World War II. Their lived experiences as U.S. soldiers resonate with the many *Boricua* men and women who feel deep nostalgia when they join the military and are transferred away from their homeland, *Borinquen*. In 1971 the song "En mi Viejo San Juan" was adopted as the official city anthem of the capital city of Puerto Rico, San Juan, because it invokes for the DiaspoRican listener multiple images of and connections with its land, fauna, food, music, traditions, and extended family on *la Isla del Encanto* (the Island of Enchantment). The following lines from the chorus, in particular, evoke connections:

Adiós (adiós, adiós)/ Goodbye (goodbye, goodbye)
Borinquen querida/ My beloved *Borinquen*
Dueña de mi amor/ Land of my love
Me voy (ya me voy)/ I'm leaving (I'm leaving now)
Pero un día volveré/ But some day I will return
A buscar mi querer/ To search for my love
A soñar otra vez/ To dream once again
En mi Viejo San Juan/ In my Old San Juan

Chicana/os also understand that music raises to consciousness the diaspora experience. While a significant part of their homeland was ceded as a condition of the Treaty of Guadalupe Hidalgo in 1848, a traditional *ranchera* song, "Mexico lindo y querido," captures for Chicana/os the same loyalty to homeland and real or imagined desire to return that are contained within the lyrics of "En mi Viejo San Juan." As a child in Puerto Nuevo, a suburb of the metropolitan area of San Juan, I heard my father play the sentimental songs of the great Mexican singer Jorge Negrete. His feelings of pride for his homeland were powerful as the following lines attest:

> Yo le canto a sus volcanes/ I sing to its volcanoes
> a sus praderas y flores/ Its meadows and flowers
> que son como talismanes/ Which are like talismans
> del amor de mis amores/ Of the greatest of my loves
> México Lindo y Querido/ My beautiful and beloved Mexico
> si muero lejos de ti/ Should I die far from you
> que digan que estoy dormido/ Let them say I am asleep
> y que me traigan aquí/ And bring me back to you

While I am no musician or singer, the lyrics of both of these songs characterize the worlds and words that describe my embodied identities as a *Puertorriqueña* living and teaching in the southwestern part of the U.S. for a considerable part of my life. These overlapping worlds of relation between and across national boundaries and cultural practices extend my repertoire of language, my epistemologies, my pedagogies, and my identities. In this chapter I describe how these movements across borders contributed to the naming of my selves as ChicaRican. In my naming I am informed by border crossers such as Anzaldúa (1987), or in more contemporary terms, transnationalists such as self-proclaimed CubaRican Jorge Duany (2011) who accepts that "contemporary migrants may develop multiple identities, lead bifocal lives, express loyalties to more than one nation, and practice hybrid cultures" (p. 24). I use this border crossing theory of construction of identities and an autoethnographic approach to tell my tale because it places me within a social context (Reed-Danahay, 1997) in an effort to "garner insights" (Goodall, 2000, p. 86) into the larger cultures or subcultures in which I have participated. As stated by Ricci (2003), "While not the traditional form of research to which we are accustomed, autoethnography makes available the bridge linking the personal with the cultural" (p. 595) worlds where authoring of identities occurs.

Why autoethnography?

> "Face" is the surface of the body that is the most noticeably inscribed by social structures, marked with instructions on how to be *mujer, macho*, working class, Chicana. As *mestizos*—biologically and/or culturally mixed—we have different surfaces for each aspect of identity, each inscribed by a particular subculture. We are "written" all over, or should I say, carved and tattooed with the sharp needles of experience. (Anzaldúa, 1990, p. xv)

In *Making Face, Making Soul,* feminist scholar Gloria Anzaldúa offered an anthology of literary works by women of color as a viable teaching tool for the (de)construction of knowledge. Each work's author takes an autoethnographic stance in their self-reflexive act to introduce the reader to ways relations of power are implicated in the construction of herstory. They examine how women of color have to change faces when the dangers are many and the options few. Anzaldúa explains that making faces is her metaphor for constructing one's identity within the structures of private and public worlds. As she states, "This book aims to make accessible to others our struggle with all our identities, our linkage-making strategies, and our healing of broken limbs" (p. xvii).

I see this framework used in *Making Face, Making Soul* as autoethnographic writing, which has been defined as an autobiographical genre of writing that "make[s] the researcher's own experiences a topic of investigation in [their] own right" (Ellis & Bochner, 2000, p. 733) and "ask[s] their readers to feel the truth of their stories and to become co-participants, engaging in storyline[s] morally, emotionally, aesthetically, and intellectually" (p. 745). This autoethnographic approach treats memories, interviews with the self, and artifacts from one's life as data to be discussed and analyzed. In each autoethnography the author presents herself as an object of ethnographic inquiry. In the autoethnographies presented in Anzaldúa's anthology, women of color sought to examine the movement from their categorization as an unmarked racial woman, or a woman marked with otherness, to becoming a "woman of color." As confirmed by a Puerto Rican many years after the publication of the anthology, the sense of otherness described in many autoethnographies is omnipresent. In the case of Chicanas such as Anzaldúa or Puerto Ricans such as myself, otherness exists regardless of our status as American citizens. For example, in the case of Vidal-Ortiz (2004), a light-skinned Puerto Rican schooled on the Island, it did not matter how much Spanish or European blood he possessed, because his otherness when he moved to the U.S. mainland is based on how *Americans* in the U.S. see all Puerto Ricans. As he poignantly states, "Light-skinned Puerto Ricans become 'people of color' in the U.S. because the term means more than 'race'" (Vidal-Ortiz, 2004, p. 190). The DiaspoRican experience of Vidal-Ortiz verifies what Stuart Hall (1991) suggested: "the notion that identity has to do with people that look the same, feel the same, call themselves the same, is nonsense. As a process, as a narrative, as a discourse, it is always from the position of Other" (p. 49). To theorize our selves, therefore, means to examine the dialectic between how we see ourselves and how others see us.

As you may have deduced by now, autoethnography is a genre that is not totally without criticism in the academy. Yet, it is a writing genre that many scholars of color utilize even though it may endanger their access to promotion and tenure. Thus, I have sought to understand the legitimacy of the tradition rather than the perils. For example, several decades ago Hayano (1979) defined autoethnography as a set of issues in anthropology relating to the researcher's study of their "own people" (p. 99). Because the insider is at the heart and center of this definition of an autoethnography, a researcher studying a group distinctly different than her own would be excluded from the rubric of autoethnography. Pratt (1992) adds, "If ethnographic texts are a means by which Europeans represent to themselves their (usually subjugated) others, autoethnographic texts are those the others construct in response to or in dialogue with those metropolitan representations" (p. 7). Pratt's term refers broadly to retrospective analysis and discussion in which "colonized subjects undertake to represent themselves in ways that *engage with* the colonizer's own terms" (p. 7, emphasis in original). Accordingly, Denzin (2006) proposes a civic, publicly responsible autoethnography that addresses the central issues of self, race, gender, class, society, and democracy (p. 259).

Caroline Ellis and Arthur P. Bochner (2000) explain that in an autoethnography, the reader is repositioned as a coparticipant in the dialogue because the intention of the researcher is to allow the reader to enter into the story and experience the moral or ethical dilemma, and to evoke a response. Ellis and Bochner also explain that a researcher does not offer "undisputable conclusions" (p. 745), rather, she uses evocative narrative. In this way, the reader can put him/herself, "within a culture of experience that enlarges their social awareness and empathy" (Ellis, 2004, p. 30) and can make connections from the personal account to the social, cultural, and political structures that influenced the identity construction of the autoethnographer.

Autoethnographic writing, then, presents a personal narrative that poses particular methodological issues in the larger context of social science research precisely because the researcher's personal life is exposed to scrutiny and critique. In spite of issues, the autoethnographic approach is evolving rapidly in disciplines such as communication, education, family therapy, sociology, anthropology, nursing, and social work (Ellis, 2004, p. 71). For this chapter I use autoethnography to connect the personal to my experiences in the Puerto Rican diaspora. I highlight the autobiographical experiences in terms of a cultural identity that was positioned as Puerto Rican on the Island. Then I describe the effects of dislocation from homeland. Finally, I present the search for belonging in and through hybridity that many authors articulate as imperative in relation to diaspora processes (Hall, 1990; Flores, 2008).

Life in Puerto Rico

My mother grew up in a poor barrio in Bayamón, Puerto Rico. She was the youngest of seven children. My father grew up Santurce, Puerto Rico. He was the oldest of thirteen siblings. I was born at the Maldonado Clinic in Hato Rey and grew up in Puerto Nuevo, Puerto Rico, currently a densely populated *municipio* in the metropolitan area of San Juan. I recall the neighborhood as a working-class community in which telling stories was the way to socialize the younger generations about the values, histories, traditions, recipes, and remedies that were often excluded from the formal structures of schools, churches, and governments. Shared memories of the past under Spanish colonization, descriptions of present American colonization, and dreams of the Island's independence from colonialism were common stories heard in day-to-day conversational exchanges among parents, neighbors, aunts and uncles, older cousins, and visitors from other parts of the Island. *Bochinche* (*chisme* for Mexican-American speakers; "gossip" for English speakers) was ubiquitous and often centered on violation of community norms—who cheated on a spouse, who got drunk and was arrested for disorderly conduct, who was ill, who lost their job, and who died. *Bochinche* also provided a sense of personal and collective pride—who bought a new car or television, who got engaged, who enlisted in the armed services, whose son/daughter earned excellent grades in school, who composed a new song. I remember hearing and being absorbed in the *bochinche* and feeling such a sense of pride when the buzz involved people I knew—that my grandfather shared his harvest with neighbors, my father was promoted to sergeant, my sister was cured of thrush with herbal remedies, or my *madrina* (godmother) made the best First Communion dresses in our neighborhood. These stories were communicated in Spanish and represent a community discourse that worked itself into my identities. This discourse was forged in community and felt deeply. Through it emerged the ideologies encompassing ideas such as nation, culture, race, class, gender, citizenship, self-determination, and human rights, among others. The stories embedded in the discourse preserve the past and assure that I can remember where my family came from in order to pass that legacy to my children and grandchildren. As stated by Sonja Z. Pérez (2002), "...one of the reasons that people in the United States tell stories is to write themselves into the discourse of nationhood, to revise the official stories of the nation, the constitution of We the People" (p. 277). This authoring became particularly poignant for me as my childhood became a diasporic experience.

I started school at La Academia Santa Monica. The bus from Puerto Nuevo would take my siblings and me to Avenida Fernández Juncos in

Santurce, where the school still stands. The school's arches are wide; they grace the outside hallways of the three-storied building. A cross near the roof's center, visible from the surrounding streets, marks the school as Catholic. The garbs the priests and nuns wear distinguish them as followers of St. Augustine.

With classes conducted in Spanish, except one course in English, I learned early about the separation of languages and about the separation of cultures. For example, I was taught that in the U.S. mainland intergenerational relations could be informal, while on the Island they could not. I also learned that Catholicism unites people even though vernaculars and social conventions may be different. I felt privileged to attend La Academia Santa Monica. It was a strict and somber beginning of my formal education, presenting all kinds of contradictions that I will discuss in the sections that follow.

It was during my years at La Academia that my brother and I were baptized and received our First Holy Communion. We were not baptized as infants because my father was angry with the Catholic Church for demanding an exorbitant stipend to marry my mother. Despite this, however, my *papá* liked the discipline and values taught by the priests and nuns. This is why my siblings and I attended many Catholic schools during my father's military career.

All the Sisters at La Academia spoke Spanish even though their heritage language may have been English. In this predominantly Spanish-speaking world I met a red-haired, freckled-faced "American" girl. While the teachers and students in the upper grades could read English, the little "American" girl in kindergarten seemed to be the only one that pronounced it like a stateside native. I adored and envied her—the way she spoke, the way she looked, even the way she acted—so entitled. She was loud and I was quiet. Her features were light; mine were darker. She was assertive; I was submissive. She was American and I was Puerto Rican. Our only bond was that we were children living in military families, but I did not know our fathers were serving the *same* nation. I thought she came from another country, even another planet—a place where all people were fair, red-haired, English-speaking, and freckled. It seemed an enviable life.

My red-haired classmate and I passed from kindergarten through 3rd grade together. In 3rd grade we were so excited to read a book in English that was 190 pages long! Our reading book, *These Are Our Friends*, written by Sister M. Marguerite, S.N.D., was part of the Faith and Freedom series whose goal was to teach reading, highlighting the virtues of love, respect, generosity, and helpfulness. David and Ann were the central characters, and a very young Sister Jean was their teacher. David and Ann did not wear uniforms at school the way we did. Comprehension questions were sometimes embedded in the stories about their lives. For example, David and Ann's parents gave their children a little white rabbit that eventually ran away. Interestingly, the rabbit talked. "I do not like to eat cookies," he said. "I like green things to eat. I will run away from here." Then the story asks, "Can you guess what kind of green things Little Rabbit wanted?"

Besides comprehension questions, there were also biblical stories and Catholic doctrine embedded within the stories. For example, one story stated: "Jesus was kind to people when they were hungry. He loves us when we are kind to others, too." These types of messages were important for the spiritual development of children like me. While it seemed nice that the father and mother bought their children a new pet rabbit when Little Rabbit ran away, it also seemed frivolous when I compared it to the needs of my immediate family and my extended family who lived in poverty. I was curious about the life of the characters portrayed in the book, the stories about Jesus and his love for everyone, but I was also perplexed by the stories of pets—dogs, cats, rabbits, and birds—whose houses, food, and other needs occupied so much of the family's time and resources. Even more curious was learning about the helpers in their neighborhood—the policeman, fireman, mailman, and priests. I was mystified that all the jobs were for men, and girls could not be altar girls or priests. However, the book affirmed: "But girls can help God, too. They can be Sisters. Every Sister helps to do God's work. And God needs many more Sisters." In this specific story the message was further elaborated with a prayer that David and Ann repeated every night: "Please, dear God, make many good boys want to be priests. Please, dear God, make many good girls to be Sisters. Give us many more priests and Sisters to do Your work." I did not know until later about the power of subliminal messages inherent in those readers, or the gendered tale that would dramatically shift with future transnational processes.

In contrast to the middle-class values represented in the book assigned to my English class, my 3rd-grade mathematics class in Spanish required a great deal of reading. The publisher made efforts to make the math problems in the book culturally relevant. For example, the page showed a black-and-white pencil drawing of a tobacco worker cutting down ripe tobacco with a machete. The review problem for addition read:

"La finca de café"
El café es uno de los productos más importantes de Puerto Rico. Se cultiva en los terrenos montañosos de la Isla. Don José tiene una finca de café. En la finca trabajan muchos obreros. Ramón trabaja con Don José. La semana pasada trabajó tres días. El lunes se ganó $1.50; el martes se ganó $0.85 y el

miércoles se ganó $1.10. No pudo trabajar los demás días de la semana debido a la lluvia. ¿Cuánto se ganó Ramón en la semana?
"The coffee plantation"
Coffee is one of the most important products of Puerto Rico. It is cultivated in the mountain regions of the island. Don José has a coffee plantation. Many workers work on the plantation. Ramón works with Don José. Last week he worked three days. On Monday he earned $1.50; on Tuesday he earned $0.85 and on Wednesday he earned $1.10. He could not work the rest of the week because of rain. How much did Ramón earn during that week?

These math problems presented the real economic circumstances of Puerto Rico. As a child I knew my grandfather worked raising and harvesting tobacco and my grandmother worked at the Lucky Strike factory making cigarettes, so these word problems provided me a way to understand the economic world in which my mother's parents lived. I was comfortable in this world of the *Isla del Encanto* and a bit anxious about leaving *Mi Viejo San Juan, Mi diosa del mar, Mi reina del palmar.*

Life on the northeastern seaboard

In March of my 3rd grade, my father was transferred to Ft. Bragg, North Carolina. Initially, life on the northeastern seaboard and at St. Patrick School was a humbling experience. My sister cried and cried during morning prayers because she did not understand English and was subsequently retained in kindergarten. One day soon after our enrollment, my brother suddenly left the school grounds, alarming my parents, school administrators, and the local and military police. Although he was bright, he was impatient when his teacher did not understand what he was trying to say. My father spent all his free time that spring and summer teaching my brother and me sufficient English to stay at grade level. He also got us a subscription to *Highlights* magazine for children. It gave us a better glimpse to the cultural ways of children on the mainland.

It was hard for my parents to live in an all-English environment. My father fared much better than my mother. They both could understand and read English fairly well, but had difficulty producing native-like pronunciation and grammatical forms that could be readily understood. When my father was at work, as the oldest child, I was designated as translator for my mother and caretaker of my siblings outside the home. I often felt inadequate as language broker in places where my mother or siblings needed assistance—the store, the school, the post office, and the doctor's office. I felt little consolation in a foreign land where spoken and unspoken words were too often misunderstood. My excellent grades in English at La Academia Santa Monica were of little value in the English-saturated world where we now lived.

There were many humbling moments. One of the first things I noticed stateside is that few people had red hair—what a disappointment! Another thing I noticed were signs separating Negroes and Whites in certain places, even from drinking from the same water fountains. This segregation scared my mother. She recounts to her great-grandchildren how when we moved stateside my father came first and the family followed. The flight from Puerto Rico to Alabama that she took with an infant and three young children was on a military cargo plane. My father was to meet us, but was detained. Thus, we boarded a bus in Alabama during the Jim Crow era. The bus driver did not want trouble, so he directed my mother to sit with her children directly behind him. We had no idea that everyone else was contemplating whether we belonged in the back of the bus or in the front. My father met us in North Carolina in full uniform, and we were so relieved.

During the initial months stateside, my mother missed San Juan because her English reading, writing, and speaking abilities, once effective on the Island, were now ineffective in North Carolina. I also noticed that my father wore his U.S. Army uniform even when he was off duty, as a way to command respect. This is how we adapted to our new life on the U.S. mainland. In time, it became more acceptable. At school the Sisters paired me up with a little White girl who acted as my language broker. Unfortunately I don't remember her name, but she helped me to become biliterate, *poco a poco*—little by little. In turn, I became a more effective language broker for my mother, the real shiny star in my life, who in her role as homemaker had fewer opportunities to develop her English.

My elementary schooling was interrupted each time my father was transferred from one military post to another. Each move brought its own necessary adjustments to life in and outside of school, and many family discussions regarding different ways of retaining island ways while acculturating to mainland ways. At that time I did not know how to name this in-between existence and the hybrid identities that emerged.

Life in the Southwest

When my father was transferred to El Paso, Texas, the disquiet that accompanies a move presented new challenges for my family and me. My siblings and I were initially enrolled at a Department of Defense (DOD) school at Ft. Bliss. Shortly afterwards, my father enrolled us at St. Joseph's School (http://www.stjoseph-school.org/) on Lamar Street. The Sisters of Loretto with the help of a few lay teachers ran the school.

One bitter memory I carried for years was inflicted by a Mexican American teacher who made fun of my Puerto Rican Spanish language variant that

I used the first day of school. When I asked her "¿Dónde puedo encontrar la parada de guaguas?" (Where can I find the bus stop?), she answered, "Speak English. And the correct word for bus is *camión*." I assumed, incorrectly, that I could use Spanish in school. I also assumed that *guaguas* (buses) referred to the same vehicle in Puerto Rico and in El Paso, where there were many Spanish speakers. I was wrong on both counts. At St. Joseph's in the 1950s there was a rule that no Spanish was to be used on school grounds, and English-only was strictly upheld. Disobeying the rule was considered a venial sin of disobedience—an offense that had to be confessed to the priest during confession time on Thursdays. Also, the issue of one "correct" word for buses was rigid. At the age of 10 I had no idea that this woman's Mexican American language variant, *camión*, could be perceived as nonstandard as mine. If the accepted Spanish translation for "bus" in many dictionaries is "autobús" or "ómnibus," then the Mexican variant *camión* should have been as acceptable as my Puerto Rican variant of *guagua*.

In Puerto Rico my Spanish heritage language was seen as a right, and an asset. On the mainland, Spanish was seen as a sin to be confessed, if not expunged. Although many Puerto Ricans were stationed at Ft. Bliss, the language ideologies of that era just did not serve our educational needs. Unlike some of our peers who grew up in El Paso, we were not accustomed to English borrowings and frequent language alternations that are awkwardly labeled Spanglish, Tex-Mex, or *pocho*. However, these bilingual-bidialectical youngsters functioned to some degree in both English and Spanish. In contrasst, my siblings and I were unfamiliar with the sophisticated language alternations of our bilingual-bidialectical peers who knew the appropriate contexts for code-switching. Schools encouraged us to lose our Spanish in order to gain English proficiency. This line of reasoning led the Sisters at St. Joseph's to advise my parents to stop using Spanish at home. As a result, my parents spoke to us in Spanish and we answered in English. In terms of biliteracy this meant we retained receptive Spanish skills and, over time, lost our productive skills. In many ways, the thinking is not different from what teachers think today—i.e., bilingualism can be acquired and maintained only sequentially, instead of simultaneously (see Baker, 2001, and Escamilla & Hopewell, 2011, for definitions and examples). Despite prevailing assumptions, my peers in El Paso acquired simultaneous bilingualism while my siblings and I came to biliteracy in a more sequential manner. Unlike our peers in El Paso, after leaving Puerto Rico we rarely lived in a community with majority Spanish speakers. As a consequence, our language development was arrested at various points in our schooling. Fragments that remained were in songs such as "En mi Viejo San Juan" that I heard on records sold in El Paso and sung by the popular

Mexican singer and actor Javier Solís. Hearing records by Solís also served as an introduction to the lyrics of "Mexico Lindo y Querido." These fragments served to shape my shifting identities in the southwestern United States.

Life overseas

From El Paso, my family traveled to the Vogelweh military complex in Kaiser-slautern, Germany, where we once again attended DOD schools. Instruction was in English, and we studied German as a subject on a daily basis. This was in the midst of the Cold War, when everyone was consumed by the threat of nuclear weapons, the threat of communism, and the decision to build the 28-mile Berlin Wall that symbolized the Iron Curtain between Western Europe and the Eastern bloc (e.g., Communist or Soviet bloc). While in Germany, the U.S. government began sending military advisers to help South Vietnam defend itself against Communist North Vietnam. That aid would later expand into a long period of U.S. involvement in Vietnam. As I continued my K–12 schooling, my languages were enriched as I sang Christmas carols in German and Latin during mass at the Catholic church, and earned excellent grades in English and other subject areas in junior high school. I also listened to nostalgic Spanish music, particularly "En mi Viejo San Juan." My father played this song over and over again as a response to the passing of his favorite sister. I think my father buried his grief in the lyrics of the song because he could not be with his extended family in his *Borinquen Querido* for the final good-bye to his sister.

During our 3 years in Germany, my father was recognized for unique talents and promoted to army warrant officer. He had developed skills as not just a bilingual soldier, but a trilingual one. His third language was Czech. In the Cold War era, proficiency in an Eastern bloc language was seen as an important military asset. He also developed important skills related to missiles and associated equipment. I tried not to learn too much about my father's military talents, because the danger of war was made real on military bases overseas. Instead, I concentrated on developing my skills in algebra, German, writing, and in track and field athletics.

Life out west

When our family returned to the U.S. mainland, my father was reassigned to a port—San Pedro, California, in the Los Angeles Harbor Area. This time, my younger sisters attended public schools. In 10th grade I attended an all-girls school, Mary Star of the Sea High School. My brother attended its counterpart, a new all-boys high school, Fermín Lasuén. Sister Nepomu-cen of the Order of the Immaculate Heart of Mary and principal of the high school I attended was strict but kind. These descriptors fit all the Sisters who taught me. At Mary Star of the Sea, I was not humiliated for any language variant I had, and the only sin that was discouraged was the sin of injustice. I also identified easily with the patronage to Mary, the Mother of Christ. The college preparatory curriculum meant all the girls could aspire to be scien-tists, doctors, lawyers, hospital administrators, or superintendents regardless of their parents' linguistic, racial, economic, or educational backgrounds. My parents were very pleased that I had access to opportunities unavailable to most Puerto Rican young women until the civil rights movement gained mo-mentum. Unfortunately, my father was transferred after 2 years in San Pedro. We moved to a rural area in the San Fernando Valley of California. At that time the Newhall-Saugus area was not very enlightened regarding the roles of young women and men; the social capital I had accumulated at Mary Star of the Sea was not valued. I graduated with my aspirations intact, but did not enjoy my last year of K–12 education.

The civil rights movement was difficult for my family. I was still in high school when the mass social mobilization with diverse political agendas from reform to revolution exhausted every single one of us. To put things in perspective: At the same time that Puerto Rican Young Lords adopted anti-imperialist political programs, my brother was training for infantry en-counters in Vietnam. Even in the Catholic Church, priests and nuns took stances to end a war that seemed to promote imperialism. While thousands of Latinas/os served in the Tet Offensive with my brother, as a newly recruited member of the Sisters of Immaculate Heart, I was at home protesting *against* the war. There were radical transformations of Latina/o identities in the U.S. mainland promoted by *El Movimiento* and liberation theology. I was attracted to these social movements, and loved the Vatican II move of the Roman Catholic Church toward ecumenism promoted by Pope John XXIII in 1962. I admired Daniel and Phillip Berrigan and Thomas Merton's efforts to create an interfaith coalition against the Vietnam War—the same war in which both my brother and my future husband would experience physical, psychological, and spiritual wounds. This backdrop provided a bitter paradox of Latinas/os dying on U.S. streets in the name of liberatory movements, while many of the young men in the U.S. military forces fought for "democracy" in Vietnam. For a very long time my family was divided about appropriate response to conflicting ideologies—nonviolent resistance or military solutions. The Viet-nam War was heartwrenching. In the midst of the turmoil my father retired from the U.S. Army and returned to his beloved *Borinquen*.

Returning to Puerto Rico

My father retired from the U.S. Army and returned to Puerto Rico to the *casita* my father had built decades before with the help of his father and neighbors. However, Puerto Nuevo was not the same. As my parents made the transition, I remained in California, my sister, Nereida, stayed in Alaska (my father's last assignment in the U.S. Army), and my brother was in Vietnam. Upon their arrival in our former neighborhood, my family occupied the ambiguous role of return migrants in the Puerto Rican imagery that Duany (2001) and other scholars discuss. For example, the neighbors questioned why my youngest sister did not speak Spanish. They equated the loss of language with voluntary choice—a response that injured my family more than any unjust experience they had endured on the mainland. With circular migration from the Island to the mainland and back to the Island, it is not news that Puerto Ricans return to *la Isla del Encanto* with mixed language abilities and cultural affiliations. Thus my father and mother returned bilingual, and my sister who had left the Island as an infant returned an English-dominant young woman. As Luis Aponte-Parés (1998) notes in his essay, my family, like many other Puerto Rican families, returned to their *casita* in Puerto Nuevo full of pride and memories that validated their Puerto Rican identity. However, our *casita* from the past was not as easy to return to as expected. A good measure of displacement had occurred in the neighborhood while my family was stateside, and *rescatando* (rescuing) my family's former life meant rebuilding the *casita* as an act of belonging to a place, reclaiming the language of that place, and affirming a heritage. My sister struggled in the public schools, not so much with academic subjects as with the banter regarding the perceived anglicization of *los que vienen de afuera* (those who come from outside)—returnees who allegedly refuse to assimilate to life in Puerto Rico and dare to bring ideas to transform its cultural (Pérez, 2004, 2005) and linguistic landscape. For that reason, she went to La Universidad de Sagrado Corazón in Santurce. There the official language is Spanish, but English is widely spoken everywhere. While all courses are taught in Spanish, written work in English is accepted in many courses. In spite of these concessions and our renovated *casita*, after 5 years on the Island my parents returned to California. They left disheartened, having experienced what scholars such as Gina M. Pérez (2005) document: "return migrants occupy an ambiguous role in the Puerto Rican imaginary and are frequently the targets of derision, ridicule and contempt" (p. 184). This condition, which my family as returnees experienced, stems from the binary characterization of Puerto Rican national identity as homogeneous or hybrid (Duany, 2001).

What do you mean, "ChicaRican"?

During our relocations my family spent many years in California (San Pedro, San Fernando, San Francisco), and these places influenced our language and cultural ways. While my parents maintained their linguistic identities as Puerto Rican speakers, my siblings and I showed more fluid linguistic markers as a result of our frequent interactions with Californians of Mexican descent. For us it was as natural to exclaim *¡Híjole!* as it was to exclaim *¡Ay Bendito!* The influence was also political. Because I had not returned to Puerto Rico with my family, staying in California, I heard about the labor organization struggles of the newly formed United Farm Workers, the political battles of the Young Lords in Chicago and New York, and the formation of the Raza Unida Party in Crystal City, Texas. The collective impact of the civil rights movement and subsequent legislation led to discussions within my social context regarding bilingual education for the nation, Chicano studies in the West, and Puerto Rican studies in the East. Since I was located in the West I became acquainted with the student struggles in California as expressed in El Plan Espiritual de Aztlán and El Plan de Santa Barbara, with their provisions for the founding of the Chicano student group Movimiento Estudiantíl Chicano de Aztlán (MEChA). The cultural nationalism of the Chicano movement was so close to me that it was easy to embrace, particularly since many of my friends were Mexican Americans from the Los Angeles metropolitan area. In contrast, cultivating an attachment with the Puerto Rican Young Lords from so far west was not so easy. So I was a Puerto Rican taking up Chicana/o causes. What I did not know then was that Indiana University, Bloomington, had Chicano Rican studies and Wayne State University had Chicano Boricua studies (Aparicio, 2003). Without this knowledge, I thought it was unique that my friends called me a "ChicaRican"—not because I had mixed parentage, but because I had mixed cultural and political affiliations.

When I began my graduate studies I was truly blessed. Although I was enrolled in classes in the Graduate School of Education at the University of California, Santa Barbara, I was also a teaching assistant for the Department of Chicano Studies. Here I had the privilege of working with Chicana/o historians such as Antonia Castañeda, Guadalupe San Miguel, and Mario Garcia. The ultimate privilege came when I was selected to be one of the two teaching assistants for César Estrada Chávez. The Department of Chicano Studies had negotiated for a number of years with the United Farm Workers union to have the civil rights leader teach a course to undergraduate students. An agreement was reached, and in spring 1992 he taught Chicano Studies 191HH, Farm Labor History in California. Readings included works by Rodolfo Acuña, Ernesto Galarza, Cletus E. Daniel, Carey McWilliams, Joan London and Harry Anderson, Ellen Cantarow, Margaret Rose, and Constance Matthiessen, among others. Each Sunday Chávez drove the 177 miles from the Forty Acres in Delano, California, to Santa Barbara in order to work with his two teaching assistants, María Ibarra, now an anthropologist, and me, an educator. We met with him every Sunday for 10 weeks to prepare for the week's upcoming class. During those 10 weeks I was astounded by the humility of César Estrada Chávez. He was very self-conscious about having left school after the 8th grade, even though that very spring of 1992 he received an honorary doctorate at Arizona State University. While I scribbled notes regarding court cases and fact-finding committees, the dates and names of specific strikes and court cases rolled easily from his memory; it was incredible how many names of judges, politicians, and large ranch owners he could retrieve. Meals shared were always light and vegetarian. He also spoke of daily meditation as well as his intimate relationship with Catholicism of the liberation theology type. Yes, I was definitely a ChicaRican, in awe at the wisdom that was imparted to me during this remarkable educational experience. For these reasons, I was delighted to learn that the place were he is buried has been declared a national historic landmark. The words used during the dedication ceremony are worthy of quoting here:

> We should all be inspired by César Chávez. His leadership, tireless work ethic, and selfless sacrifice helped forge a new era of justice for millions of farm workers and gave them hope for a better future, both for themselves and for their children. He's an American hero and one of the great civil rights icons of our country's history. By recognizing the Forty Acres site as a National Historic Landmark we are ensuring that César Chávez's story, and the story of all who struggled with him, is remembered, honored, and passed along to future generations. (Ken Salazar, Secretary of the Interior, February 21, 2011)

While the song that motivated and inspired my father and many other Puerto Ricans to bring their families back to their beloved roots is "En mi Viejo San Juan," as a farmworker, the song that always inspired César Chávez was "De Colores." While my father cherished his *casita* and longed for a Puerto Rico that is past, César lived in his *casita* on the Forty Acres, planning ways to improve the labor conditions in the production of food safe from pesticides. While my father was trained to obey, César participated in nonviolent resistance for positive change. As Latino males they have both had a great impact on the music I love, the places where I feel at home, and the values that motivate my actions in living up to the highest potential of a ChicaRican—a cultural and political hybrid.

Conclusion

As I reflect on my autoethnographic narrative and look ahead into my children's and my grandchildren's future, I am amazed at how far our family has come, yet how much further we have to go in understanding the hybridity demanded by a diasporic condition. I was rebaptized in the Southwest as ChicaRican, and accept living as a Puerto Rican with deep Chicana cultural and political affiliations; however, the case may be different for my progeny.

My life has gone beyond the literal translation of living between geopolitical borders, as described by the Aztecs. In the Puerto Rican diaspora my experience seemed to fit Anzaldúa's (1987) theoretical position of *nepantla*, or living in the middle of distinct realities. She imagined a hybrid mestizo people from diverse backgrounds and needs coexisting and working together to bring about change for social justice. Anzaldúa explained that those who are willing to embrace hybridity are *nepantleras* if they can manage multiple worlds *a la vez* (simultaneously), committing to being facilitators of change in contested spaces and developing transformative alliances (Keating, 2005, p. 7) as necessary. Such work presumes a conception of identity proposed by Hall (1990) that "lives with and through, not despite, difference" (p. 235). Accordingly, the process of cultural hybridization calls into question dualistic notions of power relations such as English dominance over Spanish or *los de acá* (native islanders) *and los de afuera* (anglicized outsiders), or between "us" and "them." Instead, the process of hybridization requires that identities be constructed across different and often intersecting and antagonistic discourses and positions, such as those of a Puerto Rican military family's constructions of identity within the sanctioning of threats of exclusion on the mainland as well as when they return to the Island of Enchantment.

For me, a diaspora consciousness emerged from the diasporic process initiated by my parents and forced on my siblings and me. Much like Duany's (2011) notion of "bifocal" lives, my hybrid identity was busy bridging two or more languages and cultures, and became a politicized mode of existence at the intersection of distinct cultures and values—those of Puerto Rico and the mainstream U.S. and Chicana. My "here" in the Southwest of the United States and my "there" in *Borinquen* was further complicated by paternal relations in New York, a sibling and nephews living for over 25 years in Maryland, a son and grandchildren permanently settling down in London, and parents, oldest son, and grandsons with decades of fervent affiliation to California. Although my sons and I have crossed the legal boundaries between our ancestral homeland and current places of residence, our webs of diasporic and transnational experiences connect our respective generations and us differently in markets, communities, and languages. Practicing and maintaining our bifocality will require tactical strategies of communication that can be expressed in our own autoethographies or other artistic reflections.

Mérida Rúa (2001) used the term *colao* subjectivities to describe Puerto Rican relations that cross, intersect, and sometimes are altered in and through interactions with other Latino populations. She discusses PortoMex (Puerto Ricanized Mexican) and MexiRican (Mexicanized Puerto Rican) identity formations. It is my hope that the important intersections with Chicana/o culture and politics that shaped my autoethnographic account of the makings of a hybrid Latina will be followed by other autoethnographies of resilient identity formations, whether they are the narratives of my sons, or the narratives of other DiaspoRicans. In this way, the complexities of the diaspora formation processes can continue to inform the current literature on the range of identities in the Puerto Rican diaspora.

Note

1. Parts of this chapter appear in Reyes, M. de la Luz (Ed.). (2011). *Words were all we had: Becoming biliterate against all odds.* New York: Teachers College Press.

References

Anzaldúa, G. (1987). *Borderlands/la frontera: The new mestiza.* San Francisco: Spinsters/ Aunt Lute.

Anzaldúa, G. E. (1990). Haciendo caras, una entrada: An introduction. In G. E. Anzaldúa (Ed.), *Making face, making soul/haciendo caras: Creative and critical perspectives by women of color* (pp. xv–xxviii). San Francisco: Aunt Lute Foundation.

Aparicio, F. R. (2003). Latino cultural studies. In J. Poblete (Ed.), *Critical Latin American and Latino studies* (pp. 3–21). Minneapolis: University of Minnesota Press.

Aponte-Parés, L. (1998). Lessons from *El Barrio* – The East Harlem real great society/ urban planning studio: A Puerto Rican chapter in the fight for urban self-determination. *New Political Science, 20*(4), 399–420.

Baker, C. (2001). *Foundations of bilingual education and bilingualism* (3rd ed.). Clevedon, UK: Multilingual Matters.

Denzin, N. K. (2006). Analytic autoethnography, or déjà vu all over again. *Journal of Contemporary Ethnography, 35*(4), 419–428.

Duany, J. (2001). *The Puerto Rican nation on the move: Identities on the island and in the United States.* Chapel Hill: University of North Carolina Press.

Duany, J. (2011). *Blurred boundaries: Transnational migration between the Hispanic Caribbean and the United States.* Chapel Hill: University of North Carolina Press.

78   MARÍA E. FRÁNQUIZ

Ellis, C. (2004). *The ethnographic I: A methodological novel about autoethnography*. Walnut Creek, CA: AltaMira Press.

Ellis, C., & Bochner, A. P. (2000). Autoethnography, personal narrative, reflexivity: Researcher as subject. In N. Denzin & Y. S. Lincoln (Eds.), *The handbook of qualitative research* (2nd ed.) (pp. 733–768). Thousand Oaks, CA: Sage.

Escamilla, K., & Hopewell, S. (2011). When learners speak two or more languages. In D. Lapp & D. Fisher (Eds.), *Handbook of research on teaching English language arts* (pp. 17–21). New York: Routledge.

Flores, J. (2008). *The diaspora strikes back: "Caribeño" tales of learning and turning*. New York: Routledge.

Goodall, H. L., Jr. (2000). *Writing the new ethnography*. Walnut Creek, CA: AltaMira.

Hall, S. (1990). Cultural identity and diaspora. In J. Rutherford (Ed.), *Identity: Community, culture, difference* (pp. 222–237). London: Lawrence & Wishart.

Hall, S. (1991). Old and new identities; Old and new ethnicities. In A. D. King (Ed.), *Culture, globalization and the world-system: Contemporary conditions for the representation of identity* (pp. 41–68). Basingstoke, UK: Macmillan.

Hayano, D. M. (1979). Auto-ethnography: Paradigms, problems, and prospects. *Human Organization, 38*, 113–120.

Keating, A. (Ed.). (2005). *Entre mundos/among worlds: New perspectives on Gloria Anzaldúa*. New York: Palgrave.

La Fountain-Stokes, L. M. (2009). *Queer Ricans: Cultures and sexualities in the diaspora*. Minneapolis: University of Minnesota Press.

Pérez, G. M. (2004). *The near northwest side story: Migration, displacement and Puerto Rican families*. Berkeley: University of California Press.

Pérez, G. M. (2005). A gendered tale of Puerto Rican return: Place, nation, and identity. In R. B. Potter, D. Conway, & J. Phillips (Eds.), *The experience of return migration: Caribbean perspectives* (pp. 183–206). Burlington, VT: Ashgate.

Pérez, S. Z. (2002). Autoethnography and the politics of recovery: Narrative anxiety in the borderlands of culture. In J. F. Aranda, Jr. & S. Torres-Saillant (Eds.), *Recovering the U.S. Hispanic literary heritage*, vol. 4 (pp. 277–291). Houston, TX: Arte Publico Press.

Pratt, M. L. (1992). *Imperial eyes: Travel writing and transculturation*. London: Routledge.

Reed-Dunahay, D. (1997). *Auto/ethnography: Rewriting the self and the social*. New York: Berg Publishers.

Ricci, R. J. (2003). Autoethnographic verse: Nicky's boy: A life in two worlds. *The Qualitative Report, 8*(4), 591–596.

Rúa, M. (2001). Colao subjectivities: PortoMex and MexiRican perspectives on language and identity. *Centro Journal, 8*(2), 117–133.

Vidal-Ortiz, S. (2004). On being a white person of color: Using autoethnography to understand. *Qualitative Sociology, 27*(2), 179–203.

Section II: Threads of diaspora through circular migration

Coca-Cola and Coco Frío

Martín Espada

On his first visit to Puerto Rico,
island of family folklore,
the fat boy wandered
from table to table
with his mouth open.
At every table, some great-aunt
would steer him with cool spotted hands
to a glass of Coca-Cola.
One even sang to him, in all the English
she could remember, a Coca-Cola jingle
from the forties. He drank obediently, though
he was bored with this potion, familiar
from soda fountains in Brooklyn.

Then, at a roadside stand off the beach, the fat boy
opened his mouth to coco frío, a coconut
chilled, then scalped by a machete
so that a straw could inhale the clear milk.
The boy tilted the green shell overhead
and drooled coconut milk down his chin;
suddenly, Puerto Rico was not Coca-Cola
or Brooklyn, and neither was he.

For years afterward, the boy marveled at an island
where the people drank Coca-Cola
and sang jingles from World War II
in a language they did not speak,

while so many coconuts in the trees
sagged heavy with milk, swollen
and unsuckled.

Finding community cultural wealth in diaspora: A LatCrit analysis

ROSALIE ROLÓN-DOW

> I still say I got yanked away from Puerto Rico, [and] I always had the desire to come back. Even after I understood why my mom had to do it, I still had that feeling that I want[ed] to come back.... You know, when I'm in the States, I feel Puerto Rico is my home. When I'm in Puerto Rico, even though I still feel Puerto Rico is my home, I miss the States. I need both. (Samuel Calderón,[1] University of Puerto Rico student)

Transnational sensibilities such as those described by Samuel Calderón are forged by Puerto Ricans in the context of an unresolved and long-standing colonial relationship between the United States and Puerto Rico. This relationship facilitates a diaspora project of grand magnitude that is characterized by ongoing circular migration patterns, the development of networks across Puerto Rican communities in the United States and Puerto Rico, and the production of hybrid identity practices (Duany, 2007; Flores, 2009; Grosfoguel, 1999). The impact of diaspora processes is wide-ranging, evident in various arenas of Puerto Rican life including schooling.

In this chapter, I explore the experiences of students who completed some or all of their schooling in the United States and returned to Puerto Rico to pursue their undergraduate studies at the University of Puerto Rico (UPR). Community cultural wealth, a conceptual framework developed by Yosso (2005), is helpful in my analysis because it allows me to focus on cultural knowledge, skills, and networks, also known as social and cultural capital, that are produced and nurtured through diasporic processes and sensibilities and that are essential in the lives of these students. I focus on the ways that diaspora processes shape the production of cultural and social capital and illustrate the ways that these forms of capital are negotiated and affirmed within the University of Puerto Rico educational context. I argue that

Latino/a critical race theory (LatCrit) should consider the ways that diaspora processes shape community cultural wealth, and that educators can draw on this community cultural wealth to provide additive schooling experiences for Latino/a students.

Theoretical framework

Critical race theory (CRT), which grew out of critical legal studies, has been utilized in the field of education (Dixson & Rousseau, 2005; Ladson-Billings, 2005; Ladson-Billings & Tate, 1995; Lynn & Parker, 2006) for almost two decades as a transdisciplinary analytic framework that acknowledges the centrality and permanence of race and racism; challenges dominant ideologies such as White privilege, objectivity, colorblindness, and equal opportunity; values the experiential knowledge of people of color; and is committed to social justice (Solórzano, 1997, 1998). Of particular relevance to my work is Latino/a critical race theory(LatCrit), a strand within CRT that has also been utilized by education scholars (Delgado Bernal, 2002; Rolón-Dow, 2005; Solórzano & Delgado Bernal, 2001; Solórzano & Yosso, 2001; Villalpando, 2003). LatCrit seeks to move beyond the confines of a Black/White binary to understand the ways that additional elements of Latino/a histories and experiences including migration, culture, language, gender, and phenotype intersect and impact the racialized experiences of Latinos/as in particular ways (Delgado & Stefancic, 2001; Espinoza & Harris, 2000; Haney-López, 1997; Valdes, 1998). LatCrit theory is a useful tool because I seek to highlight the intersections between forms of capital and diaspora processes that are of high relevance in the contemporary experiences and histories of varied Latino/a subgroups.

In education, CRT and LatCrit are powerfully utilized to counter racialized, deficit, and distorted perspectives regarding the educational histories and experiences of students of color. The concept of community cultural wealth (Yosso, 2005) is grounded in a CRT approach to education. Traditional cultural capital theory (Bourdieu & Passeron, 1977) is often applied or interpreted in ways that do not recognize or value the cultural knowledge, assets, and dispositions that marginalized groups develop within their communities (Carter, 2003; Yosso & García, 2007). Seeking to counter deficit perspectives, Yosso (2005) defines community cultural wealth as "an array of knowledge, skills, abilities and contacts possessed and utilized by communities of color to survive and resist macro and micro forms of oppression" (p. 77).

Scholars using community cultural wealth (Liou, Antrop-González, & Cooper, 2009; Yosso, 2005; Yosso & García, 2007) highlight various forms of capital that are evident in communities of color, including linguistic, aspirational, navigational, social, familial, and resistant capital, and they assert that these forms of capital create community cultural wealth that serves as a source of strength in the education of students of color. In this chapter, I utilize Yosso's community cultural wealth conceptual framework through a LatCrit perspective. In particular, a LatCrit perspective leads me to examine the ways that notions of diaspora, central to the experiences and sensibilities of Latino/a life and cultural practices, intersect with the formation of community cultural wealth. More specifically, I highlight the linguistic, navigational, social, familial, and aspirational capital that students draw on from the cultural wealth produced and nurtured in and through their diasporic experiences.

Duany (2002b) argues that acknowledging the force of diaspora in the Puerto Rican social reality allows for a redefinition of the Puerto Rican nation as "a dispersed and fragmented subject that flows across various spaces, classes, and social locations" (p. 36). Diaspora is thus more than a bounded, quantifiable group of people. Rather, as Brubaker (2005) suggests, diaspora can be conceptualized as a category of practice, project, or stance. Engaging diaspora as process or stance allows me to pay attention to the ways community cultural wealth develops in and through the realities of circular migration patterns and transnational networks and allegiances (Duany, 2002b; Flores, 2007, 2009). I also draw on constructions of diaspora that rupture essentialist notions of nation, home, and belonging, and acknowledge the ways that diasporic cultural and linguistic practices articulate hybridity, difference, and borders (Clifford, 1994; Edwards, 2001; Hall, 1990; Lukose, 2007; Villenas, 2007). Thus, I attend to the ways that community cultural wealth develops in and through the diasporic necessity to contend with barriers to full inclusion and citizenship rights in both Puerto Rico and the United States.

Diasporization processes significantly influence the educational opportunities that Puerto Ricans are able to access, as well as the type of educational experiences they encounter. For example, Nieto (2004) argues that the second-class citizenship status engendered by the Puerto Rican colonial condition is evident in the quality of educational experiences historically experienced by Puerto Rican students. Diasporization processes also influence the forms of social and cultural capital that Puerto Rican families develop and utilize as they negotiate educational endeavors. In this chapter, I analyze the experiences of Puerto Rican students by considering the connections between diaspora processes and sensibilities and the community cultural wealth that students develop. Before I present an analysis of findings, I describe the research context and methodology for the study.

Research context, data sources, and methods

The primary participants for this study were Latino/a students, mostly Puerto Rican, who graduated from U.S. high schools and then enrolled as undergraduate students at the University of Puerto Rico (UPR). A document outlining the 21st-century goals of the university mentioned the objectives of recruiting top talent to the university and establishing initiatives that would foster cooperation and exchange with Puerto Rican communities in the United States and other countries (Diez para la década, 2006). The Bilingual Initiative Program (BI) sought to address these objectives by recruiting and enrolling Latino/a students at UPR. The program started in 2003 and was offered at three of the university's eleven campuses. Approximately 50% of the students who were part of the BI in 2008 at two UPR campuses agreed to participate in the study. The residential and educational histories of the participants varied; some students had spent all their lives to that point in the U.S., and others had experienced life and schooling in both Puerto Rico and the U.S. The students had varied levels of social and academic linguistic competence in English and Spanish.

The Bilingual Initiative Program at UPR provided an institutional space that reflected the diasporic nature of the Puerto Rico/U.S. relationship. To be eligible for the program, students had to graduate from a U.S. high school, thus providing a space at the university for students who had spent all or some portion of their lives in the United States. By offering in-state tuition for these return migrants, the project, in theory, included them as part of the Puerto Rican nation and affirmed their identities as worthy of inclusion in the Puerto Rican student body that the university is committed to serve. To be accepted into the university, students were expected to meet the university's standard admissions criteria. Once accepted, the program provided some language services such as bilingual class instruction during students' freshman year, and one-on-one or small-group tutoring services for students who needed to bolster their Spanish skills. In addition, there were excursions, meetings, and events planned for the BI students in an attempt to engage students with Puerto Rican historical knowledge and cultural practices.

Ethnographic methods were appropriate for the study because I sought to document participants' experiences and perspectives. I collected the majority of ethnographic data from August 2008 to December 2008, followed by two other brief visits in 2009. My entry into the BI family was gradual, beginning with a meeting with program personnel when they were recruiting students for the program in the United States. We found common interests and commitments through our shared concern for the education of Puerto Rican students. My own identity as a Puerto Rican female with experiences living and attending school in both Puerto Rico and the United States helped me make connections that facilitated rapport with students and program personnel. I was primarily an observer, but given the hospitality and familial cultural practices prevalent in Puerto Rico, it was relatively easy to be included in events and conversations that allowed me to develop a fuller picture of the participants and the program. My own experiences as a return migrant and an educator serving Puerto Rican students in the U.S. undoubtedly impacted how I framed my study and analysis, privileging notions of diasporic inclusiveness and expanded educational opportunities for Puerto Ricans in both the United States and Puerto Rico.

The majority of data were collected during the fall semester of 2008 and included extensive field notes focusing on BI experiences. I recorded field notes as I regularly attended classes with BI students, participated in BI program meetings, attended student and faculty academic and cultural events, and spent time chatting with students and faculty in various parts of campus. I also conducted semistructured, hour-long interviews with 36[2] of the participating students, conducted 11 focus groups with BI students, and interviewed faculty administrators and staff who participated in the program in various roles. Because I want to highlight the potential of diaspora experiences in building community cultural wealth, I focus on data from the students and university personnel who were participants in the Bilingual Initiative Program. These individuals tended to support the program and saw value in the diaspora experiences of the BI students. However, I also acknowledge that I am not making claims about the perspectives of the broader university community. The goals of the program and the students' identities as Puerto Rican were also contested and fragile within the larger university context. However, that discussion is beyond the scope of this chapter.

Data gathering was conducted in English or Spanish, according to the preferences of the individual participants. In this article, English is privileged; I translated into English all the quotes from participants who used Spanish. In what follows, I define the various forms of capital that constitute community cultural wealth, and illustrate the production and negotiation of these forms of capital in and through the experiences of BI students.

Linguistic capital

Yosso and García (2007) describe linguistic capital as "the intellectual and social skills attained through communication in multiple languages and/or language styles" (p. 160). Diaspora processes in Puerto Rican communities produce varied linguistic experiences along a bilingual continuum (Zentella, 1997), and thus expose youth to dynamic and multiple forms of linguistic capital (García, 2009). The students in this study varied both in terms of their social and academic language skills in English and Spanish and in terms of the linguistic capital available to them in home, community, and school settings. Some students were proficient bilinguals, while others were English dominant and longed to improve their limited Spanish skills. Yet, all the students experienced bilingualism, in some way or other, as part of their daily lives or as influential in their identities. For example, many of the students recalled the ways that communication within their own families in the U.S. encouraged or obligated them to use Spanish, English, or Spanglish. Nadine Sánchez stated, "I spoke English to my brother and that's how we communicated, or in Spanglish, and my mom speaks to me in Spanish." Some students had parents who regularly spoke Spanish at home, often forbidding the use of English in an effort to develop their children's Spanish proficiency. Javier Santiago said:

> That's one thing my mother always told us. Outside you're going to learn English, you're going to speak English, but inside the house you talk to me in Spanish. That's why my Spanish is strong. I can write, I can read it. She always taught us that.

Beyond the linguistic capital available in their own homes, students who attended schools in both the United States and Puerto Rico reported developing language skills because they needed to use Spanish and English in their roles as students. For example, Samuel Calderón reported that completing 2 years of elementary school in Puerto Rico provided a strong foundation for him in academic Spanish, explaining that in 4th and 5th grades he learned rules of grammar such as how to properly accentuate words in Spanish. Lymari Ortiz, who spent one of her elementary school years in the United States, reported that that year was invaluable in giving her a stronger command of English. She said, "It was really good for me. When you are young, you learn the language quickly. It was a good year for my English" (translated from Spanish).

Intermittent visits to Puerto Rico during school vacations, or ongoing connections with relatives in Puerto Rico provided other avenues for nurturing students' linguistic capital. Vanessa Morales stated, "When I was little, I would write my cousin letters in Spanish to practice my Spanish. We would also come to Puerto Rico in the summer, for a month or two." Nadine Sánchez's ongoing connections with relatives in Puerto Rico nurtured her Spanish literacy. She stated, "My grandmother and my grandfather, they used to send Spanish books to Orlando [Florida] so I would read them and not forget how to read or how to speak Spanish, [and] not to lose my Spanish accent either." Diasporic experiences of travel or of maintaining relationships across geographic borders developed linguistic capital for the students.

A positive disposition for learning or improving limited Spanish skills was another form of linguistic capital developed through diasporic longings to be identified with and belong to a body of people with shared histories and cultural practices. Hector López described how his Puerto Rican identity intersected with his longing to improve his Spanish:

> I was always really proud, I was like, "I'm Nuyorican, but I am Puerto Rican." My parents are Puerto Rican. I was always really proud of my culture and I just wanted to, I guess I wanted to better my Spanish and my [Spanish] writing because it was really bad at the time.

Melissa Pérez, who had not previously lived in Puerto Rico, explained that she was particularly interested in participating in the BI because it built on the linguistic skills of second- and third-generation Puerto Rican students like herself:

> This program was specifically for me, for second- and third-generation Puerto Ricans who are interested in learning more Spanish. I knew grammar from 4 years of high school. So this is something I want to do because Spanish still is a goal that I want to attain.

A community cultural wealth construction of students' diaspora experiences of mobility, border straddling, and cultural and linguistic identity development stands in contrast to the overused perspectives that mark students with hybrid linguistic characteristics as deficient. As Melissa and other students explained, the BI afforded students the opportunity to develop their Spanish language skills. Program personnel articulated the benefits of Spanish-English bilingualism and recognized that the students had diverse linguistic experiences. Mariana Feliciano, a university faculty/staff member, explained how diasporic migration often relegates native languages to sentimental status, and how developing students' bilingualism offered students a helpful tool for the future:

> The BI looks to make Spanish more than a language of remembering, more than the language that your grandmother spoke. We want students to be able to manage the language, not only for personal reasons but also because it can serve as a helpful tool in today's workplace. (translated from Spanish)

The BI program acknowledged the linguistic profiles of students along a bilingual continuum, and offered both institutionalized and informal support services to assist students as they acquired both academic and social Spanish language skills. One of the distinguishing features of the program was that it offered bilingual courses[3] for students during their freshman year. In addition, BI program coordinators helped some students access resources that could provide more intensive language tutoring services. While BI faculty and administrators acknowledged the language challenges that some of the students faced, they supported the students' efforts and positive dispositions toward tackling linguistic barriers. The bilingual continuum produced through diaspora processes can present particular challenges in the education of Puerto Rican students. Yet, it also produces unique forms of linguistic capital that need to be understood and harnessed as assets in the education of Puerto Rican students.

Social and familial capital[4]

Social capital is evident in the knowledge and support that is available through resources and networks of people in a given community (Yosso, 2005). Familial capital develops in the context of relationships with immediate and extended family, and through community bonds that establish a sense of kinship between individuals. This type of capital includes the cultural knowledge, community history, and memory that are produced through familial bonds (Yosso & García, 2007). The interplay of social and familial capital with processes of diaspora was powerfully evident as students described how they navigated their educational experiences. Family members who resided in Puerto Rico or had direct experiences with the UPR served as resources for many of the students. For example, Richard Ríos mentioned that family members made him aware of opportunities available at UPR and helped him establish connections with BI staff. During a visit by Richard to Puerto Rico, his uncle expressed that it would be "advantageous" for him to attend UPR because it offered "one of the most advanced chemistry [programs] you can take. It's the best place to study." Once he decided to attend the university, his cousin sent him contact information for one of the BI coordinators, who subsequently guided him through the admissions process.

Richard Ríos, one of the highest achieving students in the program, was interested in the university not only because of what it offered academically, but also because of his desire to nurture the familial capital that he had developed through previous experiences in Puerto Rico. This familial capital was expressed by his desire to return and live with his grandmother in Puerto Rico and through his strong sense of kinship with his cousins. He stated that in the United States he "was kind of alone with just my brothers. Over here, since I got like 20 cousins, I can be with them, share the holidays. I couldn't do none of that [in the States]." Students drew on familial capital to more fully incorporate themselves as members of the university community and the Puerto Rican student body. For students like Richard, who had strong bonds with family on the Island, this transition was often seamless as they drew on their experiences and familiarity with multiple homeplaces. For example, Soledad Méndez stated,

> I was born and raised in Miami all of my life, but I've been coming to Puerto Rico since I was 4, so Puerto Rico has always been to me like a second home. So, you know, I've always traveled back and forth. So, for me, moving from Miami was not that much of a big deal because I'm already used to this place, and it's part of who I am. So, there was no problem with me adjusting.

Lymari Ortiz's explanation for why she decided to stay at the university seemed to account for the familial capital that was nurtured on her return to Puerto Rico:

> Puerto Rico is home. That's one of the reasons I decided to stay here. It's because over there you're Latina. Here you're *Boricua* with everybody who's *Boricua*. So I find more identity here and this is home. *El campo* (the country) is home. Over there, the instant you get in, you're a Latino…. Culture wise, America is different than Puerto Rico.

The strength of ties with relatives and friends on the Island varied among students, but both recent and distant connections with family and community members sometimes facilitated the re-entry of students into different contexts. For example, Emily Ramírez described interactions with former classmates:

> The other day when school started I found people [at the university] that I hadn't seen since kindergarten. And I hadn't seen them in 12 years and they're like, "oh my God, it's Emily." And it felt good to know that they remembered me when they saw me. It's a shock that they still remember me, but then we have something that connects us.

Similarly, Enid Rivera stated, "When I'm in *el pueblo* (the town), just walking around, people are like, 'You're the granddaughter of Julian Rivera, right?' Like people know who my family is." Enid stated that these family connections helped her gain entry into the social scene. She said,

> I love my cousins, they'll call me up and be like, "we're going to lunch, we're going to pick you up in 45 minutes, get dressed. You're going with us." And then we meet people and go dancing and stuff.

Not all students, however, had direct ties with families or friends on the Island. Yet, many of them felt a sense of attachment to the Island that was nurtured through stories from parents or grandparents who grew up in Puerto Rico, and through stories of migration experiences and a connection to a shared Puerto Rican history or cultural practices. Despite students' diasporic longings, sometimes their claims to a shared history and their positionality as part of a Puerto Rican community were precarious and contested. While U.S. Puerto Ricans often identify the Island as a homeland, this identification is sometimes challenged in Puerto Rico (Flores, 2007). Enid stated, "People just think that we're American, that because we didn't live all our lives in Puerto Rico then we're not Puerto Rican, that we're American gringos."[5] The students' identities as Puerto Ricans were challenged to varying degrees, often depending on how much time they had spent in Puerto Rico as children and youth, their level of comfort with using Spanish, and whether they had relatives and friends on the Island. Given this context, students found ways to negotiate their familial capital in Puerto Rico. For example, Melissa Pérez, who had spent limited time in Puerto Rico, drew on the ties that her family had to particular places on the Island as useful evidence to position herself as a member of a Puerto Rican community. She stated:

> I feel like Puerto Ricans need to hear where my grandparents are from to validate that I'm Puerto Rican. I tell them, "Look, my grandfather's from Arecibo[6] and my grandmother's from Humacao, all right?" So that they know that I know about the *pueblos* (towns).

Clifford (1994) asserts that "Diaspora cultures thus mediate, in a lived tension, the experiences of separation and entanglement, of living here and remembering/desiring another place" (p. 311). For Melissa and other students, coming to Puerto Rico provided the opportunity for their remembering and desire to be tempered by the reality of negotiating their identity as Puerto Ricans in a new context.

The BI affirmed the claims to social and familial capital that students made by asserting that students seeking to make familial connections were part of the Puerto Rican student body that the university serves. Carmen Vega, a university faculty/staff member, stated,

> Part of the current [university] president's goals was to pursue initiatives that foster diversity, and that includes recruiting students in U.S. Latino communities as well as in other countries. We have generations of Puerto Ricans who want to understand the experiences of their parents or grandparents. (translated from Spanish)

The goal of fostering diversity in the university was repeatedly mentioned by BI faculty and administrators as an important impetus for developing the BI program. While the university clearly articulated the broader goal of fostering diversity, BI personnel specifically acknowledged and saw value in the diversity of "Puerto Rican" experiences that BI students embodied. Mariana Feliciano, university faculty/staff, described ways that the presence of BI students at the university provided an opportunity for other students to connect their own histories with those of Puerto Ricans who had experienced migration, essentially extending their sense of kinship to be more inclusive of diasporic connections and networks. She said,

> It's really interesting to watch how the students, having the BI students in the same classroom, they begin to notice and to think about how that other Puerto Rico is part of the Puerto Rican chapter. And the island of Puerto Rico can't stop at Vieques and Culebra,[7] even though psychologically and through education or academically they have made you think that. So in that sense, the program opens a reflection on that history. When they begin to hear about the experiences of the parents of those BI students, what it was like for them to leave Puerto Rico for what they thought was a better place, then they begin to make connections in history, and history begins to be repaired. (translated from Spanish)

The BI sought to nurture deeper connections between students with varied Puerto Rican experiences. Additionally, it drew on and further developed connections with Puerto Rican communities in the United States. For example, some of the students learned about the BI program through connections with Puerto Rican community organizations in the United States. These community organizations provided an extended network within the Puerto Rican community that served as a resource in recruiting and supporting students. Additionally, BI faculty and administrators hoped that some of the BI students would be able to return to Puerto Rican communities in the United States after their graduations and contribute to the development of those communities. As Carmen Vega, university faculty/staff, stated, "We also understand that we contribute to their educational development but also to the development of leaders to serve Hispanic communities in the U.S." Nancy Ramos, university faculty/staff, also spoke of the reciprocal relationships that could be developed by nurturing the social and familial capital produced by Puerto Rican diaspora proceses. She stated:

> Like these administrators from [a community organization in] New Jersey came precisely because they feel that now it's the third generation, they're losing the language, they're losing the links with the culture, they need community activists, they need people that are more entrenched in the culture and the language of Puerto Rico so the new immigrants can be served. So this is that third generation that is going to be professional, but they felt that they have distanced themselves. How are they going to serve this community? They came here, four of them came here to Puerto Rico because they heard

about the BI program and they wanted to give scholarships to students in the community.... They spoke to us, they explained what they were looking for, they needed professionals, well-prepared professionals to serve their communities and be activists of their communities.

The social and familial capital of students developed through diaspora processes was a source of cultural wealth utilized in a range of ways, from the recruiting efforts of the BI in the United States to the efforts to integrate students into university and community life in Puerto Rico.

Resistant capital

Diaspora consciousness partially develops as individuals and communities continually face and resist exclusion, racialization and socioeconomic constraints (Clifford, 1994). As individuals and communities oppose inequities, they develop particular skills, dispositions and knowledge known as resistant capital (Yosso, 2005). This intersection of resistant capital with the development of a diaspora consciousness and diaspora processes was evident among some of the students. That is, parents and/or community leaders sought to educate youth on historical and contemporary struggles faced by Puerto Rican communities, and they nurtured skills and dispositions to help them resist inequality. Hector López, who attended a predominantly White high school, recounted several instances where he experienced either subtle or overt prejudiced or racist actions and attitudes. He stated:

> Like, there's this one teacher and me and her used to fight a lot. She [would say things] like, "oh, did you hear they are making new low-income apartments? Now there's going to be all these minorities in this school?" Or the students [would say], "oh there's more Black people, it's getting darker." These people would tell me these things and I'm like, do you realize I'm a minority as well. "Yeah, but you're different" [they'd say].

Hector explained that these prejudiced and racist perceptions of Puerto Ricans and other people of color were countered by his family's active engagement in a Puerto Rican community in a nearby city. His perspective was shaped by his family's regular visits to a Puerto Rican community to shop, attend church, participate in a cultural organization, and spend time with Puerto Rican family and friends. It was his ongoing connections with Puerto Ricans in diasporic communities that helped him develop a critical perspective of what some students and teachers were saying about Puerto Ricans.

For Samuel Calderón, it was involvement in the local chapter of the ASPIRA[8] organization that was instrumental in helping him develop a critical understanding of the predominantly Puerto Rican community where he lived. He said:

Over there in the States, you know, there's always the thing about everyone's equal; but there's always something in the back of everybody's head that is completely the opposite. You know, [there are] differences, stereotypes, whatever. It would be subtle, but it's still, you can tell it's still racist, or racism. And I also saw it in the way people referred to Puerto Ricans, there were subconscious differences.

RR: Tell me a little bit more about that, how you felt that, how you experienced that.

SC: It's not the racism that people always alienate others, from like the South kind of racism. It's not like that. It's more like, who to blame. Like when people say, "You guys don't try enough." Like the leader in ASPIRA, he was telling me he was talking to a state senator about trying to get funds for ASPIRA, and he said "Your people don't vote so why should I help you?" Those kind of comments.

Samuel's conversations with a community leader helped him interpret contemporary ways that racism is manifested towards Puerto Rican and other Latino/a communities. Students offered a range of understandings on how racism impacted them personally or Puerto Rican communities generally. Where there seemed to be the most shared experience among students was in regards to racism along linguistic dimensions. As students spoke of how they sought to maintain or nurture their linguistic capital, it was evident that they also developed skills and knowledge to resist racism. Nadine Sánchez recounted the following experience:

I remember in middle school there was this teacher who told me that I shouldn't speak Spanish. [She said,] "You're in America, and you should speak English." And that's when I'm like, "I don't think so. I think I have the right to express myself in any language." And that's the reason why I started looking for an answer. Can we talk Spanish? Are we allowed? It really bugged me. And I started reading more books about it. I just started to read about everything like civil rights and Martin Luther King. And I even called up my grandfather since he was a lawyer. I'm like *Abuelo* [Grandpa], what do I do?" And he's like, you have the right to talk any language that you want in the United States [be]cause it's in the constitution. It doesn't state a specific language. And after that, it made me want to study law.

Many students had similar experiences of prohibited Spanish language use. Nadine's motivation to "look for an answer" was fostered by her personal experiences of racism and nurtured through her familial diasporic ties. Yosso (2005) writes that "maintaining and passing on the multiple dimensions of community cultural wealth is also part of the knowledge base of resistant capital" (p. 80). Students who had access to diasporic linguistic capital were thus also receiving resistant capital. Students also shared frustrations about not having Spanish classes in high school that took into account their bilingual skills. In one case,

Adamary Muñiz, along with some friends, managed to advocate for a special Spanish class that considered their advanced Spanish language skills:

> They taught grammar (in high school). And the grammar was like, "cat is *gato.*" I didn't learn any Spanish while I was in Spanish, and I graduated from the highest level of Spanish my school had to offer. Actually, we made them open a higher level than what they had. There was three of us, we took the highest level there was junior year, and senior year we would have had nothing to take and we made them offer [Spanish] in the higher level for us.

Some of the students were frustrated and sometimes surprised that they continued to face linguistic borders when they came to Puerto Rico. Neftalí Irizarry spoke of the ways that this linguistic othering mirrored what he had felt in the United States:

> Maybe some towns [in Puerto Rico] are more exposed to English, but people still have that same notion that if you talk English, you're gringo. Even if they are exposed to English, that's the idea they have. I see that both sides see the other as the stranger, as inferior. If you are here and talk English, it's like you are invading. If you are over there [in the U.S.] and you talk Spanish, it's like you are invading as well.

Some of the BI faculty members explained that living and studying in Puerto Rico provided students more critical, resistant perspectives on the challenges of "othering" that they faced both in the United States and Puerto Rico. Nancy Ramos (university faculty/staff) stated:

> In the U.S. they are inserted in a country where the Puerto Rican and Latin Americans are the minority, and there's a dominant discourse of stereotypes and prejudices against these minorities that permeates everything. They're inserted in that, and even if you are the minority that the prejudices are against, you hear that discourse so much that you are assimilated in some shape or form. You have to be alert day and night to the discourse that is being used for you to always be challenging them. There are times where you relax and that enters your cognitive unconscious. Here they insert themselves in a community where the majority are Puerto Ricans. That doesn't mean that the dominant discourse does not function here; it functions here also. But they are here and they are seeing and they are experiencing it; they are experiencing what it is to live here and looking at the problems of the Puerto Ricans here. They are going to be talking about that immigration and why do people leave, what are the circumstances. So they are going to have a more critical, not only a more academically critical view, a more embodied critical view because they are living these experiences and not just reading about them.

The BI nurtured resistant capital rooted in diaspora experiences through its acknowledgement of the challenges that hybrid identity and linguistic practices presented for students. It thus provided a form of resistant capital to students by challenging essentialized notions of who belonged, and acknowledging diaspora experiences in the construction of Puerto Rican identities.

Aspirational capital

Aspirational capital refers to "the ability to maintain hopes and dreams for the future, even in the face of real or perceived barriers" (Yosso, 2005, p. 77). Clifford (1994) writes that "Diaspora consciousness lives loss and hope as a defining tension (p. 312)." In communities that have historically been underserved by educational systems, the hope engendered by aspirational capital can help students break historical patterns as children are encouraged to advance to occupational and academic trajectories that their parents or grandparents have not experienced. As students recounted their educational journeys, it was repeatedly evident that aspirational capital was nurtured in their homes and communities. While social class and quality of educational experiences mediated the barriers that the students faced, it was not uncommon for students to advance beyond their parents' educational achievements by the time they graduated high school and enrolled in the university. Students, such as Héctor Camacho, described how his father encouraged him to work to create more opportunities for himself and subsequent generations.

> My dad tells me, "In my house, my father was the only one that worked and he told me what he could give me. I am giving you what I can give you son and it's a lot more than what my father could give me. I only ask you to do better than me." It's hard because every time I try to do something, he says, "try to do better than me so that you can give your children something better than what I gave you. If you think that I have failed you in any way, do it better than me." You know, [he means] give them a better life (portions of this quote translated from Spanish).

Lymari Ortiz talked of the hopes that her parents had for quality educational opportunities in the United States and the ways these hopes and dreams were constructed in light of her mother's limited schooling and career experiences.

> My dad has always, it was always one of my expectations to go to America and study there; my dad always wanted me to go there and study too because maybe it would give me more opportunities... They want me to do my bachelor's and from there carry on studying and have a profession. My mom wants me to have a profession so bad because she never had that, she never had it. Women need to study and be able to support themselves; she's always told me that. (portions of this quote translated from Spanish)

It was out of her mothers' limited educational and occupational experiences that Lymari was taught lessons of self-reliance (Villenas & Moreno, 2001) that nurtured aspirational capital. Jessica Figueroa learned similar lessons.

My mom would like me to be more than her. She tells me that she didn't have the support I have or the opportunities I have. She tells me to take advantage of those opportunities because if she had been in my position she would have done what I am doing and much more. (translated from Spanish)

The vast majority of the students felt that their parents supported their educational pursuits and, in particular, the attainment of a high school diploma. Students also reported that their parents encouraged them to attend college even if they were unsure how they would cover the costs of higher education. Over and over, most of the students explained that the Bilingual Initiative Program provided the most viable option for them to afford college, making the dream of going to college a reality. For example, Jessica Figueroa stated:

It wasn't easy because I only count on my mom to help me economically and I always thought that paying for college would be an obstacle. Here [in Puerto Rico] I have more opportunity because going to the university is a little more accessible. Paying for college was one of the major obstacles I faced, but despite all that, there was always support, there was always love, the only thing was the economic piece.

Aspirational capital did not eliminate the stresses of determining how students would overcome obstacles to achieve their hopes and dreams. Lymari Ortiz fully understood the aspirations her parents held for her, and she realized that UPR was the best option to help her pursue those aspirations after receiving a tuition bill from a university in the United States:

When we were there, we saw it was so expensive. So I got myself a scholarship but when the bill came my dad said, "where is the scholarship?" And I'm like, "right there, don't you see it?" And it was a lot of pressure because it was $15,000 every semester and we couldn't pay that. I thought that because I had a 3.6 GPA that I would get a really good scholarship, but the scholarship didn't even cover a fourth of what I had to pay. (portions of this quote translated from Spanish)

Nurturing the hopes and dreams of students sometimes involved finding alternative routes to pursue educational goals. For many of the students, the Bilingual Initiative Program became this alternative route, nurturing a culture of possibility grounded in the realities of lives shaped by Puerto Rican diaspora processes. These realities include suppressed economic opportunities on the Island and a primarily poor and working-class migrant experience. Nancy Ramos, university faculty/staff, explained that her hope for the program was that it would remove some of the barriers to higher education that Puerto Rican students continue to face because of poverty and inequitable educational systems in the United States:

There is a big Latino population in the United States. And studies have shown that the Latinos are way at the bottom in terms of college education. It's been shown in the studies that without a college degree, the jobs that you get are jobs below sustenance level, [and] that means that the cycle of poverty will never end for the Latinos. Never. Never. They are stuck in poverty. The University of Puerto Rico is the state university, it is the public university. It's here to serve the Puerto Rican population. So we have broadened our definition of the Puerto Rican population to include the Puerto Ricans that are not from the Island, millions that are not on the Island. We're making that definition broader so that they can come and receive quality education at a very low cost, making higher education accessible to them, because at this moment it is not.

Leslie Mercado, university faculty/staff, asserted that a more inclusive perspective on "the Puerto Rican community" would help Hispanic communities in Puerto Rico and the United States:

My impression is that many people have different visions of what this type of student is. I understand that I am serving the Puerto Rican community [in the BI].... We need to make education accesible to the Hispanic community in the United States so that they may be an asset in their society, be it here or there, it doesn't matter. That's my vision.

This broader vision of the role of UPR in improving the educational conditions of Puerto Ricans was inherently tied to an acknowledgement of the central role of diaspora processes in shaping Puerto Rican history. For these faculty members, there was a sense of a collective "we" in defining the Puerto Rican community, and an acknowledgement of the inextricable link between the U.S. and Puerto Rico. They asserted that it was in the best interests of both Island and mainland Puerto Ricans to be inclusive of one another in efforts to improve educational and social conditions, that is, in playing a role in nurturing the aspirational capital of diaspora students. Several faculty/staff members stated that this idea was contested, but they believed the university had an obligation to this segment of the Puerto Rican community. Julio Díaz, a faculty/staff member, described it as "a historic responsibility of something we owe because these are the grandchildren of that immigration of the 1950s to the United States." They explained that extending the boundaries of Puerto Rico would benefit Puerto Rican communities on the Island and in the United States. Nancy Ramos stated:

I think that everything that allows us to connect with the Puerto Rican community in the States, anything that helps us understand each other better and understand the contexts in which we are raised, is an extraordinary benefit. There are differences and we can accept them as differences, not as deficits.

> I think the students that come here are going to make connections, and I think that's enriching. By including these students in the university, we can also contribute to the development of leaders in those U.S. communities.

Individuals who had leadership roles in the BI were likely to be highly supportive of the idea behind the program, and were deeply committed to the success of students in the program. In this way, they nurtured the aspirational capital of students.

Conclusions and implications

In this chapter, I highlight the linguistic, navigational, social, familial, and aspirational capital that is evident as a group of Puerto Rican students negotiates educational experiences in the Bilingual Initiative Program at the University of Puerto Rico. I illustrate the ways that diaspora processes and sensibilities intersect with the development of community cultural wealth for Puerto Rican students. Articulating the intersections between diaspora processes and community cultural wealth provides one example of the ways Latino/a critical race theory can be enhanced through attention to diasporization. LatCrit theory and practice will benefit by carefully considering the workings of dynamic and ongoing diaspora processes of migration, homeland orientation, identity development, exclusion, and resistance as these intersect with racial projects and practices.

Yosso (2005) argues that "one of the most prevalent forms of racism in U.S. schools is deficit thinking" (p. 75), and she advances community cultural wealth to acknowledge the cultural and social capital of marginalized communities. Understanding the ways that diaspora processes intersect with the formation and deployment of community cultural wealth is one way educational researchers can counter racism that is manifested through deficit perspectives and dominant (mis)representations of Latino/a students. This is an important contribution to the literature on social and cultural capital because, as Carter (2003) asserts, scholars have paid scant attention to nondominant forms of capital. A diasporic perspective can provide an alternative lens for constructing and investigating the cultural and social capital that exists in the communities, networks, and institutions of (im)migrant families. An important line of inquiry is investigating how diaspora processes shape the assets and cultural wealth of Latino/a groups, as well as the (mis)representations and deficit perspectives that are constructed about students. I thus advance the LatCrit concept of diasporic community cultural wealth because it offers potential to researchers examining the relationship of social capital and education across Latino/a subgroups.

This work also has practical implications. Duany (2002a) asserts that the constant mobility and circulation that characterizes Puerto Rican migration "does not entail major losses in human capital for most Puerto Ricans, but rather often represents an occupational, educational, and linguistic asset" (p. 365). Focusing on the assets or capital produced in and through Puerto Rican migration opens up ways to be responsive to the particular realities of students who are impacted by diasporic processes. Most importantly, building on the diasporic community cultural wealth of varied Latino/a subgroups can help educators, policy makers, and reformers conceptualize and provide additive schooling experiences (Valenzuela, 1999) in Latino/a communities. The Bilingual Initiative Program highlighted in this study contained some elements of an additive schooling experience for Puerto Ricans returning to the Island for their postsecondary schooling. I suggest that the BI provided additive schooling experiences when it promoted practices and polices that considered and built on the diasporic community cultural wealth of students. Other Latin American countries that are impacted by diaspora processes might consider how their educational programs and policies can build on the knowledge, skills, and sensibilities engendered by their own diaspora histories and contemporary circumstances. Additionally, educators and reformers in the United States ought to investigate how to draw on the diaspora community cultural wealth of both individual Latino/a subgroups and the larger panethnic Latino/a group. Many models of educational reform for Latino/a students focus on giving students access to dominant, powerful forms of capital (i.e., middle- and upper-class cultural practices and values). While I believe this remains important, it is also imperative to notice and utilize the unique forms of capital that Latino/a communities develop in and through diasporic processes and histories. Seeking to understand the potential assets found in diasporic paths and sensibilities can open up new possibilities for conceptualizing who students are, what they can offer in a school setting, and the types of skills and curriculum that might be relevant to their lives. This investigation of diasporic community cultural wealth as a site for additive schooling experiences is timely, given the increasing ways that the lives of Latino/a youth from various subgroups are shaped by diaspora sensibilities born of their transnational experiences across literal and figurative borders.

Acknowledgments

This project was made possible through funding from a Ford Foundation Postdoctoral Diversity Fellowship and funding from the Center for International Studies, University of Delaware, International Research Award. The author would like to acknowledge the generosity and hospitality provided by her research participants at the University of Puerto Rico.

Notes

1. Names of participants are pseudonyms. At times, I slightly alter details about their histories to provide anonymity. When university faculty, staff, or administrators are quoted, I identify them only as university faculty/staff in order to provide minimal information about their roles at the university and ensure anonymity.
2. In this chapter, I consider the experiences of the Puerto Rican students. There were a small number of Latino/a students in the BI who were from other subgroups, and students who did not claim any Latino/a heritage but were attracted to the program because of previous experiences in other Spanish-speaking countries.
3. BI faculty informally recruited instructors willing to teach these courses. There was a range of ways that faculty implemented a bilingual model in their classrooms.
4. I present social and familial capital together because they were produced in inextricable ways.
5. In Puerto Rico, "gringos" refers to foreigners, most usually people from the United States. It is sometimes, but not always, intended as a disparaging term.
6. Arecibo and Humacao are cities in Puerto Rico.
7. Vieques and Culebra are small islands that are part of Puerto Rico.
8. ASPIRA is an organization founded in the 1960s to address educational needs and challenges in Puerto Rican communities in the United States.

References

Bourdieu, P., & Passeron, J.-C. (1977). *Reproduction in education, society and culture.* London: Sage.
Brubaker, R. (2005). The "diaspora" diaspora. *Ethnic and Racial Studies, 28*(1), 1–19.
Carter, P. (2003). Black cultural capital, status positioning, and the conflict of schooling for low-income, African American youth. *Social Problems, 50*(1), 136–155.
Clifford, J. (1994). Diasporas. *Cultural Anthropology, 9*(3), 302–338.
Delgado, R., & Stefancic, J. (2001). *Critical race theory: An introduction.* New York: New York University Press.
Delgado Bernal, D. (2002). Critical race theory, Latino critical theory, and critical raced-gendered epistemologies: Recognizing students of color as holders and creators of knowledge. *Qualitative Inquiry, 8,* 105–126.
Diez para la década. 2006. University of Puerto Rico. Retrieved from http://www.upr.edu/?type=page&id=la_upr_diez_para_la_decada&ancla=diez_para_la_decada
Dixson, A. D., & Rousseau, C. K. (2005). And we are still not saved: Critical race theory in education ten years later. *Race, Ethnicity and Education, 8*(1), 7–27.
Duany, J. (2002a). Mobile livelihoods: The sociocultural practices of circular migrants between Puerto Rico and the United States. *International Migration Review, 36*(2), 355–388.
Duany, J. (2002b). *The Puerto Rican nation on the move: Identities on the island and in the United States.* Chapel Hill: University of North Carolina Press.

Duany, J. (2007). Nation and migration: Rethinking Puerto Rican identity in a transnational context. In F. Negrón-Muntaner (Ed.), *None of the above: Puerto Ricans in the global era* (pp. 51–63). New York: Palgrave Macmillan.

Edwards, B. H. (2001). The uses of diaspora. *Social Text, 19*(1), 45–73.

Espinoza, L., & Harris, A. (2000). Embracing the tar-baby: LatCrit theory and the sticky mess of race. In R. Delgado & J. Stefancic (Eds.), *Critical race theory: The cutting edge* (2nd ed.) (pp. 440–447). Philadelphia: Temple University Press.

Flores, J. (2007). The diaspora strikes back: Nation and location. In F. Negrón Muntaner (Ed.), *None of the above: Puerto Ricans in the global era* (pp. 211–216). New York: Palgrave Macmillan.

Flores, J. (2009). *The diaspora strikes back: Caribeño tales of learning and turning.* New York: Routledge.

García, O. (2009). *Bilingual education in the 21st century.* Malden, MA & Oxford: Wiley/Blackwell.

Grosfoguel, R. (1999). Puerto Ricans in the USA: A comparative approach. *Journal of Ethnic and Migration Studies, 25*(2), 233–249.

Hall, S. (1990). Cultural identity and diaspora. In J. Rutherford (Ed.), *Identity: Community, culture, difference* (pp. 222–237). London: Lawrence & Wishart.

Haney-López, I. F. (1997). Race, ethnicity, and erasure: The salience of race to LatCrit theory. *La Raza Law Journal, 10*, 57–125.

Ladson-Billings, G. (2005). The evolving role of critical race theory in educational scholarship. *Race, Ethnicity and Education, 8*(1), 115–119.

Ladson-Billings, G., & Tate, W. (1995). Toward a critical race theory of education. *Teachers College Record, 97*(1), 47–68.

Liou, D., Antrop-González, R., & Cooper, R. (2009). Unveiling the promise of community cultural wealth to sustaining Latino/a students' college-going information networks. *Educational Studies, 45*, 534–555.

Lukose, R. (2007). The difference that diaspora makes: Thinking through the anthropology of immigrant education in the United States. *Anthropology and Education Quarterly, 38*(4), 405–418.

Lynn, M., & Parker, L. (2006). Critical race studies in education: Examining a decade of research on U.S. schools. *The Urban Review, 38*(4), 257–290.

Nieto, S. (2004). Puerto Rican students in U.S. schools: A troubled past and the search for a hopeful future. In J. A. Banks & C. A. McGee Banks (Eds.), *Handbook of research on multicultural education* (2nd ed.) (pp. 515–541). San Francisco: Jossey-Bass.

Rolón-Dow, R. (2005). Critical care: A color(full) analysis of care narratives in the schooling experiences of Puerto Rican girls. *American Educational Research Journal, 42*(1), 77–111.

Solórzano, D. (1997). Images and words that wound: Critical race theory, racial stereotyping and teacher education. *Teacher Education Quarterly, 24*, 5–19.

Solórzano, D. (1998). Critical race theory, racial and gender microaggressions, and the experiences of Chicana and Chicano scholars. *International Journal of Qualitative Studies in Education, 11*, 121–136.

Solórzano, D. G., & Delgado Bernal, D. (2001). Examining transformational resistance through a critical race and LatCrit theory framework: Chicana and Chicano students in an urban context. *Urban Education, 36*(3), 308–342.

Solórzano, D. G., & Yosso, T. J. (2001). Critical race and LatCrit theory and method: Counterstorytelling Chicana and Chicano graduate school experiences. *International Journal of Qualitative Studies in Education, 14*(4), 471–495.

Valdes, F. (1998). Foreword: Under construction—LatCrit consciousness, community and theory. *La Raza Law Journal, 10,* 1087–1142.

Valenzuela, A. (1999). *Subtractive schooling: U.S.-Mexican youth and the politics of caring.* Albany: State University of New York Press.

Villalpando, O. (2003). Self-segregation or self-preservation? A critical race theory and Latina/o critical theory analysis of findings from a longitudinal study of Chicana/o college students. *International Journal of Qualitative Studies in Education, 16*(5), 619–646.

Villenas, S. (2007). Diaspora and the anthropology of Latino education: Challenges, affinities and intersections. *Anthropology and Education Quarterly, 38*(4), 419–425.

Villenas, S., & Moreno, M. (2001). To *valerse por si misma* between race, capitalism, and patriarchy: Latina mother-daughter pedagogies in North Carolina. *International Journal of Qualitative Studies in Education, 14*(5), 671–688.

Yosso, T. (2005). Whose culture has capital? A critical race theory discussion of community cultural wealth. *Race, Ethnicity and Education, 8*(1), 69–91.

Yosso, T. J., & García, D. G. (2007). "This is no slum!" A critical race theory analysis of community cultural wealth in Culture Clash's *Chavez Ravine. Azlán: A Journal of Chicano Studies, 32*(1), 145–179.

Zentella, A. (1997). *Growing up bilingual: Puerto Rican children in New York.* Malden, MA: Blackwell.

Educated entremundos (between worlds): Exploring the role of diaspora in the lives of Puerto Rican teachers

SANDRA QUIÑONES

So, the word *educación* was so much in my household since we didn't speak very much English in my household. I only spoke English with my sisters because we were at school and we were learning English. So, to me, the word *educación* just held all that and then when I actually graduated from college, it kinda solidified the meaning for me. I think that *educación* is not just going to school and succeeding, but it's about overcoming. A lot of the time when we look at successful Puerto Ricans in the media, or just anywhere, I'm sure they didn't have a peachy clean picket-fence childhood. I mean, I didn't live in a two-story house with a picket fence and the dog. We were working check to check. My mom was on welfare for a long time, so it was a struggle to get to where I am today. My roots is what pushed me to where I am, so the word *educación* represents attributes of home life and school life merging into the success of what I am today. (Interview with Liana Roldán[1])

In the quote above, Liana Roldán, a 27-year-old Puerto Rican bilingual education teacher, shares her experiences and perspectives around *educación*[2] and education. Liana was one of six Puerto Rican teachers at Gordon Elementary School[3] in Lakeview,[4] New York, who participated in a qualitative study[5] I conducted about the role of *educación* in the life histories and outlook of Puerto Rican diaspora teachers, and how teachers connect Latino family values about *ser bien educado*[6] with teaching and learning in and outside of schools.

Given my experience as an elementary school teacher and a member of the Puerto Rican diaspora community of Lakeview for 16 years, Liana's response intrigued me. What I found particularly interesting in Liana's response was how she stated that *educación* "is not just going to school and succeeding, but it's about overcoming." Although she framed her discussion of *educación* and education within the dominant American narrative of "triumphing against the odds," (Flores, 2009), she also addressed structural issues of poverty and inequity related to individual and collective obstacles in the journey toward success (Acosta-Belén & Santiago, 2006; Marzán, 2009; Whalen & Vázquez-Hernández, 2005). Moreover, Liana affirmed her primary language and culture by noting that being raised in a Spanish-speaking Puerto Rican household played a significant role in her development as a well-educated person: "My roots is what pushed me to where I am, so the word *educación* represents attributes of home life and school life merging into the success of what I am today." In doing so, she espoused an additive and equity-minded view of education that valued "the histories, resources, strengths and cultural and linguistic practices present in Puerto Rican communities" (De Jesús & Rolón-Dow, 2007, p. 5). Liana, who was born in Cayey, Puerto Rico, and moved to Lakeview, New York, as a toddler, actively negotiated language, culture, and power in multiple geographic settings over her lifetime. She helped me understand how being raised in a Spanish-language, working-class Puerto Rican household within a U.S. mainland setting informed her bilingual and bicultural understanding of *educación* and what it means to be a well-educated person.

The purpose of this chapter is to highlight how diaspora processes intersect with the life histories of six Puerto Rican teachers living and working in western New York. I draw from Darder's (2012) critical biculturalism framework and use the notion of diaspora as a stance (Brubaker, 2005; Rolón-Dow, 2010) to theorize the role of diaspora in the lives of the teachers as I examine how diaspora processes have shaped their experiences as educators. Two questions frame the research: (1) How do diaspora-forged experiences (Flores, 2009) contribute to the development of critical bilingual-bicultural social identities and practices? (2) How do participants mediate historical and ongoing sociocultural dissonance amidst multiple roles and changing contexts? I highlight four themes in the findings, and argue that diaspora processes contribute to the development of critical bilingual-bicultural stances over time, across generations and geographic locations, and in relation to other groups. By highlighting the role of diaspora in the lives of these teachers and how diaspora processes informed their teaching and learning, this chapter contributes to a better understanding of how in-service Puerto Rican educators "bring knowledge and wisdom centered in their own ways of knowing and being" to their teaching and learning profession (Darder, 2012, p. 100).

Theoretical framework

Diasporas can be viewed as a group of people, or bounded entities, who are dispersed in locations outside of their homelands or heritage nation-states, yet hold emotional and social ties (i.e., sense of belonging) to real or imagined homeland communities (Braziel & Mannur, 2003; Brubaker, 2005; Flores, 2009; Whalen & Vázquez-Hernández, 2005). A more active orientation of diaspora emphasizes cultural and linguistic practices and identities, while remaining mindful of essentialist notions of cultural membership. In line with Rolón-Dow & Irizarry (this volume), I conceptualize diaspora "as a set of historically grounded processes and sensibilities which are continually produced, negotiated, and/or resisted in relation to other groups, across generations and geographic locations and in and through the sociopolitical, historical, and cultural conditions germane to a particular group." This diachronic and processual approach to diaspora accounts for the relationship between individuals and society in a way that is dynamic, contextual, and nuanced, rather than unchanging, ahistorical, unidirectional, and devoid of power, tension, and struggle (Brinkerhoff, 2009; Cohen, 1997; Grosfoguel, 2003; Negrón-Muntaner, 2007; Rolón-Dow, 2010; Torres & Velázquez, 1998).

Puerto Ricans living in the U.S. mainland have distinct and complex historical, sociocultural, and sociopolitical experiences that need to be taken into account as part of a growing body of Latina/o education research (De Jesús & Rolón-Dow, 2007; Nieto, 2000, 2004; Rolón-Dow, 2005, 2010). According to Duany (2002), Puerto Rico represents a translocal community "with its own territory, history, language, and culture" (p. 83), with sociopolitical ties to the United States as a territory:

> The prevailing juridical definition of the Island as neither a state of the Union nor a sovereign republic has created an ambiguous, problematic, and contested political status for more than a hundred years. Paradoxically, it has also strengthened the sense of peoplehood among Puerto Ricans. (Duany, 2002, p. 4)

The complexity and distinctiveness of the Puerto Rican diaspora, with its strong sense of peoplehood, is grounded in ongoing transnational migration patterns amidst long-standing colonial politics (Duany, 2002, 2011; Flores, 1993, 2009; Grosfoguel, 2003; Negrón-Muntaner & Grosfoguel, 1997).

Given Puerto Rico's sociopolitical context and legacies of colonialism, I utilize Darder's critical biculturalism framework to explore the ways that participants (re)negotiate their identities around cultural constructs that shape role expectations, views of education, and social interactions:

Biculturalism speaks to the process wherein individuals learn to function in two distinct sociocultural environments: their primary culture, and that of the dominant mainstream culture of the society in which they live. It represents the process by which bicultural human beings mediate between the dominant discourse of educational institutions and the realities that they must face as members of subordinate cultures. (Darder, 2011, p. 20)

Darder associates four major response patterns with the process of biculturalism: alienation, dualism, separatism, and negotiation. These four responses reflect modes of engagement, or patterns of interactions that move a person closer toward, or away from, bicultural affirmation. This, in turn, relates to the extent that a person's cultural identity (individual and social/collective identity) is negotiated with the primary culture, dominant culture, or a combination of both cultures. Hence, Darder's (2012) critical biculturalism framework is a tool for examining to what extent participating teachers' diasporic experiences and perspectives reveal a strong relationship between bicultural social identity development and critical social consciousness (p. 204). This lens is also helpful for considering how home, school, and community conditions support, complicate, or hinder the development of critical biculturalism (Darder, 1993, 1995).

Utilizing a diaspora framework combined with a critical approach to biculturalism provides a useful interpretive lens for theorizing the role of diaspora in the lives of the teachers in this study, and for considering how diaspora processes have shaped their experiences as educators. By emphasizing resistance to subjugation at the individual and collective levels, this combined interpretive framework facilitates a deeper understanding of how participants mediate historical and ongoing sociocultural dissonance amidst multiple roles and changing contexts.

Research design

The findings in this chapter are part of a qualitative research study blending life history and narrative research methods to examine how bilingual Puerto Rican teachers in an urban elementary school conceptualize and enact what it means to be *bien educada/o* and well educated. In the larger study, I drew from Chicana/Latina feminist theory (Delgado Bernal, Elenes, Godinez, & Villenas, 2006) grounded in a critical bicultural framework (Darder, 2012). The research design was inspired and informed by the metaphorical and theoretical concept of *trenzas* (braids), which allowed me to explore how personal, professional, and community knowledge shaped teachers' perspectives and experiences (Delgado Bernal, 2008). Through a series of in-depth interviews and focus groups with participant reflections, I studied the lives of six teachers who told me stories about their home-family-community upbringings, family values, schooling, and professional-occupational experiences. I viewed their stories and the details of their lives "as a way of knowing and understanding" individual and collective meaning-making around a shared concept (Seidman, 2006, p. 1). This methodological approach facilitated a deeper understanding of the life histories and outlook of Puerto Rican teachers, and how teachers connected views to teaching and learning in and outside of schools.

Research site

The research took place in Lakeview, a mid-sized city in western New York where Puerto Ricans historically represent a large and fast-growing Latino population, particularly since the great migration period of 1945 to 1960 (McCally, 2007; Saenz, 2011). Similar to other Puerto Rican diaspora communities in the United States, Puerto Ricans in Lakeview were actively involved in creating their sense of place, space, and belonging (Acosta-Belén, 2009; Flores, 2009; Walsh, 2000). The school site, Gordon Elementary School, is a large elementary school in the Lakeview City School District (PreK–6) with nearly 700 students. Nearly 100% of the students at Gordon Elementary School were eligible for free or reduced lunch, and the student population was predominantly Hispanic/Latino (60%), followed by African American (38%), and White (2%). The school had partnerships with several community organizations to support literacy, character education, extended learning opportunities, and mentoring programs. A local health management organization provided on-site medical and mental health services.

I gained access to the school site through Roger, a White male bilingual teacher who had been working at Gordon for more than 25 years. I met Roger at a local Spanish-speaking church and told him about my research interests and objectives. He then spoke with Miguel, a Puerto Rican administrator at Gordon Elementary School, about my research project. Miguel immediately requested to meet with me. He was excited about the study because he felt it was timely and relevant to the everyday practices of Puerto Rican teachers at Gordon Elementary School.

Participant selection criteria

During a series of meetings and school visits in early spring 2011, Miguel introduced me to the school staff, with particular attention to teachers who met the participant selection criteria. Initially, I wanted a purposive sample of participants who self-identified as Puerto Rican and had advanced degrees and professional teaching certification(s). Beyond the initial criteria, I sought diversity in terms of age, place of birth, migration patterns, and generational status, in an effort to account for transnational and diaspora-related factors between participants.

Of the twelve teachers who met the participation selection criteria, six approached me personally during the school visits and expressed their interest in being interviewed for the study (see Table 1). Ariana was the first teacher to approach me. She and I had met through a mutual friend of more than 10 years. I was also excited when Maribel, Patricia, and Helena volunteered to participate. I had previously worked with them at a local bilingual charter school, and this research project afforded us the opportunity to reconnect and expand our personal and professional relationships. Brenda and Liana were new contacts that were pleased to hear that I had teaching experience in the same district, and was a Puerto Rican doctoral candidate focusing on the perspectives and experiences of Puerto Rican diaspora teachers. They eagerly approached me to participate in the study, even though they were deeply immersed in a collaborative capstone project and were completing their graduate degrees in bilingual education while working full-time at the time of data collection.

Table 1. Sample Teacher-Participant Demographics.

Participant and Age Range	Place of Birth	Places Lived	Degrees & Certifications	Years Teaching	Children
Liana 21–30	Puerto Rico	Puerto Rico Connecticut New York	Ms.Ed. Bilingual Ed. Elementary Education and Bilingual PreK–6	1–5	No
Brenda 21–30	New York	New York Puerto Rico	Ms.Ed. Bilingual Ed. Inclusion/Special Ed. Elementary Education Bilingual Education	1–5	Yes
Ariana 31–40	Puerto Rico	Puerto Rico New York	Ms. Ed. Bilingual Ed. Early Childhood and Elementary Education	7–14	Yes
Maribel 41–50	New York	New York Puerto Rico	Ms. Ed. Literacy Elementary Education Bilingual Education	6–9	Yes

Participant and Age Range	Place of Birth	Places Lived	Degrees & Certifications	Years Teaching	Children
Patricia 41–50	Puerto Rico	Puerto Rico New York	Ms. Ed. Literacy Elementary Education Bilingual Education	7–14	Yes
Helena 51–60	New York	New York	Ms. Ed. Bilingual Education (in process) Inclusion Elementary Education Bilingual Education	20 or more	Yes

As shown in Table 1, the participants varied in age, certifications, and years of teaching experience. They also varied in terms of where they were born, where they were raised, and where they went to school and college. However, all participants were women who self-identified as Puerto Rican and were raised in Spanish-dominant households with parents who were born in Puerto Rico. Moreover, all of the teachers were first-generation college students at the undergraduate and graduate levels.

Data collection and analysis

I collected data from multiple data sources between March and July 2011. I combined individual and focus-group interviews together in data gathering to emphasize social reciprocity and collectivist forms of knowledge construction (Delgado Bernal, Elenes, Godinez, & Villenas, 2006). In the development of the semistructured individual interview protocol, I drew from Seidman's (2006) approach, which incorporates life history methods and narrative inquiry and focuses on lived experiences around a particular phenomena or concept. The first interview emphasized home, family, and education history, the second interview highlighted details of experience, and the third interview elicited reflections on the meaning of lived experiences.

After conducting individual and focus-group interviews, I followed a multilayered process in thinking about the research data. The data analysis process included initial and focused coding, with a thematic analysis of the narrative profiles of the participants (Saldaña, 2009; Seidman, 2006). Interpretative procedures required relating categories and themes to relevant literature and considering ways of using pre-existing theory to build cumulative theory.

Overall, a thematic narrative analysis of multiple data sources revealed key elements within U.S. Latino family epistemology, including the primacy of family, shared cultural values, and resistance to subjugation (Delgado Gaitán, 2004; Hidalgo, 2005; Villenas, 2002). More specifically, the analytic process pointed to important ways that teachers took on critical bilingual-bicultural stances that reflected experiences and perspectives anchored in primary cultural socialization practices (Darder, 1991, 1995, 2011, 2012). In what follows, I discuss four themes that highlight how diaspora processes contribute to the development of critical bilingual-bicultural social identities and practices over time, across generations and geographic locations, and in relation to other groups.

Thematic findings

Puerto Rican teachers as domestic foreigners

Regardless of the varying reasons and circumstances for their dispersion to the U.S. mainland, most of the teachers shared experiences about dealing with cultural differences between the Island and U.S. mainland contexts. Ariana and Patricia, who moved from Puerto Rico to New York in their early twenties, shared experiences that reflected long-standing issues of Puerto Ricans positioned as racial/colonial subjects and domestic foreigners (Duany, 2002; Negrón-Muntaner, 2007; Rolón-Dow, 2010; Urciuoli, 1996). In the following narrative vignette, Patricia tells a story about being asked for a green card at a community college campus:

> I remember one time in college…*y yo nada más llevaba como dos años aquí, todavía mi inglés no era tan perfecto y la mujer viene y me dice* (and I had only been living here for about 2 years, my English was still not quite perfect, and the woman comes and says to me),"Where's your green card?" *Yo le dije* (I said to her), "Excuse me? I am Puerto Rican. Just in case you don't know history and you don't know anything about Puerto Rico, I'm a citizen, so I don't need a green card. Do you?" I was so mad! *Solamente porque te ven que eres hispano pues tiene que ser que vienes de otro sitio y que necesitas un* green card (Just because they see that you are Hispanic they assume you are a foreigner and need a green card).

Patricia's story reveals how she negotiates changing views of citizenship. In Puerto Rico she was never asked for a green card. Yet, as a Puerto Rican in the U.S. diaspora context, she was positioned as a foreigner who needed a green card. She resisted this positioning and informed the staff person of her citizenship status in relation to the history of Puerto Rico. In so doing, she reaffirmed her cultural identity and repositioned herself as an educator of the shared history *de nuestra gente* (of our people).

Later in the interview, Patricia also talks about her growing aware-ness of her Spanish- and English-speaking brown body within dominant, English-speaking, Black-White racialization practices in the U.S. For instance, she shared stories about being treated differently at restaurants when she spoke in Spanish, and she questioned these experiences over time: "So when things like that happen, I really have to question why this is happening. Is it a racial thing, or would they do this to anybody?" From her perspective, she went from a broader ethnic- and culture-based racialization experience in Puerto Rico to a more narrow, phenotype- and language-based racialization experience in New York. As a result, Patricia was very conscious of the need to question and challenge negative assumptions about Puerto Ricans in the dominant, mainstream U.S. culture.

Patricia's experiences living and working in Lakeview for more than 20 years and being positioned as a domestic foreigner informed her role as a bilingual teacher and reading-intervention specialist. For instance, Patri-cia spoke about helping other newcomer families and their children navi-gate *choque cultural* (culture shock, see Vega de Jesús & Sayers, 2007) and racism, not only in the school setting, but also in the Lakeview community setting. Although her primary role as a reading specialist emphasized English language learning, and she participated in schooling practices underscoring Anglo-American cultural values, she encouraged parents and students to con-tinue speaking Spanish while also learning English. Such efforts served not only to mediate the process of bilingualism and biculturalism, but also to counteract assimilative pressures and inequities that the children and families may have experienced as Puerto Ricans living in the U.S. mainland diaspora context. Consequently, she viewed herself as "an agent of change," and let her students know ways "that they could become agents of change as well." To this extent, Patricia took a socially conscious stance of affirming aspects of the Spanish language and Puerto Rican culture. In this way, she asserted more inclusive notions of belonging for Puerto Rican students at her school and in the larger community setting. In the next theme, I elaborate on socially con-scious ways that the participants confront, negotiate, and create productions of being well educated (Levinson, Foley, & Holland, 1996).

Puerto Rican teachers as socially conscious

Another way that the data illustrated the development of critical bilingual-bicultural social identities and practices was in the ways teachers discussed what being well educated meant to them. When I asked the participating teachers to identify and describe a person whom they considered to be well educated, all six chose individuals whom they considered to be *bien educado*

and well educated in the "combined" and "blended" ways that they conceptualized this construct. An analysis of the exemplar narratives using Darder's
(2011) critical bilingualism framework suggests that teachers did not prefer
dominant views, promote the subjugation or domination of their primary
culture, or deny the existence of prejudice and racism. Rather, the teachers
took a stance grounded in the process of cultural negotiation. Throughout
the research process, their conceptions of being well educated demonstrated a
bilingual-bicultural understanding and engaged tensions due to cultural differences or to changing and conflicting values around these constructs. To
illustrate this theme, it is helpful to discuss Brenda and Helena's interview
responses in this focus area.

Brenda, who was born in New York City and moved to Puerto Rico as an
elementary school student, reflected a critical mode of engagement in her response when asked whom she considered to be a well-educated person. In the
passage below, Brenda takes into account what it means to be well educated
in terms of credentials and professional accomplishments as well as what it
means to be *bien educado* in terms of a person's character and way of relating:

> I would consider my husband well educated. I'm going to be honest, what
> first comes to mind when I think of well educated—I don't think of my im-
> mediate family. Instead, I think of these people who have these big old titles.
> Then, I kind of have to think back and think: What made them get there?
> Why are they well educated, and why couldn't you be? and your husband be?
> Why can't your mom be? or whoever. So, usually we think of all those people
> who I was with at the PC Foundation Advisory Board. "Oh, these people are
> all well-educated people. It's an honor to have been chosen to be here" and
> all of that. But then, eventually, I think "my husband is well educated!" He is
> very knowledgeable in very different areas. He's also very good with technol-
> ogy and computers. Whenever I need help with something, he helps me. Not
> only with that, but he is very good with numbers and vocabulary and defining
> words and all of that. And, in the cultural sense, then, *also*, because he is very
> respectful, he treats others kindly and with respect. He has very good man-
> ners. So, as I think about it now, I think, "Well yeah! He is well educated!"
> from *my* criteria, as what I see not only the cultural, Hispanic perspective of it,
> but also, from what I think in the American perspective of it. He has a degree
> in computer science. He fits criteria for both.

Brenda's thought process demonstrates critical thinking about biculturalism
in relation to asymmetric power relations, larger social structures, and access to resources. In the process of negotiating linguistic and cultural notions, Brenda moves away from subordinate thinking in this area toward a
repositioned affirmative stance inclusive of bilingual-bicultural conceptualiza-
tions of what it means to be a well-educated person. She recognizes cultural

differences and also engages with tensions around what being a well-educated person means for her at an individual and collective level.

Helena, who was born in New York City and raised on Long Island, initially stated that it was "so hard" to think of a person who she considered to be well educated in the way that she understood it. However, her eventual response to this question was also grounded in the process of cultural negotiation. Helena described two civic- and equity-minded individuals. First, she described Roberto, a community leader who served as the CEO of AVANCE, a nonprofit human services and advocacy agency dedicated to improving the quality of life of Latinas/os in Lakeview. Second, Helena described her daughter Jackie, a bilingual social worker working in the state capital. In the passage below, Helena described Roberto as well educated and *bien educado*:

> I think if I were going to look for a combined definition it would be Roberto Cerrano. He was the first Hispanic male that I met that was very involved in the community. He was very proud of his cultural heritage and he was very well respected in the community as a Hispanic. Roberto was very well educated, yet he carried that *educado* that [complemented his] education, and what he said had validity and credibility. It had weight. He represented the community and was visible in the community. He is respectful and was respected and admired in the community. He was confident that what he was seeing and what he was expressing for us is a true representation of the needs of the people. He would be able to talk to others outside the Hispanic community and be heard. He represented us and was unrelenting.

For Helena, Roberto exemplified a well-educated person who effectively and respectfully engaged in civic-minded and justice-oriented practices as a representative of—and as part of his commitment *to*—the Puerto Rican diaspora community in Lakeview. The idea of being committed to the Puerto Rican community in Lakeview exemplified a socially conscious orientation, and underscored how diaspora community conditions relate to the development of critical bicultural-bilingual social identities and practices.

As Helena reflected on the qualities that made Roberto a well-educated person, she connected her perspectives with some of her own lived experiences that contributed to her evolving and agentive thinking in this area. In doing so, she did not negate or move away from the tension, conflict, and contradictions that result from cultural differences around what it means to be a well-educated person. For instance, in the following passage, Helena notes that individuals like Robert were influential in her growing social consciousness and developing bicultural social identity:

> These things were all things that were new to me because I wasn't raised in a Hispanic community. I didn't even know the plight of the Hispanic, in many

ways, until I came to Lakeview. Even after I graduated and got married—it wasn't really until I started working at AVANCE that I became more conscious—it was a whole other world for me…. You know, where have I been? I was raised in a "whitebread" setting.

Over time, Helena reflected on her experiences of discrimination and exclusion in multiple locations in New York State, and the process of becoming more socially conscious about the positioning of Puerto Ricans as racialized, domestic foreigners. Her responses in relation to her life history reveal how she negotiates language, power, and culture amidst multiple roles and in changing diasporic contexts.

Considered together, Brenda and Helena's responses reflect socially conscious perspectives that combine primary and dominant cultural views in a critical manner that accounts for power and difference. Again, their responses do not seek to move away from tensions in constructions of what it means to be a well-educated person. Instead, Brenda and Helena's responses reflect the development of critical bicultural-bilingual social identities and practices over time, across geographic contexts, and in relation to other groups.

Puerto Rican teachers living between worlds

The teachers in this study revealed peculiar ways that they were educated *entremundos* (between worlds). That is, they were born, socialized, and educated between two (or more) geographic localities, languages, cultures, identities, and "contending and sometimes dissident experiences" (Zavala-Martínez, 1994, as cited by Zavala, 2000, p. 119). This *entremundos* experience, as proposed by Zavala-Martínez (1994), "is part of an ongoing polemic on national identity that has permeated Puerto Rico's colonial history" and forms "part of a complex, dynamic process which is also influenced by other variables such as gender, social class, race, personal values, political forces, and generational status" (p. 30). Although it is beyond the scope of this chapter to engage in a thorough discussion of the many variables that Zavala-Martínez points out,[7] I do want to connect the notion of being educated *entremundos* with diasporic circular migration and the experience of feeling out of place.

In the following narrative vignette, Brenda describes circulation migration patterns between New York and Puerto Rico that contributed to the experience of being educated between two worlds:

> I was born in New York City, in Queens, but lived in Brooklyn. I attended kindergarten over there. I was in a general education classroom. From there we moved to Puerto Rico. I completed 1st through 6th grade in Puerto Rico. It was all Spanish and one English class as a foreign language. Then in middle

school we moved here. We moved because my mom wasn't doing well economically. At the time, she was a single parent in Puerto Rico. It was tough for us, economically, so she was just looking for the better life. She was in New York City for a couple of months and then came to Lakeview. We have family in New York City, but my mom didn't want to live again in New York City. Originally we left because of the crime and drugs and everything that was rising, in the 90s pretty much. So, she had a cousin here who had told her about Lakeview and how there were jobs, the schools were pretty good, and all of that. She left me with my maternal grandparents in Humacao [Puerto Rico] for a year while she came here, settled, and then sent for me. My mom and I, we are really close. My siblings and I are really close, too. So it was definitely tough for me because I missed them. But, she [mom] went to my graduation. I went [to New York] during Christmas and things. It was tough, but I understood her reasoning. When I came here to Lakeview City School District, they tested me for my language and I tested out of bilingual. I wasn't placed in bilingual. They did place me in ESL (English as a Second Language), but I was in a general education program. It was definitely very different from what I was used to in Puerto Rico. I remember looking for those students that I could relate to—like looking for other Puerto Ricans, or Hispanic students. I think they were mostly all in my ESL class. Still, I struggled with the culture shock type of thing, but I had a lot of support from my mom when I went home. My teachers were all really supportive and understanding, [too].

Brenda's life history narrative is characteristic of "working-class and economically based migratory movements" (Flores, 2009). She reflected on her experiences as a circular migrant student, and noted that she looked for other bilingual Latina/o students as she negotiated linguistic and cultural differences between Puerto Rico and New York.

During separate (one-on-one) interviews with me, Liana and Helena spoke about feeling out of place, and both struggled with ambiguous and changing cultural identities. Both used the expression "like a fish out of water" on several occasions, and shared stories of rejection and disillusionment (Flores, 2009). For instance, Liana stated that she had become "very Americanized." This experience made the otherwise familiar feel unfamiliar, and led to her feeling out of place when she visited her extended family in Puerto Rico:

As kids, we went to Puerto Rico a lot. I remember one summer my mom actually sent just the three of us for 3 months—for like the whole summer vacation. We spent the summers there, so as a kid I went a lot. I went less in high school. After my parents got divorced, money was tighter and it was more difficult to get over there. It's almost kinda weird because though I felt like we were really really Puerto Rican here—you go to Puerto Rico, and you're really not that Puerto Rican there! You're definitely the "American kid" in the middle of like all of your family. To this day, that's how we feel. It becomes surreal to realize how different it is there in the Island and how it is here. My family lives in the center of the Island. Pure *campo* [countryside/rural area]. And we're just very Americanized. I'm definitely a *fish out of water* there.

Liana's feeling of being more or less Puerto Rican, and the desire for belonging, influenced her decision to become a bilingual teacher in Lakeview. She noted that many of the students at Gordon, like her, came from working-class families who traveled "back and forth" between the mainland and Island. Consequently, she felt that an important part of her role as a Puerto Rican diaspora teacher was to interact with students in ways that affirmed bilingual and bicultural ways of being and knowing. She understood that some of her students, and their families, struggled with complex and changing sociocultural identities associated with distinct Puerto Rican diaspora experiences anchored in historical and constant sociocultural dissonance.

Accordingly, Liana recognized that an integral part of the process of biculturalism is to take into account "the daily struggle with racism and other forms of cultural invasion" (Darder, 2011, p. 20). For instance, Liana reflected on how the research process helped her to realize that even though she spent most of her childhood and adult life in Lakeview, "more things" from her primary culture "came to the surface" during the individual and focus-group interviews. Most notably, she reflected on assumptions and cultural differences around what it means to be a well-educated person, as well as the need to reframe deficit views about Puerto Rican teachers in Lakeview. During a focus-group interview, Liana shared some of the stereotypes and misrepresentations that she resisted:

> Oh these Latina/o teachers, they all just stick together and they don't talk to anybody else. They talk Spanish all day long and they talk to their kids all day long and their kids don't learn English….And, you know, there are a lot of things that we're fighting against by being Puerto Rican teachers in this district.

The extent to which she shared her own experiences in order to connect with her students during instruction is an area that can be explored further (Irizarry, 2007; Irizarry & Raible, 2011).

Similar to Liana, Helena also spoke about feeling like "a fish out of water." She was born in the Bronx and was raised on Long Island. However, unlike Liana, Helena did not visit Puerto Rico until she was an adult. In the following narrative vignette, Helena speaks about feeling like a fish out of water in relation to situations with other Puerto Ricans in Lakeview who questioned her cultural/ethnic authenticity:

One time at the bilingual charter school, I was going down the elevator, and a girl in the elevator asked me, "Are you Hispanic?" I said, "Yes, I'm Hispanic, why?" She said, "because you don't act Hispanic," and I was like, "what?" What did she mean by that? What do you mean I don't act Hispanic? I did engage her, and she said, "Well, you don't look Hispanic. You don't talk with an accent." Then, I'm like, "Ok?" So, how does that make me not Hispanic? Does that mean I have to adopt your accent? That experience solidified for me the way I already felt: I felt like a *fish out of water* amongst my own kind because of my own rearing. I didn't even really speak Spanish at that time. I could understand it, but I hadn't been hearing it for years! There was no such thing as bilingual education at that time in Long Island. Do I have to go to Puerto Rico and come back? There's no way I can just become Hispanic on her terms!

These kinds of experiences informed Helena's views on the role of bilingualism in relation to being well educated. Below, she notes how she encourages the maintenance of Spanish for her students and their families:

I think learning English matters, but don't forget your Spanish. Being bilingual is definitely part of being well educated. I tell my students: I don't want you to stop speaking Spanish, even though our model is subtractive—well, I don't tell them that, but... I tell the parents, "Do not stop speaking to your child in Spanish, even if it seems at this point in time that it's holding them back from transitioning to English." They need to have that exposure to both languages. I give the students examples—like when you go to the store, do you ever translate for your mom? I try to bring those situations [to the forefront] to show that what they're doing is important. I don't want them to give up that part of who they are, because of my own experience. I don't want them to feel like a *fish out of water*. I want them to be able to function in both those worlds.

As a Puerto Rican diaspora educator, one of Helena's primary objectives was to affirm her students' bicultural-bilingual existence. Her hope was that the students did not feel out of place, but rather had the ability to critically negotiate "both those worlds."

Migration and resettlement between New York and Puerto Rico forged diasporic experiences of living between two distinct worlds in which Brenda and Helena were born, socialized, and educated. For Helena and Liana, the expressions of Puerto Rican cultural identity seemed to be motivated by a simultaneous sense of belonging and a lack thereof, "in response to feelings of marginalization" in the Island and mainland context (Brinkerhoff, 2009, p. 41). At a broader level, feeling like a "fish out of water" reflects a kind of *entremundos* experience that mimics the ambiguous "belongs to but is not a part of" unincorporated U.S. territory status of Puerto Rico (Duany, 2011,

p. 232). In other words, Liana and Helena's lived experiences speak to a collective diaspora consciousness grappling with ongoing sociopolitical dynamics between Puerto Rico and the United States (Aranda, 2007; Duany, 2011; Flores, 1993, 2009; Otero, 2008; Torres-Padilla & Rivera, 2008).

Puerto Rican diaspora teachers: Bilingual and proud

Despite pressures to subjugate their primary cultural and linguistic experiences and perspectives, all of the teachers in this study engaged in practices intended to counteract deculturalization, or "the process of stripping away the culture of a conquered people and replacing it with the dominant culture" (Zavala, 2000, p. 115). However, it is important to point out that all six teachers in this study had lived in Lakeview for more than 12 years, and none of them mentioned a future return and resettlement to Puerto Rico. Instead, they spoke about going to Puerto Rico to visit family and friends. This commonality of a prolonged separation from Puerto Rico also marked their experiences as educators.

Hence, the fourth theme represents a common thread in the participant narratives about having pride in being bilingual and Puerto Rican, both in spite of and because of their diasporic reality(ies). For example, Maribel, who was born and raised mostly in Lakeview, felt blessed because of several factors that contributed to ethnic pride and a strong sense of bilingualism-biculturalism:

> When I was little I lived a couple of years in Puerto Rico; I want to say, 2 years shortly after I was born, we lived in San Juan. But most [of my childhood] was here in Lakeview. Actually, we lived right here in the Latino neighborhood. We lived in a double-occupancy home. I lived with my parents and my brothers, but next door, I had my grandparents. Since my mother worked the night shift, my grandmother took care of us. So, I would say that I was raised with my parents, but also with my grandparents. She [my grandmother] was very important in my life in that, I think that we were able to maintain our home language because she was one that didn't speak any English at all. [So there was Spanish spoken in the home] every day, and it wasn't an option. She didn't speak English and she didn't want to learn how to speak English. She was not going to have you speak in English to her. She was not going to have it! My mother is another one! It took her a long time to learn English. So, even to this day, I don't speak English to my mom. The conversations that we have are in Spanish. I've been bilingual all my life, but I know what it's like to learn another language. We speak both languages.... I think that my father purposefully put us in bilingual education because he didn't want us to lose the Spanish language. I think that was a smart move on his part. I went right here to Gordon Elementary School. But I think that what helped, too, was having my grandparents and my mother who didn't speak any English. I grew up in the neighborhood. I lived on *La Avenida* [Avenue] Cooper. A lot

of my neighbors were Latinos.... I was very blessed in that sense, blessed that I was surrounded with people like me. I think that that helps. It helped me with self-esteem and embracing who I was as a person. To be proud of who I am, in terms of my culture.

In addition to the importance of being in close proximity with extended family and growing up in a supportive Latino diaspora neighborhood, Maribel helped me to understand also how a family's migration history interacts with the educational history and positive cultural identity development of multiple generations in a diaspora setting. For example, she was particularly cognizant that her father valued bilingual education because he didn't want his children "to lose the [Spanish] language." Maribel felt that this "was a smart move on his part." She understood this move not only as a way to honor the family's historical migration legacy, but also as a way to enrich the family's future legacies as well-educated, bilingual, and proud Puerto Ricans in the U.S. mainland setting:

> In terms of my father, education was very important for him. We had to finish school. That was [it]. No ifs, ands, or buts. It's not negotiable. He could not emphasize more the importance of having an education. I think it absolutely had everything to do with his own struggles—with his father coming to this country. It took him many years to realize that grandpa came not for other reasons that he thought at the time [migrant farm labor], but more so because he wanted to provide more opportunities for his children and more opportunities meant access to a better education. My father understood that later. For him, that [a better education] was important for us, for our generation. And he clearly saw the picture. Growing up, in elementary school, my father was obtaining his bachelor's degree. So, he not only said it, he too, was doing it.... And now that I have a master's degree, he tells me he's proud of me. Of all of his children, I'm the one that finished and went all the way.

Now as a bilingual elementary teacher with a specialization in literacy, Maribel was conscious that "knowing what it's like to learn another language" was really helpful for understanding her own students as emergent bilinguals (see García & Kleifgen, 2010). Interestingly, she worked in the same elementary school that she had attended as a bilingual student. During the interviews she emphasized the significance of having strong relationships with parents as part of enhancing the schooling experiences of students in the bilingual program. She drew from her lived experiences as a bilingual student in Lakeview, not only in order to relate to parents and students, but also as a means of fostering the development and expression of bicultural-bilingual social identities. In a critical manner, she also shared personal and professional conflicts associated with situations where she felt that primary cultural values served to reinforce invisibility, silence, passivity, and complacency (see Quiñones, 2012).

Discussion and implications for teacher education

The findings in this study suggest that diaspora-forged experiences have stable and emergent characteristics that result in dynamic meaning-making and potential forms of resistance. As bilingual education Puerto Rican teachers, the participants in this study drew from a diaspora consciousness that included negative experiences of discrimination and exclusion as well as positive experiences and identification with a shared historical heritage and language (Darder, 1993, 1995; Vertovec, 1997). Thus, further underscoring these findings is the need to find meaningful ways to "create school and home partnerships that truly respect and work from the power of relationships, commitments, wisdom, and sensibilities born of a life's work of straddling fragmented realities" (Villenas et al., 2006, p. 5). To this extent, the teachers benefitted from having historically grounded processes and sensibilities associated with the cultural identities and practices of the children and families they served.

A growing number of studies suggest that students of color benefit academically from having teachers of color (Achinstein & Ogawa, 2012; Villegas & Irvine, 2010). Yet, in high-minority urban schools, there is a shortage of teachers of color (Villegas & Davis, 2007). More specifically, there is a critical shortage of Latina/o teachers (Irizarry & Donaldson, 2012). Although nearly one in five students in public schools is Latina/o, about 7% of our nation's teachers are Latina/o. (Irizarry & Donaldson, 2012, p. 156). In light of the persistently low academic performance of Puerto Ricans in U.S. schools (De Jesús & Rolón-Dow, 2007; Nieto, 2000), it is crucial that teacher educators and multiple educational stakeholders leverage the lessons learned from the experiences of these teachers to inform collective efforts (Pedraza & Rivera, 2005) aimed at recruiting, preparing, and developing critical Puerto Rican diaspora teachers who are willing to serve as role models (Darder, 1995; Ochoa, 2007) in the same or similar urban school communities in which they lived and went to school as youths (Irizarry, 2007, 2011a, 2011b; Mercado, 2011).

One model worthy of considering for increasing the number of community-based and equity-oriented teachers of color in urban school districts is the "Grow Your Own" (GYO) approach to teacher education (Irizarry, 2007; Oliva & Staudt, 2003; Skinner, Garretón, & Schultz, 2011). In Illinois, California, and Texas, for instance, collaborative partnerships between schools, districts, community agencies, and universities facilitate strategic pathways for successfully recruiting and preparing Latina/o high school youth into the teaching profession.

In addition to cultivating a new generation of Puerto Rican teachers who will work to improve the educational outcomes of all students (particularly in urban schools), there is a need to support and learn from in-service Puerto Rican teachers who might otherwise be rendered invisible or misrepresented amidst a predominantly White, middle-class, monolingual English-speaking population in America's teaching force. In this chapter, I show how a small group of teachers redraw and blur the lines (Duany, 2011) between Puerto Rico and New York, and merge their home and school experiences to confront, mediate, and enact lives as bilingual-bicultural educators inspired by their roots. I invite my readers to engage with this line of inquiry, and invite future researchers to draw from a larger sample of Puerto Rican teachers from multiple locations in an effort to examine the life histories of teachers working to ameliorate the education of the Puerto Rican diaspora.

Notes

1. Names of participants are pseudonyms.
2. In Latino family epistemology, the concept of *educación* (cognate for education) takes on broader and distinct meanings associated with cultural-heritage values and moral education; in addition to its academic/schooling components, cultural constructions of *educación* encompass expectations and socialization practices around being moral, responsible, respectful, and well behaved. (For a literature review of scholarly research in this focus area, see Quiñones, 2012.)
3. The name of the school is a pseudonym.
4. The name of the city is a pseudonym.
5. This research was supported by a Cultivating New Scholars of Color Research Grant, National Council of Teachers of English, awarded to Sandra Quiñones.
6. The expression "to be well educated" is typically interpreted as *ser bien educado*, which is a derivative of *educación* (refer to footnote 3). As many scholars have noted, the Spanish expression takes on different meanings, and points not so much to school-based knowledge or formal credentials, but to family values and home- and community-based expectations about a person's civil comportment and proper demeanor, including how they interact with others both in and out of school (see Quiñones, 2012).
7. For an insightful analysis on the role of gender in transnational migration, see Mahler and Pessar (2001) and Pessar and Mahler (2003).

References

Achinstein, B., & Ogawa, R. T. (2012). *Change(d) agents: New teachers of color in urban schools*. New York: Teachers College Press.

Acosta-Belén, E. (2009). Haciendo patria en la metrópoli: The cultural expressions of the Puerto Rican diaspora. *Centro Journal 21*(2), 49–83.

Acosta-Belén, E., & Santiago, C. E. (2006). *Puerto Ricans in the United States: A contemporary portrait*. Boulder, CO: Lynne Rienner.

Aranda, E. (2007). *Emotional bridges to Puerto Rico: Migration, return migration and the struggles of incorporation.* Lanham, MD: Rowman & Littlefield Publishers.

Braziel, J. E., & Mannur, A. (2003). *Theorizing diaspora.* Malden, MA: Blackwell Publishing.

Brinkerhoff, J. M. (2009). *Digital diasporas: Identity and transnational engagement.* Cambridge and New York: Cambridge University Press.

Brubaker, R. (2005). The "diaspora" diaspora. *Ethnic and Racial Studies, 28*(1), 1–19.

Cohen, R. (1997). *Global diasporas: An introduction.* Seattle: University of Washington Press.

Darder, A. (1993). How does the culture of the teacher shape the classroom experience of Latino students? The unexamined question in critical pedagogy. In S. W. Rothstein (Ed.), *Handbook of schooling in urban America* (pp. 95–121). Westport, CT: Greenwood Press.

Darder, A. (1995). Buscando America: The contributions of critical Latina/o educators to the academic development and empowerment of Latina/o students in the United States. In C. E. Sleeter & P. L. McLaren (Eds.), *Multicultural education, critical pedagogy, and the politics of difference* (pp. 319–348). Albany: State University of New York Press.

Darder, A. (1991). *Culture and power in the classroom: A critical foundation for bicultural education.* New York: Bergin & Garvey.

Darder, A. (1995). *Culture and difference: Critical perspectives on the bicultural experience in the United States.* New York: Begin & Garvey.

Darder, A. (2011). *Dissident voices: Essays on culture, pedagogy, and power.* New York: Peter Lang.

Darder, A. (2012). *Culture and power in the classroom: Educational foundations for the schooling of bicultural students* (rev. 20th anniversary ed.). Boulder, CO: Paradigm Publishers.

De Jesús, A., & Rolón-Dow, R. (2007). The education of the Puerto Rican diaspora: Challenges, dilemmas, and possibilities. *Centro Journal, 19*(2), 4–11.

Delgado Bernal, D. (2008). La trenza de identidades: Weaving together my personal, professional, and communal identities. In K. P. González & R. V. Padilla (Eds.), *Doing the public good: Latina/o scholars engage civic participation* (pp. 135–148). Sterling, VA: Stylus.

Delgado Bernal, D., Elenes, C. A., Godinez, F. E., & Villenas, S. (2006). *Chicana/Latina education in everyday life: Feminista perspectives on pedagogy and epistemology.* Albany: State University of New York Press.

Delgado Gaitán, C. (2004). *Involving Latino families in schools: Raising student achievement through home-school partnerships.* Thousand Oaks, CA: Corwin Press.

Duany, J. (2002). *The Puerto Rican nation on the move: Identities on the island and in the United States.* Chapel Hill: University of North Carolina Press.

Duany, J. (2011). *Blurred borders: Transnational migration between the Hispanic Caribbean and the United States.* Chapel Hill: University of North Carolina Press.

Flores, J. (1993). *Divided borders: Essays on Puerto Rican identity.* Houston, TX: Arte Público Press.

Flores, J. (2009). *The diaspora strikes back: Caribeño tales of learning and turning.* New York: Routledge.

García, O., & Kleifgen, J. A. (2010). *Educating emergent bilinguals: Policies, programs, and practices for English language learners.* New York: Teachers College Press.

Grosfoguel, R. (2003). *Colonial subjects: Puerto Ricans in a global perspective.* Berkeley: University of California Press.

Hidalgo, N. M. (2005). Latino/a families' epistemology. In P. Pedraza & M. Rivera (Eds.), *Latino education: An agenda for community action research* (pp. 375–402). Mahwah, NJ: Lawrence Erlbaum.

Irizarry, J. G. (2007). "Home-growing" teachers of color: Lessons learned from a town-gown partnership. *Teacher Education Quarterly, 34*(4), 87–102.

Irizarry, J. G. (2011a). En la lucha: The struggles and triumphs of Latino/a preservice teachers. *Teachers College Record, 113*(12), 2804–2835.

Irizarry, J. G. (with Project FUERTE). (2011b). *The Latinization of U.S. schools: Successful teaching and learning in shifting cultural contexts.* Boulder, CO: Paradigm Publishers.

Irizarry, J. G., & Antrop-González, R. (2007). RicanStructing the discourse and promoting school success: Extending a theory of culturally responsive pedagogy for Diasporicans. *CENTRO Journal, 19* (2), 37–59.

Irizarry, J. G., & Donaldson, M. L. (2012). Teach for América: The Latinization of U.S. schools and the critical shortage of Latina/o teachers. *American Educational Research Journal, 49*(1), 155–194.

Irizarry, J. G., & Raible, J. (2011). Beginning with el barrio: Learning from exemplary teachers of Latino students. *Journal of Latinos and Education, 10*(3), 1–18.

Levinson, B. A., Foley, D. E., & Holland, D. C. (1996). *The cultural production of the educated person: Critical ethnographies of schooling and local practice.* Albany: State University of New York Press.

Mahler, S. J., & Pessar, P. R. (2001). Gendered geographies of power: Analyzing gender across transnational spaces. *Identities: Global Studies in Culture and Power, 7*(4), 441–459.

Marzán, G. (2009). Still looking for that elsewhere: Puerto Rican poverty and migration in the Northeast. *Centro Journal, 21*(1), 101–117.

McCally, K. (2007). Building the barrio: A story of Rochester's Puerto Rican pioneers. *Rochester Historical Society, 70*(2), 1–28.

Mercado, C. I. (2011). Successful pathways to the teaching profession for Puerto Ricans. *Centro Journal, 23*(11), 114–135.

Negrón-Muntaner, F. (Ed.). (2007). *None of the above: Puerto Ricans in the global era.* New York: Palgrave Macmillan.

Negrón-Muntaner, F., & Grosfoguel, R. (Eds.) (1997). *Puerto Rican jam: Rethinking colonialism and nationalism.* Minneapolis: University of Minnesota Press.

Nieto, S. (2000). *Puerto Rican students in U.S. schools.* Mahwah, NJ: Lawrence Erlbaum Associates.

Nieto, S. (2004). A history of the education of Puerto Rican students in U.S. mainland schools: "Losers," "outsiders," or "leaders"? In J. A. Banks & C. A. McGee Banks (Eds.), *Handbook of research on multicultural education* (2nd ed.) (pp. 388–411). San Francisco: Jossey-Bass.

Ochoa, G. (2007). *Learning from Latino teachers.* San Francisco: Jossey-Bass.

Oliva, M., & Staudt, K. (2003). Pathways to teaching: Latino student choice and professional identity in a teacher training magnet program. *Equity & Excellence in Education, 36,* 270–279.

Otero, S. (2008). Getting there and back: The road, the journey, and home in Nuyorican diaspora literature. In J. L. Torres-Padilla & C. H. Rivera (Eds.), *Writing off the hyphen: New critical perspectives on the literature of the Puerto Rican diaspora* (pp. 274–292). Seattle: University of Washington Press.

Pedraza, P., & Rivera, M. (2005). *Latina/o education: An agenda for community action research.* Mahwah, NJ: Lawrence Erlbaum.

Pessar, P. R., & Mahler, S. J. (2003). Transnational migration: Bringing gender in. *International Migration Review, 37*(3), 812–846.

Quiñones, S. (2012). *Educated entremundos: Understanding how Puerto Rican diaspora teachers conceptualize and enact ser bien educado and being well educated.* (Doctoral dissertation). Retrieved from ProQuest Dissertations and Theses. (Accession Order No. 3508563).

Rolón-Dow, R. (2005). Critical care: A color(full) analysis of care narratives of the schooling experiences of Puerto Rican girls. *American Education Research Journal, 42*(1), 77–11.

Rolón-Dow, R. (2010). Taking a diasporic stance: Puerto Rican mothers educating children in a racially integrated neighborhood. *Diaspora, Indigenous, and Minority Education, 4,* 268–284.

Saenz, J. (2011). *Rochester's Latino community.* Images of America Series. Charleston, SC: Arcadia Publishing.

Saldaña, J. (2009). *The coding manual for qualitative researchers.* Los Angeles: Sage.

Seidman, I. (2006). *Interview as qualitative research: A guide for researchers in education and the social sciences.* New York: Teachers College Press.

Skinner, E. A., Garretón, M. T., & Schultz, B. D. (2011). *Growing your own teachers: Grassroots change for teacher education.* New York: Teachers College Press.

Torres, A., & Velázquez, J. E. (Ed.). (1998). *The Puerto Rican movement: Voices from the diaspora.* Philadelphia: Temple University Press.

Torres-Padilla, J. L., & Rivera, C. H. (2008). *Writing off the hyphen: New perspectives on the literature of the Puerto Rican diaspora.* Seattle: University of Washington Press.

Urciuoli, B. (1996). *Exposing prejudice: Puerto Rican experiences of language, race, and class.* Boulder, CO: Westview Press.

Vega de Jesús, R., & Sayers, D. (2007). Voices: Bilingual youth constructing and defending their identities across borders, a bi-national study of Puerto Rican circular migrant students. *Multicultural Education, 14*(4), 16–19.

Vertovec, S. (1997). Three meanings of diaspora exemplified among South Asian religions. *Diaspora, 6*(3), 277–299.

Villegas, A. M., & Davis, D. E. (2007). Approaches to diversifying the teaching force: Attending to issues of recruitment, preparation, and retention. *Teacher Education Quarterly, 34*(4), 137–147.

Villegas, A. M., & Irvine, J. J. (2010). Diversifying the teaching force: An examination of major arguments. *Urban Review, 42*, 175–192.

Villenas, S. (2002). Reinventing *educación* in new Latino communities: Pedagogies of change and continuity in North Carolina. In S. Wortham, E. T. Murillo, & E. Hamann (Eds.), *Education in the new Latino diaspora: Policy and the politics of identity* (pp. 31–49). Westport, CT: Greenwood.

Villenas, S., Godinez, F. E., Delgado Bernal, D. D., & Elenes, C. A. (2006). Chicanas/Latinas building bridges: An introduction. In D. Delgado Bernal, C. A. Elenes, F. E. Godinez, & S. Villenas (Eds.), *Chicana/Latina education in everyday life: Feminista perspectives on pedagogy and epistemology* (pp. 1–9). Albany: State University of New York Press.

Walsh, C. E. (2000). The struggle of "imagined communities" in school: Identification, survival and belonging for Puerto Ricans. In S. Nieto (Ed.), *Puerto Rican students in U.S. schools* (pp. 93–114). Mahwah, NJ: Lawrence Erlbaum Associates.

Whalen, C. T., & Vázquez-Hernández, V. (2005). *The Puerto Rican diaspora: Historical perspectives*. Philadelphia: Temple University Press.

Zavala, M. V. (2000). Puerto Rican identity: What's language got to do with it? In S. Nieto (Ed.), *Puerto Rican students in U.S. schools* (pp. 115–136). Mahwah, NJ: Lawrence Erlbaum Associates.

Zavala-Martínez, I. (1994). *Quien soy?* Who am I? Identity issues for Puerto Rican adolescents. In E. Salett & D. R. Koslow (Eds.), *Race, ethnicity and self: Identity in multicultural perspectives*. Washington, DC: National Multicultural Institute Publications.

Ballin' and becoming Boricua: *From Roxbury to Rio Piedras and back again*

SHABAZZ NAPIER WITH JASON G. IRIZARRY

A big part of life is figuring out who you are, crafting an identity that is influenced by your past, is performed in the present, and moves toward becoming the kind of person you want to be in the future. People who have the means, travel the world looking for inspiration. Some read books trying to learn more about themselves. Others spend time in meditation. For me, my search for self and many of the "ah ha" moments that inform my identity have occurred on the 94'x 50' hardwood floor of a basketball court. It is in this space that I have learned many life lessons, opened doors to academic institutions that are typically out of reach for many in my community, and crafted an identity as a student athlete. The value of playing team sports has been touted in research and in popular media, and there is a general consensus that playing sports can have a positive impact on kids' physical, social, and emotional development. While I can certainly speak to these benefits, I have recently spent a significant amount of time reflecting on how basketball has created an opportunity for me to develop a more robust, emerging sense of my own racial/ethnic identity as a DiaspoRican. In this narrative, I share how my participation on the Puerto Rican national basketball team allowed me to embrace my identity as a Puerto Rican in the diaspora, how my identity is complicated by identity politics within the U.S. context, and how my sense of self is evolving as a result. In short, I document how my journey from Roxbury, Massachusetts, to Rio Piedras, Puerto Rico, and back again shaped how I see myself and other Puerto Ricans in the diaspora.

Coming of age in the diaspora: Racialization and the politics of identity

As a person of mixed raced, identity has always been a complicated construct for me. I am Puerto Rican and African American, and I grew up in a predominantly Black neighborhood in Boston, Massachusetts. Most of my neighbors did not see culture or ethnicity as a marker of identity, but rather focused on color. To them, either you were Black or you were White. There really was no schema for multiracial/multiethnic people like myself. I lived primarily among African Americans, and felt accepted by this community. We shared similarities beyond skin color, including being poor and living in the projects. I, too, experienced the depressed expectations of teachers and others who assumed that I would never amount to anything in life. I looked like other African Americans in my community, was treated similarly, and identified closely with this group.

However, deep inside, I also valued my Puerto Rican heritage, although I did not seem to get positive recognition for that outside of my Puerto Rican grandmother's house. I often felt as if I could not claim my Puerto Rican identity, in part because I did not speak Spanish. Also, I was living in Boston, and had never been to Puerto Rico. I felt more "urban" than Puerto Rican, and communicated using Ebonics—also referred to as African American Language (see Paris, 2011) rather than Spanish or Spanglish. My inability to effectively communicate in Spanish created a wedge between my Puerto Rican family members and me. I was looked at differently by many Puerto Ricans because they raced me as African American, and in many cases I felt looked down upon because I did not speak the language and knew little about the culture.

I heard stories about the Island and always imagined it as a tropical paradise, juxtaposed against the concrete jungle of my home city of Boston, Massachusetts. I often wondered why people would leave the Island to settle in neighborhoods like Roxbury. Why leave the warm weather for cold New England winters? Why leave a place where people value being Puerto Rican to come to a new land where Puerto Ricans are viewed as foreigners, outsiders, and forced to deal with xenophobia and other forms of discrimination? These questions remained largely unanswered, ignored by schools and often lost in the daily struggle of my Puerto Rican family members to survive and make it through each day.

As a teenager trying to figure out my identity, I felt an increasing desire to learn Spanish. I began to imitate words I heard from Puerto Rican, Spanish-speaking classmates. I spent hours trying to figure out how to pronounce these new words the right way, doing all I could to sound like a native speaker of the language. I drove my mother crazy asking her to constantly translate for me. Moving through my high school years, my strength of identity as a Puerto Rican began to grow, and some of my peers even began to identify me as such. Nevertheless, I felt a constant tension between being Black and Puerto Rican, as if the two identities could never rest harmoniously in my adolescent body. The tensions played out in all aspects of my life, especially in my sports career.

Basketball is not exempt from the racial politics of U.S. society. The majority of the players in the National Basketball Association (NBA) are Black, and most of the owners, general managers, and coaches are White. For many youth of color, basketball is one of the few avenues available for professional success. It is a sad but true reality that most of my friends and I saw the NBA, which employs only approximately 400 players, as a more realistic option than becoming doctors, lawyers, or business professionals. Like many other young men in my city and in cities across the United States, I invested my heart and soul into basketball, not only because of my love for the sport but also because of the opportunities that success on the court could afford me and my family. Despite the odds, a professional basketball career seemed more likely than a career in business or law. The narrowing of career opportunities is most certainly influenced by racial politics in the United States, as educational opportunities are often distributed based on class and race. As a young man of color growing up in an economically depressed community, it was clear that the traditional public school system was unlikely to prepare me to become a successful professional, and I am grateful for the doors that basketball has opened for me. Many of my friends have not been as fortunate.

Finding myself through basketball

Basketball opened the doors to a college education, and I acknowledge that had I not been able to play basketball at a high level, schools such as the University of Connecticut and others would not have been recruiting me to join their student body. Nevertheless, I value the opportunity for a college education that my basketball skills have helped to provide, and I am excited about completing my degree requirements. In fact, I am even contemplating graduate school after my playing career is over. In addition to the obvious benefits of an athletic scholarship and the educational opportunities it provides, basketball has also given me opportunities to travel across the country and abroad, and to interact with diverse individuals. While each of these experiences has been interesting and instructive, perhaps the most significant experience has been my time spent in Puerto Rico playing with the Puerto Rican national team.

When I was first approached to try out for the team, my primary consideration was not basketball, as crazy as that might sound. For a brief moment, I wondered if I could qualify as Puerto Rican, given that I have never lived on the Island and do not have a Spanish surname. Despite my reservations, I immediately recognized that the chance to travel to Puerto Rico and play for the national team was a great opportunity to hone my basketball skills and simultaneously connect with my cultural roots. While I knew relatively little about Puerto Rican history or life on the Island, my family at home in the States had always told me that the people on the Island were very friendly and always helpful. I wondered how helpful they would be with someone who did not speak Spanish. Unlike in the States, where I could speak English or African American English, languages with which I felt most comfortable, on the Island I would have nowhere to run. I would have to confront the cultural disconnect and tensions that I was able to avoid in Boston. Demonstrating the generous spirit my family had described, my teammates and Puerto Ricans on the Island embraced me, and neither language nor geographic differences could prevent me from maximizing this experience and learning more about my Puerto Rican roots.

Wearing the national team jersey gave me a renewed sense of pride. Once I put on the jersey, I was, in the eyes of my teammates and the many fans that came out to watch us practice, Puerto Rican. They made me feel as if I had returned "home," and that Puerto Rico was always part of my heritage. The Puerto Rican parts of my soul that had for many years remained dormant or unnourished were now awake and restless. With each new person I met and each welcoming smile, I felt more Puerto Rican.

While many teams practice in isolation, practice for the Puerto Rican national team was a public event, with more than 100 fans attending many of the practices. Their national pride was contagious, so much so that I was uncharacteristically nervous when I first stepped on the court. With each cheer from the fans, I became increasingly comfortable. The familiarity of the basketball court, my haven throughout my life, and the support of my teammates, coaches, and fans allowed me to quickly settle in and immerse myself in the experience. While most people are proud of who they are, of their national origins, Puerto Ricans express that pride in ways that are audile and visible to anyone on the Island and beyond. That pride was contagious, and motivated my continued search for my Puerto Rican self.

Each day I worked on trying to improve my ability to speak Spanish. My desire to learn the language grew each day. I would tell my teammates to speak Spanish to me whenever we were on the court to help me get the words down. Interestingly, for some reason I understood it better on the court because of the context. Although the words were unfamiliar, the concepts were not, and I was able to catch on pretty quickly. One of my good friends whom I met while playing for the Puerto Rico national team was J. J. Barea, who now plays for the Minnesota Timberwolves in the National Basketball League. He was fluent in both Spanish and English, which made him easy to talk to and an invaluable resource as a translator. Most basketball players want to play in the league when growing up, and J. J. is certainly a role model for aspiring Puerto Rican players. More personally, his passion for the game and dedication to play at the highest levels resonated with me, as I have the same goals.

Living in Puerto Rico, I felt so comfortable, and despite my original reservations, I never felt like an outsider or foreigner. I felt wanted and included in ways that I could not possibly have anticipated. Although few Island residents knew who I was prior to my arrival, they welcomed me nevertheless as one of their own. While I love my community at home in Roxbury and am proud of my African American heritage as well, my time in Puerto Rico made me feel as if I had found a new way home.

Understanding diaspora

Unfortunately, my time in Puerto Rico and participation on the national team was cut short as a result of an injury I sustained. While I was certainly disappointed, the benefits of the experience far outweigh any negative feelings stemming from my being sidelined. Upon leaving Puerto Rico, I felt like a different person. It was like leaving my new home, a small piece of utopia. I departed the Island and returned to the States with an even stronger passion to embrace my Puerto Rican identity. For the first time in my life, I wanted everybody to know that I was Puerto Rican and that being Puerto Rican meant a lot to me. Coming home, I wanted to learn more about the Island's history and the process through which my family left that beautiful oasis to settle in Massachusetts. I returned filled with questions and eager to search for the answers.

In addition to seeing myself as connected to Puerto Ricans on the Island, I also returned feeling more connected to Puerto Ricans in what I have come to learn is the diaspora. I know there are many Puerto Ricans in Massachusetts, New York, and Connecticut, but I was shocked to learn that there are more of us in the United States than on the Island. My thinking about identity prior to my time in Puerto Rico was narrow. I just assumed your identity is determined solely by where you are in the present, and did not think about all of the reasons that force or encourage people to leave their homelands. Moreover, I started to think about how people, including my family members, carry a part of the Island in them no matter where they live. Not even the freezing cold New England winters can dampen the warmth from the Island that I now carry in my soul.

Further speaking to this notion of diaspora, I understand now that identity is complicated for most, if not all, people. Being disconnected from one's homeland—a theme common to my Puerto Rican as well as my African American ancestors—shapes how people think about themselves in a lot of ways, some more positive than others. As a child I felt forced to choose between being Black and Puerto Rican, and my disconnect from the Island, my inability to speak Spanish fluently, and the fact that basketball in the states is "raced" as a Black sport (whereas Latinos are better represented in baseball) all pushed me to suppress my Puerto Rican identity. That, in my opinion, is a function of diaspora or displacement. It was not until my pilgrimage to the Island that I was able to reconcile my identities and develop a deeper understanding of who I am. This deeply personal journey was made possible because of basketball. That is, it was through ballin' in the diaspora, connecting with the Island and its people, and returning home—moving full circle from *Roxbury to Rio Piedras and Back Again*—that I have become more fully *Boricua*, a label that I will always embrace and wear proudly!

References

Paris, D. (2011). *Language across difference: Ethnicity, communication, and youth identities in changing urban schools.* New York: Cambridge University Press.

Section III: Threads of diaspora in established Puerto Rican communities

Tony went to the bodega but he didn't buy anything

MARTÍN ESPADA

Para Angel Guadalupe

Tony's father left the family
And the Long Island city projects,
Leaving a mongrel-skinny Puertorriqueño boy
Nine years old
Who had to find work.

Makengo the Cuban
Let him work at the bodega.
In grocery aisles
he learned the steps of the dry-mop mambo,
banging the cash register ,
like piano percussion
in the spotlight of Machito's orchestra,
polite with the abuelas who bought on credit,
practicing the grin on customers
he'd seen Makengo grin
with his bad yellow teeth.

Tony left the projects too,

With a scholarship for law school.

But he cursed the cold primavera

in Boston;

the cooking of his neighbors

left no smell in the hallway,

and no one spoke Spanish

(not even the radio).

So Tony walked without a map

through the city,

a landscape of hostile condominiums

and the darkness of white faces,

sidewalk-searcher lost

till he discovered the projects.

Tony went to the bodega

but he didn't buy anything:

he sat by the doorway satisfied

to watch la gente (people

island-brown as him)

crowd in and out,

hablando español,

thought: this is beautiful,

and grinned

his bodega grin.

This is a rice and beans

Success story:

Today Tony lives on Tremont Street,

above the bodega.

from *Trumpets of their Islands of their Eviction*

El Grito de Loisaida: DiaspoRicans, educational sovereignty, and the colonial project

JASON G. IRIZARRY & ENRIQUE FIGUEROA

The education of Puerto Ricans in the diaspora, hereafter referred to as *DiaspoRicans*, has been the focus of an emerging body of scholarship, as researchers have sought to understand and remedy the persistently problematic educational outcomes of Puerto Ricans on the U.S. mainland. Puerto Ricans residing on the Island complete high school and attend and graduate from institutions of higher education at significantly higher rates than their counterparts on the mainland (Fry, 2010), which suggests that the impact of diaspora processes on academic access and achievement should be examined more closely. Beginning with the Puerto Rican Study examining the educational attainment of DiaspoRican youth in New York City between 1953 and 1957 (Cayce, 1972) and continuing with more recent research, a plethora of explanations have been forwarded to explain the underachievement of minoritized students, including DiaspoRicans, in U.S. schools. The most popular theories and remedies offered through educational policy and pedagogical practice are often deficit based, suggesting that Puerto Ricans and other minoritized groups in the U.S. lack the characteristics that lead to school success (Bourdieu & Passeron, 1977; Cayce, 1972; Glazer & Moynihan, 1963; Payne, 2001).

Often obscured in the discussion of DiaspoRican education is the colonial status of the Island and, more specifically, how colonialism is manifested in the lives of Puerto Ricans in the diaspora. Using narrative and demographic data regarding two schools in Loisaida, the historically Puerto Rican neighborhood on the Lower East Side of Manhattan, New York City, we critically examine how educational access and opportunities have been restricted for Puerto Ricans in this neighborhood.

New York City, like many other urban communities, has been the target of countless school reform efforts. The dominant narrative trope regarding these efforts, and others across the country, suggests that urban school reform policies, like those manifested in Loisaida, are designed in the best interests of students and aimed at improving opportunity and academic achievement, especially for students from groups that have been historically marginalized in schools. Rarely, if ever, are the communities targeted in these reforms meaningfully included as partners in the reform efforts and allowed to shape policy and practice in these spaces. In an attempt to critique and destabilize these majoritarian perspectives and offer a more robust race- and culture-conscious analysis that is grounded in the lived experiences of DiaspoRicans, we offer two counter-narratives that unearth the deleterious impact of school reform efforts in two Loisaida schools. In contrast to race-neutral analyses of school reform initiatives that continue to pathologize students and their communities, we offer community-centered counternarratives to document how forms of oppression including but not limited to racism, linguicism, and xenophobia are manifest in educational policy. More specifically, we critically examine the ways in which these policies and practices have served to deny educational sovereignty (Moll & Ruiz, 2005) to DiaspoRicans and extend the far-reaching grip of U.S. colonialism. In keeping with the centuries-old tradition of Puerto Rican resistance of colonialism, the inception of which is marked by *El Grito de Lares*, an insurrection against Spanish rule initiated in the town of Lares, Puerto Rico, we see this work as a verbal coup, or *grito*, emerging from one of the most famous and influential Puerto Rican barrios in the diaspora—Loisaida.

This *grito* is rooted in our lived experiences as DiaspoRicans in Loisaida, as Jason calls this community home and Enrique has close familial ties to the neighborhood. We have witnessed firsthand the systematic marginalization of Latino neighborhood residents and the multifaceted ways that DiaspoRicans have resisted their positioning and the subsequent impact their experiences have had on shaping their understanding of their cultural identities. Just as DiaspoRicans engage in resistance to combat the multiple, interrelated forms of oppression aimed at this community, we see this essay as a method of speaking truth to power, honoring the emic perspectives of DiaspoRicans in understanding how educational opportunities are structured in this neighborhood. In addition to the responses to oppression, diaspora processes, too, speak to the multifaceted ways DiaspoRicans consistently negotiate and renegotiate their sense of self and belonging in the diaspora (Brubaker, 2005; Clifford, 1994). This essay is, for us, a way to narrate, critique, and push back against the marginalization we and other DiasporRicans have experienced in

Loisaida. While we draw from existing archival data and research literature, this essay has as a primary goal honoring the often silenced, subaltern voices of Puerto Ricans in the diaspora and inserting them into the discussion of school reform efforts, particularly those targeting schools in their communities.

Loisaida: The making of a DiaspoRican barrio

Although it is now synonymous with the Puerto Rican diaspora, the Lower East Side was a last-resort destination, a space where local government policy and real estate interests conspired to corral what they deemed "the Puerto Rican problem" (Mele, 2000). From these dubious origins, the Lower East Side became a cultural focal point of Puerto Rican identity in New York and the United States in general, and is now synonymous with Puerto Ricans, much like Chinatown is synonymous with Chinese New Yorkers and Harlem with African Americans. However, this wasn't always the case.

For the greater part of the 20th century the Lower East Side was a neighborhood whose streets teemed with immigrants from Russia and other European countries, scraping out a community within the context of a newly industrialized New York City. The neighborhood was created as an urban space for speculative real estate brokers to profit from the housing needs of the working poor. As low-skilled manufacturing jobs and an unskilled immigrant population increased, city planners parceled the Lower East Side into "shoebox-sized lots" in order to develop a "profitable housing market" (Mele, 2000, p. 40).

With its densely spaced tenements and narrow streets, the Lower East Side remained an immigrant stronghold. First, Germans inhabited the small apartments; they were later replaced by Irish and Eastern European Jews (Mele, 1994). All told, "approximately one third of the 6 million immigrants arriving from Europe between 1881 and 1889 settled on the Lower East Side" (Patterson, 2007, p. 90). The neighborhood remained a "working-class ghetto" throughout the early 20th century (Mele, 2000).

As the United States enacted laws to curb immigration for fear that "Anglo Saxon" Americans were being outnumbered by White ethnics, by the 1920s the Lower East Side saw a precipitous decline in its immigrant population (Abu-Lughod & Mele, 1994). As a consequence of a simultaneous shift from manufacturing to white-collar occupations, massive urban renewal projects were steamrolling over neighborhoods, making way for New York's new economy (Brodkin, 2004, p. 28). Around the city, "old housing stock" was being demolished to make way for newer apartment complexes (Abu-Lughod, 1994). However, the Lower East Side was conspicuously omitted from urban renewal plans, and landlords were left without new immigrant populations to rent their apartments during the latter part of the 1920s and the 1930s. Further aggravating the decline in population in the Lower East Side was the development of suburban America. At the end of World War II, returning soldiers, including newly incorporated White ethnics, were given handsome benefits in the GI Bill, which allowed for the upward mobility of children of immigrants. This precipitated a move to the suburbs, leaving the Lower East Side depopulated (Mele, 2000).

From the Lower East Side to Loisaida

The passage in 1900 of the Foraker Act, which made Puerto Ricans citizens of Puerto Rico, a territory controlled by the United States, and the Jones Act (1917), which made Puerto Ricans citizens of the United States, codified Puerto Rico's colonial relationship with the United States. While Puerto Ricans on the Island were not empowered as full citizens—Puerto Ricans on the Island are unable to vote in federal elections, and do not have a voting representative in Congress, for example—their citizenship afforded them the ability to travel to the United States without restrictions. Initially, Puerto Ricans came to the United States in small groups as a consequence of the annexation in 1898. The 1920s saw the first large wave of Puerto Rican (im)migrants, and small pockets of Puerto Ricans appeared throughout Manhattan. However, their initial settlement patterns never allowed for the establishment of large communities, as seen with European ethnic immigrants (Mele, 2000). Larger waves of Puerto Ricans arrived on the mainland after World War II. On the Island, forced urbanization created overpopulated cities, and high unemployment coupled with a weak economy resulted in extreme poverty for many Island residents. Stateside, post-wartime industrial jobs provided opportunities for unskilled workers, and Puerto Ricans found ample opportunity in New York City (Larsen, 1973). In 1940, 61,463 Puerto Ricans lived in New York City; by 1950, the number had jumped to 254,880 (López, 2007, p. 64).

Urban policy began to focus on Puerto Ricans, which greatly impacted their lives for generations. For instance, "[Robert] Moses' policy of dismembering old, working-class neighborhoods and creating new 'communities' segregated by class, ethnicity, and race offered a default solution to what was referenced by social scientists as the 'Puerto Rican problem'" (Mele, 2000, p. 42; see also Nieto, 2000). In the manufacturing of elite communities in New York City, Moses used "land-use policy to determine those areas where [Puerto Ricans] could and could not afford to live" (Mele, 2000, p. 131).

The breaking up of Puerto Rican enclaves throughout New York City, and particularly on the West Side of Manhattan, worked to the benefit of the real estate industry in the Lower East Side (Glazer & Moynihan, 1963). A long-time hub for immigrants, the Lower East Side by the 1950s was depopulated and its housing in disrepair. Landlords seeking to replace the income lost from increasingly aged and dispersed Eastern European populations, rented dilapidated small apartments at high rents to the displaced Puerto Ricans desperate for housing in an increasingly unaffordable housing market (Abu-Lughod & Mele, 1994). These early "urban renewal" policies facilitated the establishment of a colony on the Lower East Side which came to be known as "Loisaida," drawing from the phonetic pronunciation of "Lower East Side" by Spanish-speaking Puerto Ricans.

These demographic shifts also presented significant implications for schools. From the very beginning, Puerto Ricans were depicted as students who were unwilling and unable to learn (Flores, 2005; Nieto, 1995, 2000). In Loisaida, schools were structured to assimilate rather than accommodate this growing group of students. Schools had not had large numbers of English language learners since the United States capped the flow of immigrants from Eastern Europe at the beginning of the 20th century (De Jesús & Pérez, 2009). This changed with the "great migration" of Puerto Ricans to the U.S. mainland in the 1950s and 1960s. Today, the crisis continues as "Puerto Rican youth...have the highest high school dropout rate in New York City, and share the highest unemployment rates with African American young men" (Mora, 2011). A plethora of school reform efforts, including high school redesign and the establishment of small learning communities, have been adopted throughout the city. In what follows we examine the results of school reform efforts in two Loisaida schools, but first we provide an overview of the theoretical framework and methods used to inform this work.

Methods: LatCrit theory and the centrality of counternarratives

The experiences of Puerto Ricans on the mainland have been highly racialized (Rolón-Dow, 2005). Consequently, it is crucial that analyses of DiaspoRican educational experiences and outcomes be grounded in theoretical frameworks that account for the pervasiveness of race while allowing for consideration of other interrelated systems of oppression, including classism, linguicism, and sexism, among others. Because colonialism is a racialized process, LatCrit is especially relevant. To that end, our analysis draws on both Critical Race Theory and Latino/a Critical Race Theory, otherwise known as LatCrit.

Latino/a Critical Race Theory (LatCrit) builds on and extends Critical Race Theory (also known as CRT) to address issues that were often previously excluded in CRT. LatCrit extends the scope of CRT to address how variables other than race (including gender, class, immigration status, language, accent, ethnicity, and culture) intersect to shape the experiences of racialized peoples (Delgado & Stefancic, 2001; Yosso, 2006). LatCrit challenges the standard Black/White binary that tends to limit considerations of race and racism to the power relations between African Americans and European Americans, thereby creating more discursive space for Latinos/as, who can be of any "race," as well as for individuals who identify as multiracial or multiethnic. The focus on diaspora and racialized space also make LatCrit an essential analytical tool. Building upon and extending the focus of CRT to account for these experiences is crucial to understanding the complexity of the context enveloping DiaspoRican youth in schools today. Moving CRT to more accurately speak to the complexity of race and racism for Latinos, Daniel Solórzano and Dolores Delgado Bernal (2001) advanced five themes that underpin a LatCrit framework in education. These include: (a) the centrality of race and racism, and intersectionality with other forms of subordination; (b) the challenge to dominant ideologies; (c) the commitment to social justice; (d) the centrality of experiential knowledge; and (e) the interdisciplinary perspective (pp. 312–315). These five tenets shaped all aspects of our study from data collection through analysis, as will be shown.

Counterstorytelling and testimonios

Because both LatCrit and CRT are concerned with understanding power relations that lead to subordination, we use counterstories developed by culling data from privileged sites such as research databases and scholarly texts, as well as from sites that are often subordinated, such as the narratives of DiaspoRicans connected to Loisaida. Because of our positionality as DiaspoRican scholars connected to this community, and the knowledge base we have developed as a result of our formal study and lived experiences, these narratives are deeply personal. Storytelling is understood as central to the process of meaning-making, and reflective of culturally informed epistemologies. More than simply ways of knowing, epistemologies are more effectively viewed as "systems of knowing," since they are connected to worldviews, discourses, and ideologies that influence the material conditions of students' lives (Ladson-Billings, 2000). In this case, we employ counternarratives as a "tool for exposing, analyzing, and challenging the majoritarian stories of racial privilege" (Solórzano & Yosso, 2002). LatCrit and CRT point out that majoritarian stories, like purportedly race-neutral school reform efforts, are commonly accepted as unquestioned truth, when in fact, they are infused with subjective biases that serve to mask relations of domination. Critical race theorists ground their analysis in nonhegemonic and typically marginalized systems of knowledge and "integrate their experiential knowledge, drawn from a shared history as 'other,' with their ongoing struggle to transform" the conditions of their lives (Barnes, 1990, pp. 1864–1865). The perspectives of DiaspoRicans are necessary for an authentic understanding of educational opportunities and access in their communities. Therefore, we draw from CRT and LatCrit and use counternarratives in an attempt to insert these heretofore silenced voices into the discussion on education in the diaspora.

Counternarratives from Loisaida

In this section we present two counternarratives that draw on our experiences as DiaspoRicans connected to this community, interactions with community members, newspaper reports, and archival data to demonstrate how school reform efforts have served to further marginalize DiaspoRicans living on the Lower East Side. The first describes Loisaida Elementary School (a pseudonym) and the Latino community's struggle to gain access to quality bilingual education programs for Latino/a youth. Highlighting the impact on DiaspoRicans, it critically examines the role of whiteness in the school's response to shifting demographics in Loisaida.

The second counternarrative focuses on Loisaida High School (a pseudonym) and demonstrates how school restructuring can, and often does, result in limiting opportunities for DiaspoRican youth. In this case, the demographics of a newly redesigned school physically located in the heart of a Puerto Rican barrio (actually walking distance from a housing project that is home to thousands of DiaspoRican youth) are analyzed to document the underrepresentation of Latino students in a "community school." We also unearth how policies and practices in this school, whose mission focuses on increasing access to higher education for city students, reinscribe the "overwhelming presence of whiteness" (Sleeter, 2001) and restrict access to quality schooling opportunities for DiaspoRican youth in their own neighborhood.

Loisaida elementary

Loisaida Elementary, like the neighborhood it serves, has a long history as a haven for (im)migrant students. One of the oldest schools in New York City, it was first charged with educating the neighborhood's primarily Jewish community. More recently, Latino students have constituted the majority population of the school, with Puerto Ricans being the largest group of Latinos in this demographic. Today, Latinos—the majority of whom are of Puerto Rican descent—account for approximately 65% of students at Loisaida Elementary.

While their proportionate representation has declined slightly after peaking at 66% in 2007–2008, Latinos have constituted more than 50% of all students at Loisaida Elementary since the 1960s. The mission of the school has always spoken to the diversity of its student body and framed cultural and linguistic diversity as a strength rather than a deficit to be overcome. In theory, Loisaida was a haven for (im)migrant students, a place where their cultural identities and diverse linguistic repertories could be affirmed. In practice, Latino families struggled to gain access to quality maintenance bilingual education programs.

Long heralded by researchers as a model approach for bilingual education, dual language programs—which are designed to foster not only the development of "standard" English literacies, but also the development and maintenance of students' native languages—remain the minority in the country. Far more popular and palpable for the mainstream, transitional bilingual education programs—established with the goal of "transitioning" students into the "mainstream" as quickly as possible—are the dominant model across the country, and until recently, in Loisaida Elementary School. The research regarding language acquisition is clear: It takes approximately 5 to 7 years to gain academic proficiency in another language (Crawford, 2004; Cummins, 1979, 1981; Krashen, 1996). Nevertheless, in 1988 federal legislation limited transitional programs to 3 years, the underlying rationale being that the primary function of schools is to support students' language development in English, the unofficial language of the country. Several states with sizeable populations of Latino students for whom English is not a native language, including California and Arizona, have limited their programs to 1 year, implementing a sheltered immersion model where the students can receive some native language instruction while they are in the process of learning English. The goal, once again, is to facilitate the acquisition of English as quickly as possible, even if knowledge development in other subjects such as history, science, and so on is compromised.

Latino families' struggles for an authentic, pedagogically sound bilingual education is a long one, dating back centuries to the colonization of northern Mexico, which now constitutes the southwestern United States. Local struggles for bilingual education in New York City were led by Antonia Pantoja and ASPIRA, and have continued into the present. DiaspoRican and other Latino families in Loisaida have implored Loisaida Elementary to develop a dual language program where their children would have the opportunity to become biliterate—able to communicate effectively in both Standard English and Spanish. For years, their cries have fallen on deaf ears. As one DiaspoRican resident put it, "They want to make us White, like them, but we are not

White, we are Puerto Rican. I want to be Puerto Rican. I want my children to be Puerto Rican. Our language is a big part of that."

With efforts to gentrify the neighborhood, which are well documented (Abu-Lughod, 1994; Mele, 2000; Sites, 2003; Smith & DiFillippis, 1999), the White population in Loisaida has grown considerably in recent years. White students comprised 1% of the school enrollment in 2010, and now represent almost 6% of all students. While 6% is far from a majority, the power and privilege they have exerted to positively influence the educational opportunities available for their children suggests that being a member of the numeric majority is insufficient in and of itself to get one's needs seriously considered. As the number of Whites at the school has grown, policy and practice in Loisaida Elementary has shifted to meet their needs, moving from a stance of assimilation of Latinos to the accommodation of White students. Evidence of this shift is perhaps best represented by the comments of a Latino educator at the school who, reporting on a faculty meeting where the shifting demographics of the school were discussed, said the following:

> Can you believe it? The principal just came out and said, "We have White families here now, so we can't just do what we want, what we have been doing. We have to listen to what they want. That is just what it is. Maybe it isn't right, but that is what it is. They have power, clout. You know? Any questions?" Can you believe it? Puerto Rican kids and Dominican kids, their families, have been speaking with nobody listening to them…for years. We get some White kids in here and all of a sudden we all need to bend over backwards? What about our kids? Our Puerto Rican and Dominican kids? Why didn't we have to bend for them?

This shift in attention, from ignoring or placing on the back burner the needs of DiaspoRican and other Latino youth to deploying schoolwide efforts to meet the needs of the minority White population, reflect the power dynamics that have governed Loisaida Elementary and informed a larger agenda in regards to DiaspoRicans on the U.S. mainland. The principal's admonition to faculty at the meeting clearly let faculty and staff know that they would be catering to the needs of White students in ways that were distinct from the school's interactions with DiaspoRican families.

Interestingly, dual language programs have been sought by many White families who value multilingualism and recognize the academic and social benefits that accrue to students who learn multiple languages in these programs. In addition, Asian families, who began sending their children to Loisaida Elementary as the borders of the city's Chinatown neighborhood were expanding, also wanted their children to learn English while maintaining and developing their native language skills. White families, seeking to positively influence the education of their children, approached the administration of Loisaida Elementary as well as district-level administrators to request the establishment of a dual language bilingual education program for their children. Based on their recommendation and lobbying by parents, the first dual language program was established at the school in 2010. However, while the most popular language spoken by students and families in the school was overwhelmingly Spanish, White families and a growing number of Asian families wanted their children to learn Mandarin Chinese. While the reasons underlying their decision to choose Mandarin over Spanish are certainly varied, it is important to note that there are 450% more Spanish speakers than Mandarin speakers in the United States and that Latino Spanish speakers represented a much larger portion of the school population (U.S. Census Bureau, 2011). In addition, the decades-long struggle Latino families engaged in for educational programs that develop students' Spanish-language proficiency suggests that the motives for choosing Mandarin over Spanish might be questionable and worthy of further study. While we cannot speak for those White or Asian families or their underlying motivations, our experiences as DiaspoRicans connected to Loisaida and personal familiarity with this struggle allow us to confidently assert that we view the differential response times and changes in policy as reflective of long-standing deficit views of Spanish and Latino youth and families. The "model minority" myth, which elevates Asians, because of their purported academic and financial success in the United States, as a model for other minoritized groups to follow, was most likely at play here. Instead of having their children learn with and from Latino students, White families would prefer to have their children work with Asian students, as their work ethic, school success rates, and "values" are positioned as more congruent in the popular media.

As of writing this chapter, DiaspoRican students and families have access to Mandarin Chinese but not Spanish as a mode of instruction and tool for learning. The elusive quest for equal and appropriate education for DiaspoRicans in Loisaida continues.

Loisaida High School

Schools on the Lower East Side are some of the most racially/ethnically segregated in the city (Frankenberg & Lee, 2002). Under the guise of school reform, many large comprehensive high schools have been transformed into smaller learning communities or "schools within schools," as multiple schools share the same physical space. Loisaida High School (LES High) is a recently redesigned school located in the heart of the neighborhood, surrounded by a large housing project that is home to many of the neighborhood's DiaspoRican residents. Central to the redesign was breaking down large comprehensive high schools into smaller schools within the same building. As educational experiences and outcomes for DiaspoRicans on the Lower East Side, and nationally, are often problematic, Loisaida High School serves as a beacon of hope, foregrounding a mission of academic success and access to higher education. With fewer than 13% of all Latinos in the United States having competed bachelor's degrees, the college-going mission of the school is well aligned with the needs of the community. However, a closer look at the demographics of the school suggests that the school population does not reflect the racial/ethnic demographics of the neighborhood of Loisaida or the city at large.

Latinos represent more than half of all students in many of the high schools on the Lower East Side. In Loisaida High School, Whites account for more than half the population, while Latinos account for approximately 18% of the student body. Conversely, Latinos comprise almost half of the population of Loisaida. The majority of White students who are attending Loisaida High are coming from other parts of the city, converging in a still very "brown" space.

The racial/ethnic composition of Loisaida High, an island of white in a sea of brown, is particularly interesting because of its physical location—within the context of the housing projects. Housing projects have been a source of low-income housing in the Lower East Side since their creation, and many Puerto Rican families who were desperate for housing that was better than the cramped tenement apartments to which they had been relegated flocked to fill the projects abandoned by White ethnics by the mid-1960s (Mele, 2000). Housing projects have not been gentrified the way that the tenements have been. Instead, they remain a stronghold for Puerto Rican families in an ever-changing neighborhood.

The founding principles of the school also seem incongruent with the reality of the demographics of the student body. Initially funded in part by one of the big funding families who pledged money to better public education in New York, Loisaida High was founded with the notion that all "students should be able to choose a postsecondary institution on the basis of what best suits their talents and interests, without being tracked by race and income" (Hoffman, 2003, p. 44). That is, this school distinguishes itself from others in the city in that it positions itself as a vehicle for students from the city to secure a quality education that makes college accessible. At the heart of the school's mission is providing access to quality educational experiences that adequately prepare all students, especially those who come from communities that, because of their race/ethnicity or socioeconomic status, have been traditionally underserved by schools. In schools across the country, many minoritized students are essentially disqualified from participation in institutions of higher education because of their lack of rigorous educational experiences. According to an official who worked on the nationwide initiative under which LES High was founded, these new schools "are aimed mainly at the underserved and the underrepresented...low-income students, minority students and first-generation college students" (Feemster, 2003).

The demographics of the school are not a chance occurrence. Rather, they are the by-product of policies and practices manifested in the admissions criteria for Loisaida High and other specialty high schools in the city. Unlike elementary and middle school, high school admission in New York City is based on an application process. The admission process to Loisaida High has been recently compared to New York City's other elite public schools which use entrance exams that often eliminate the vast majority of applicants. Sources indicate that only those students scoring in the 99th percentile will have their choice of elite schools (Herszenhorn, 2005). Racial and class disparities in performance on these tests, as well as other standardized measures of achievement, have been well documented (Altshuler & Schmautz, 2006; Lee, 2007; Steele, 1997).

There are a host of hurdles that a potential applicant must clear before being able to take an admission test for the few places available at Loisaida High. First, "successful applicants," according to the school, must have a minimum grade point average of 85. The relatively high grade point average eliminates a large number of neighborhood Puerto Ricans, who statistically and historically have not been provided access to the types of educational experiences in their elementary and middle school careers that would make them "successful applicants."

Applicants are also required to have met or exceeded the New York State standard on the English Language Arts (ELA) and math exams, which also limits the presence of Puerto Rican students in Loisaida High School. New York State averages indicate that of students in grades 3 through 8, 55% and 64.8% met or exceeded the standard in ELA and math, respectively. In Manhattan, only 40.7% of students tested in 8th grade scored a 3 and 1.2% scored a 4 (on a scale of 1–4) in English Language Arts, meaning that only approximately 4 in every 10 students in Manhattan were eligible to make application to the school. The results were similar in math, where only 38.4% of 8th graders in Manhattan scored a 3 and 19.9% scored a 4 on the test (NYS Education Department, 2012). Eligible applicants to LES High are a small fraction of New York City middle school students as a whole. Those in the best position to gain access to this school are those who have had the resources to ensure that they meet or exceed the scoring requirements on the state exam. Once students have demonstrated that they have met the initial requirements for admission to LES High, they can then take the school-based assessment exam and be interviewed.

Accounts from school insiders and mainstream education critics shed light on the exclusivity of LES High. On the one hand, the mission and vision statements of LES High claim that the schools seeks to recruit diverse students and help them all achieve at high academic levels. On the other hand, in the same publication, a school insider says that "finding good students has not been simple." He continues, saying that finding qualified students is not an easy process, and that in the past, students who did not succeed after admission were asked to transfer to other schools. These statements can be taken in a variety of ways. The definition of a "good student" depends on the criteria, and to this, the insider says they want students who see learning as the primary focus of high school. Still, a popular online education information hub seems to revel in the exclusivity of LES High. Its initial review of the school is that its "demanding, fast-paced curriculum has attracted some of the city's best students"; later, it states that "the pace is too much for some." Consequently, the demographics of the school more closely resemble those of suburban high schools in predominantly White communities than the racial/ethnic texture of Loisaida.

Educational sovereignty and the colonial project

The island of Puerto Rico is the oldest colony on the face of the earth. Beginning with Spanish colonial rule in 1493, and later, colonization by the United States as a spoil of war in 1898, the Island and its residents have been part of a centuries-long and ongoing colonial project aimed at meeting the needs of their colonial masters. Although their second-class U.S. citizenship denies Puerto Ricans on the Island all the rights enjoyed by other citizens, Puerto Ricans can travel to the United States without restriction. (Im)migration from the Island has resulted in a population of DiaspoRicans on the mainland that now surpasses the Island's population. Just as schools on the Island have been used to assimilate Puerto Ricans and as an extension of a colonial project, educational opportunities in DiaspoRican communities on the mainland reflect a similar trend. Linguistic imperialism—the positioning of Spanish as subordinate to English and unworthy of meaningful inclusion in pedagogical practice—perhaps best describes the approach to educating DiaspoRicans in Loisaida Elementary School. Despite their long-standing presence in the community, DiaspoRicans were never able to realize their dream of a dual language (Spanish-English) bilingual education program; less effective transitional or sheltered immersion models were favored. The marginalization of Spanish harks back to the approach to education implemented by the U.S. government during the early colonization of the Island. To "Americanize" the Island's inhabitants, English was imposed as the language of instruction in schools, despite the fact that the overwhelming majority of teachers and students did not speak the language. According to a report created by the first North American commission to investigate the Island's civil affairs, the primary goal of Puerto Rican education was to "Americanize" Island residents:

> ...the public school system which now prevails in the United States should now be provided for Porto Rico[1] and the same education and same character of books now regarded most favorably in this country should be given to them.... Porto Rico is now and henceforth to be a part of the American possessions and its people are to be American. (Negrón de Montilla, 1975, p. 238)

These colonial objectives have not been limited to the Island, but have followed Puerto Ricans throughout the diaspora.

Diaspora processes such as linguicism and racism, while common to the experiences of many immigrant groups, have been particularly insidious for DiaspoRicans, who, unlike other immigrants, are U.S. citizens by birth. Citizenship, however, has not resulted in equal educational opportunities. To understand the colonial function of mainland education, an examination of education on the Island is required. Part of the function of the Island's public education system was to create an expendable, low-wage labor force. In fact, tax-free havens for American businesses allowed the exploitation of Puerto Rican land and its people for corporate gains. By the 1940s, the effect of these exploitive educational and economic policies on the Island led Luis Muñoz Marin, who later became Puerto Rico's first elected governor, to describe the Island as "Uncle Sam's second largest sweatshop" (Rogler & Cooney, 1984, p. 37). Similarly, the social reproductive function of schools on the mainland, and the denial of access to high-achieving schools in their neighborhoods, have portended a pessimistic future for many DiaspoRican residents of Loisaida. Approximately half of all DiaspoRicans fail to complete high school (Fry, 2010), severely compromising their chances to participate in an increasingly knowledge-based economy. Unemployment rates on the Island hover close to 20%—nearly one-fifth of the entire workforce—and the rate for DiaspoRicans on the mainland is among the highest of any minoritized group in the United States (United States Census Bureau, 2012).

Unquestionably, DiaspoRicans have asserted and continue to assert agency in their struggle for "educational sovereignty," the power for communities to design and inform their own educational experiences (Moll & Ruiz, 2005). Educational sovereignty, according to Moll and Ruiz (2005), speaks to "the need to challenge the arbitrary authority of the 'white' power structure and reestablish within Latino/a communities themselves the structures and norms by which to determine the essence of education for Latino/a (and other minority) students" (p. 296). Instead of an approach to education grounded in the lived experiences and sociocultural realities of communities, schools in Loisaida, and across the country, often resort to top-down, "one-size-fits-all" approaches to educating racially/ethnically and linguistically minoritized students. The denial of educational sovereignty for DiaspoRicans reflects a continuation of the colonial project, where Puerto Rican culture is maligned or ignored, and education becomes a vehicle for socializing DiaspoRican youth for a particular role, typically as surplus labor, in a capitalist economy.

The cases of these two neighborhood schools illustrate the potential challenges that minoritized groups face when their neighborhoods gentrify. With an influx of White, economically privileged residents into Loisaida, shifting demographics have presented significant implications for schools. The denial of educational sovereignty to DiaspoRicans in Loisaida illustrates the continued marginalization of Puerto Ricans. One can argue that the denial of educational sovereignty, along with a larger effort to gentrify the neighborhood and its schools, serves to disperse and displace DiaspoRicans from Loisaida. For some, the whitening of the neighborhood has turned this space into an "oasis," as described by a faculty member at Loisaida High. The racialized undertones in this metaphor are not lost on DiaspoRicans in this neighborhood. The image of an oasis is that of water and palm trees within the context of dry, arid, brown sand. By exalting whiteness through privileged access to quality schools or linguistically appropriate and culturally responsive education, these two schools have created an oasis for many White students and families who long for White spaces in a city and neighborhood that is still overwhelmingly Brown and Black. Gentrification, a recent manifestation of diaspora processes, is resulting in the dispersion and displacement of DiaspoRicans from Loisaida. Accompanying the recent influx of White residents into the neighborhood is the emergence of "oases," predominantly White spaces that are inaccessible to DiaspoRicans or, minimally, where non-White residents are made to feel unwelcome and unwanted. Each morning one can see White high school students walking to LES High. Within a sea of brown, reflected in both the shades of the people as well as the colors of the brownstones and housing projects that are common to the neighborhood, are waves of White students occupying spaces and leveraging opportunities that are inaccessible to DiaspoRican families who have inhabited the neighborhood for generations. If educational opportunities and outcomes for DiaspoRican youth are ever to be improved, it is imperative that the colonial objectives of education be replaced by culturally responsive policies and practices that emanate from members of this community asserting educational sovereignty. The futures of DiaspoRican youth depend on it.

Notes

1. As part of their efforts to Americanize the Island, the U.S. anglicized the spelling of Puerto Rico. For more information, see Fernández, 1994.
2. The parentheses in reference to (im)migration or (im)migrants are employed to signal the diverse immigration experiences among individuals and communities who journey to the United States, specifically underscoring potential differences in citizenship status. For example, Puerto Ricans born on the island of Puerto Rico, a colonial possession of the United States for over a century, are U.S. citizens by birth. Subsequently, their move from the island to the mainland can be viewed as "migration" rather than "immigration." However, Spanish is the dominant language on the island and when Puerto Ricans, who are free to travel throughout the United States without restriction, migrate to the United States, their experiences share many similarities with those of other immigrants from Latin America, especially in their encounters with xenophobia, racism, and linguicism. Nevertheless, there are certain benefits that are conferred upon Puerto Rican (im)migrants that are not extended to immigrants who are not U.S. citizens. Therefore, we use the parentheses in this first reference to call attention to the complexities of immigration across groups that is often overlooked. We also use it throughout the article when specifically referencing (im)migration from Puerto Rico.

References

Aaron G. (n.d.). Loisaida (Alphabet City). Retrieved from http://www.mapsites.net/gotham/sec8/tour2ajgibralter1

Abu-Lughod, J. L. (Ed.). (1994). *From urban village to East Village: The battle for New York's Lower East Side*. Oxford: Blackwell.

Altshuler, S. J., & Schmautz, T. (2006). No Hispanic student left behind: The consequences of "high-stakes" testing. *Children & Schools, 28*, 5–14.

Barnes, R. (1990). Race consciousness: The thematic concept of racial distinctiveness in critical race scholarship. *Harvard Law Review, 103*, 1864–1871.

Bourdieu, P., & Passeron, J. (1977). *Reproduction in education, society and culture*. London: Sage.

Brodkin, K. (2004). *How Jews became White folks & what that says about race in America*. New Brunswick, NJ: Rutgers University Press.

Brubaker, R. (2005). The "diaspora" diaspora. *Ethnic and Racial Studies, 28*(1), 1–19.

Castles, S., & Miller, M. J. (2003). *The age of migration* (3rd ed.). New York: Guilford Press.

Cayce, M. J. (1972). *The Puerto Rican study, 1953–1957: A report on the education and adjustment of Puerto Rican pupils in the public schools of the city of New York.* New York: Oriole Editions.

Center for Community Development and Civil Rights, Arizona State University. (2007). *Pathways to prevention: The Latino male dropout crisis.* Retrieved from http://cdcr.asu.edu/publications/pathways-to-prevention/

Center for Latin American, Caribbean and Latino Studies. (2011, April). *The Latino Population of New York City, 2009.* Latino Data Project—Report 43. Retrieved from http://web.gc.cuny.edu/lastudies/latinodataprojectreports/The%20Latino%20Population%20of%20New%20York%20City%202009.pdf

Chang, B., & Au, W. (2007–2008). You're Asian, how could you fail math?: Unmasking the myth of the model minority. *Rethinking Schools, 22*(2), 14–19.

Clifford, J. (1994). Diasporas. *Cultural Anthropology, 9*(3), 302–338.

Crawford, J. (2004). *Educating English learners: Language diversity in the classroom* (5th ed.). Los Angeles: Bilingual Education Services.

Cummins, J. (1979). Cognitive/academic language proficiency, linguistic interdependence, the optimum age question and some other matters. *Working Papers on Bilingualism, 19,* 121–129.

Cummins, J. (1981). Age on arrival and immigrant second language learning in Canada. A reassessment. *Applied Linguistics, 2,* 132–149.

De Jesús, A., & Pérez, M. (2009). From community control to consent decree: Puerto Ricans organizing for education and language rights in 1960s and '70s New York City. *Centro Journal, 21*(2). Retrieved from http://centropr.hunter.cuny.edu/sites/default/files/Journal/2007-2010/Vol_21_2_2009_fall/3_DeJesusPerez_pg6-31.pdf

Delgado, R., & Stefancic, J. (2001). *Critical race theory: An introduction.* New York: New York University Press.

Duncan, I. (2011, August 4). Local Hispanic population declines. *New York Times.* Retrieved from http://eastvillage.thelocal.nytimes.com/2011/04/08/local-hispanic-population-declines/

Feemster, R. (2003). Early colleges: Innovative institutions attempt to reshape the transition from high school to college. *National Crosstalk.* Retrieved from http://www.highereducation.org/crosstalk/ct0103/news0103-early_colleges.shtml

Fernández, R. (1994). *Prisoners of colonialism: The struggle for justice in Puerto Rico.* Monroe, ME: Common Courage Press.

Flores, B. (2005). The intellectual presence of the deficit view of Spanish-speaking children in the educational literature during the 20th century. In P. Pedraza & M. Rivera (Eds.), *Latino/a education: An agenda for community action research* (pp. 75–98). Mahwah, NJ: Lawrence Erlbaum.

Flores, J. (2009). *The diaspora strikes back: Caribeño tales of learning and turning.* New York: Routledge.

Frankenberg, E., & Lee, C. (2002). *Race in American public schools: Rapidly resegregating school districts*. The Civil Rights Project. Cambridge, MA: Harvard University.

Fry, R. (2010). Hispanics, high school dropouts, and the GED. Washington, DC: Pew Hispanic Center.

Glazer, N., & Moynihan, D. P. (1963). *Beyond the melting pot: The Negroes, Puerto Ricans, Jews, Italians, and Irish of New York City*. Cambridge, MA: MIT Press.

Gonzalez-Cruz, M. (1998). The U.S. invasion of Puerto Rico: Occupation and resistance to the colonial state, 1898 to the present. *Latin American Perspectives, 25*(5), 7–26.

Good, F. (2007). The origins of Loisaida. In C. Patterson (Ed.), *Resistance: A radical social and political history of the Lower East Side* (pp. 21–36). New York: Seven Stories Press.

Hays, E. (2009, February 5). N.Y.C. so costly that you need to earn six figures to make middle class. *New York Daily News*. Retrieved from http://www.nydailynews.com/news/money/n-y-costly-earn-figures-middle-class-article-1.389003

Herszenhorn, D. (2005, November 12). Admission test's scoring quirk throws balance into question. *New York Times*. Retrieved from http://www.nytimes.com/2005/11/12/nyregion/12exam.html?pagewanted=all&_r=0

Hoffman, N. (2003, July/August). College credit in high school: Increasing college attainment rates for underrepresented students. *Change*, 43–48. Retrieved from http://www.jff.org/sites/default/files/collegecreditNH.pdf

Information and Reporting Service, New York State Education Department. (2012). *English language arts (ELA) and mathematics assessment results*. Retrieved from http://www.p12.nysed.gov/irs/ela-math/

Kapralov, Y. (2007). Christodora: The flight of a sea animal. In C. Patterson (Ed.), *Resistance: A radical social and political history of the Lower East Side* (pp. 99–121). New York: Seven Stories Press.

Kochhar, R., Fry, R. & Taylor, P. (2011, July 26). *Wealth gap rises to record highs between Whites, Blacks and Hispanics*. Pew Research Social & Demographic Trends. Retrieved from http://www.pewresearch.org/pubs/2069/housing-bubble-subprime-mortgages-hispanics-blacks-household-wealth-disparity

Krashen, S. (1996). *Under attack: The case against bilingual education*. Culver City, CA: Language Education Associates.

Ladson-Billings, G. (2000). Fighting for our lives: Preparing teachers to teach African-American students. *Journal of Teacher Education, 51*, 206–214.

Larsen, R. J. (1973). *The Puerto Ricans in America*. Minneapolis, MN: Lerner Publications.

Lee, J. (2007). The testing gap: Scientific trials of test-driven school accountability systems for excellence and equity. Charlotte, NC: Information Age.

López, M. E. (2007). Investigating the investigators: An analysis of the Puerto Rican study. *Centro Journal, 19*(2), 60–85.

Lower East Side (LES) neighborhood in New York, New York (NY), 10002 detailed profile. (n.d.). Urban Mapping. Retrieved from http://www.city-data.com/neighborhood/Lower-East-Side-New-York-NY.html

Maantay, J. (1990). *The geography of race and income in New York City*. Retrieved from http://www.lehman.cuny.edu/deannss/geography/race_and_income_adjusted.htm

Mele, C. (1994). Neighborhood "burn out": Puerto Ricans at the end of the queue. In J. L. Abu-Lughod (Ed.), *From urban village to East Village: The battle for New York's Lower East Side* (pp. 124–140). Oxford, UK: Blackwell.

Mele, C. (2000). *Selling the Lower East Side: Culture, real estate, and resistance in New York City*. Globalization and Community vol 5. Minneapolis: University of Minnesota Press.

Moll, L. C., & Ruiz, R. (2005). The educational sovereignty of Latino students in the US. In P. Pedraza & M. Rivera (Eds.), Latino education: An agenda for community action research (pp. 295–320). Mahwah, NJ: Erlbaum.

Mora, E. (2011, March 11). Changes and challenges for Puerto Ricans in the U.S. *People's World*. Retrieved from http://www.peoplesworld.org/changes-and-challenges-for-puerto-ricans-in-the-u-s

Morales Carrión, A. (1983). *Puerto Rico: A political and cultural history*. New York: W. W. Norton & Company.

Negrón de Montilla, A. (1975). *Americanization in Puerto Rico and the public school system, 1900–1930*. Río Piedras, PR: Editorial Universitaria.

Nieto, S. (1995). A history of the education of Puerto Rican students in U.S. mainland schools: "Losers," "outsiders," or "leaders"? In J. A. Banks & C. M. Banks (Eds.), *Handbook of research on multicultural education* (pp. 388–411). New York: Macmillan.

Nieto, S. (Ed.). (2000). *Puerto Rican students in U.S. schools*. Mahwah, NJ: Lawrence Erlbaum.

Padilla, E. (1958). *Up from Puerto Rico*. New York: Columbia University Press.

Patterson, C. (Ed.). (2007). *Resistance: A radical social and political history of the Lower East Side*. New York: Seven Stories Press.

Payne, R. K. (2001). *A framework for understanding poverty*. Highlands, TX: aha! Process.

Roberts, S. (2007, August 28). Census: New York region has widest income gap. *New York Times*. Retrieved from http://www.cityroom.blogs.nytimes.com/2007/08/28/census-new-york-region-has-widest-income-gap/

Roberts, S. (2011, July 28). Slower racial change found in census of city. *New York Times*. Retrieved from http://www.nytimes.com/2011/07/29/nyregion/census-finds-slight-stabilizing-in-new-york-city-racial-makeup.html?_r=0

Rogler, L. H., & Cooney, R. S. (1984). *Puerto Rican families in New York City: Intergenerational processes*. Maplewood, NJ: Waterfront Press.

Rolón-Dow, R. (2005). Critical care: A color(full) analysis of care narratives in the schooling experiences of Puerto Rican girls. *American Educational Research Journal, 42*(1), 77–111.

Ševčenko, L. (2001). Making Loisaida: Placing Puertorriqueñidad in lower Manhattan. In A. Lao-Montes & A. Davila (Eds.), *Mambo montage: The Latinization of New York* (pp. 293–318). New York: Columbia University Press

Sites, W. (2003). *Remaking New York: Primitive globalization and the politics of urban community.* Globalization and Community vol. 12. Minneapolis: University of Minnesota Press.

Sleeter, C. E. (2001). Preparing teachers for culturally diverse schools: Research and the overwhelming presence of whiteness. *Journal of Teacher Education, 52*(2), 94–106.

Smith, N., & DiFillippis, J. (1999). The reassertion of economics: 1990s gentrification in the Lower East Side. *International Journal of Urban and Regional Research, 23,* 638–653.

Solórzano, D. G., & Delgado Bernal, D. (2001). Examining transformational resistance through a critical race and LatCrit theory framework: Chicana and Chicano students in an urban context. *Urban Education, 3,* 308–342.

Solórzano, D. G., & Yosso, T. (2002). Critical race methodology: Counterstorytelling as an analytical framework for education research. *Qualitative Inquiry, 8,* 23–44.

Steele, C. M. (1997). A threat in the air: How stereotypes shape intellectual identity and performance. *American Psychologist, 52,* 613–629.

Treschan, L. (2010). *Latino youth in New York City: School, work, and income trends for New York's largest group of young people.* Community Service Society. Retrieved from http://www.cssny.org/publications/entry/latino-youth-in-new-york-cityoct2010

Trías Monge, J. (1997). *Puerto Rico: The trials of the oldest colony in the world.* New Haven, CT: Yale University Press.

U.S. Census Bureau. (2012). Puerto Rico and the Island Areas. Washington, DC: Author.

U.S. Census Bureau. (2011). Native North American Languages Spoken at Home in the United States and Puerto Rico: 2006–2010. Washington, DC: Author.

Yosso, T. J. (2006). *Critical Race Counterstories along the Chicana/Chicano Educational Pipeline.* New York: Routledge.

A DiaspoRican critical pedagogy: Redefining education for Puerto Rican youth

ENID M. ROSARIO-RAMOS

Many scholars argue that the negative educational experiences of Puerto Rican children in the United States are related to the history of migration of the Puerto Rican people, the colonial status of Puerto Rico, and their experiences as a minoritized[1] community in the United States (De Jesús & Rolón-Dow, 2007; Irizarry & Antrop-González, 2007; Nieto, 1998, 2000; Rolón-Dow, 2005). A lack of understanding of the social conditions that promoted the Puerto Rican migration to the United States, of the political relationship between the United States and Puerto Rico, and of the cultural values, beliefs, and practices of the Puerto Rican people, have resulted in educational programs that have failed to address the needs of Puerto Rican students living in the United States.

Educating children from Puerto Rican communities requires teachers who understand the experiences of their students, who maintain high expectations for all students and support their learning, and who are willing to work with students in the process of social change (Irizarry & Antrop-González, 2007). This commitment also involves an understanding of their experiences as members of a transnational diaspora that has historically negotiated identities, political actions, and cultural productions across geographic and cultural borders. Yet, schools in the United States have traditionally underserved Puerto Rican students, in part by ignoring these diaspora experiences.

The *DiaspoRican* experience (Antrop-González & De Jesús, 2006), which locates Puerto Ricans in a complex social space where multiple discursive, cultural, political, and economic systems intersect, is characterized by experiences of exclusion and oppression caused by socioeconomic and political structures that relegate Puerto Rican people to second-class citizenship status. The DiaspoRican experience has also been defined by a sense of agency and a tradition of resistance that is visible in the development and negotiation of hybrid identities and cultural practices, in the creation of educational programs that affirm Puerto Rican youths' experiences (Antrop-González, 2003; Ramos-Zayas, 1998), and in Puerto Rican communities' commitment to contributing to positive social change (Marquéz & Jennings, 2000; Padilla, 1987; Whalen, 2005).

In this chapter I highlight the work of Puerto Rico High,[2] an alternative Puerto Rican high school in the U.S. Midwest, to discuss how attending to diaspora experiences is central to the creation of culturally sustaining (Paris, 2012) and effective educational programs for Puerto Rican students. Drawing from interviews with teachers and field notes of classroom instruction and school events, I discuss how teachers' practices at the school reflected a uniquely DiaspoRican critical pedagogy. Central to this approach to teaching was an effort to understand and attend to the colonial situation of Puerto Rico and the resulting oppression of the Puerto Rican diaspora, and a commitment to using education to encourage students to challenge and reconstruct disparate sociopolitical relationships.

Background literature

I draw from Puerto Rican education scholarship for its contribution to the education of Puerto Rican communities. This scholarship is grounded in an understanding of the Puerto Rican diaspora's histories and experiences with discrimination, oppression, and colonialism. Moreover, many Puerto Rican scholars and other scholars addressing educational issues within minoritized communities of color have used critical pedagogy as a framework for addressing educational and other social inequities. Thus, critical pedagogy is central to this work, as it provides a model of education that emphasizes the need for academic development to be tied to a project of social justice. In the case of Puerto Rican students, education should also be grounded on a commitment to inviting and critically examining students' experiences as members of a transnational diaspora.

Puerto Rican migration and transnationalism

The Puerto Rican experience challenges traditional views about migration that focus on how people move to a host society and assimilate into its culture by severing ties with their sending country. Instead, Puerto Rican migrants have often participated in transnational social fields (Schiller, 2005) where they constantly renegotiate and redefine their ties to both the host society and their home country. Social fields are constituted by "a set of multiple interlocking networks of social relationships through which ideas, practices, and resources are unequally exchanged, organized, and transformed" (Levitt & Schiller, 2004, p. 1009). As people move between sending and host societies, they often develop ways to participate in the economic, social, and political lives of multiple nations, thus making transnationalism a central part of their own lives.

Even though Puerto Rico is not a sovereign state, scholars argue that Puerto Rican migration may be understood from a transnational perspective as the Puerto Rican diaspora in the United States crosses sociocultural borders, if not political ones. As Duany (2002) explains, "differences in geography, climate, religion, race relations, and other customs are sufficiently large to create symbolic frontiers between the United States and Puerto Rico" (p. 356; see also Duany, 2003, 2007). This denaturalization of the nation-state allows researchers to take their attention away from processes and expectations related to immigrants' assimilation to host societies, and to explore the complexity of the lives and identities that immigrant communities negotiate across geopolitical spaces (Villenas, 2007).

In discussing the diaspora, I am not merely referencing a group of people settled in the United States, but also paying attention to the ways that they construct livelihoods that cross sociopolitical boundaries and are constantly shaped by economic, political, social, and personal events occurring in transnational social fields. Thus, it is important to understand how lives in Puerto Rico and the United States interact as transnational communities use their understandings of these (and other) geopolitical spaces to negotiate their identities, their participation in social and political contexts, and, in this case, the educational experiences of their children.

Colonialism and local oppression

Rinaldo (2002) argues that colonialism may serve as a framework for examining the lives of the Puerto Rican people (see also Dobles & Segarra, 1998). She argues that in the case of Puerto Rico, colonialism refers to the political relationship between the United States and Puerto Rico, which is based on the United States' control of the Puerto Rican government, as well as the position of the Puerto Rican diaspora as a colonized people within the United States. This position as a colonized people means that Puerto Ricans, even though they have been United States citizens since 1917, continue to live as second-class citizens, as evidenced by their limited access to quality education, to well-paid jobs, and to other socioeconomic resources.

Colonialism has served for some Puerto Rican scholars as a framework for understanding the oppressive educational experiences of Puerto Rican children, and for addressing their disparate access to quality education (Ramos-Zayas, 1998). The colonial relationship between Puerto Rico and the United States is characterized by efforts to Americanize and assimilate the Puerto Rican population, which is argued to be central to their integration as citizens of the United States (Negrón de Montilla, 1975; Solís-Jordán, 1994). Furthermore, the project of Americanization of the Puerto Rican people has continued, both in the Island and the mainland, through a curriculum that silences Puerto Rican culture and privileges American culture by foregrounding American White middle-class values.

Despite their economic, social, and political struggles, the history of the Puerto Rican diaspora has been characterized by a commitment to activism and social change (Padilla, 1987; Whalen, 2005). Community organizing has been one avenue for Puerto Rican communities to gain political power despite low participation in electoral politics (Marquez & Jennings, 2000). Ramos-Zayas (2003) explains that for some Puerto Rican communities, the ideological beliefs underlying community activism are tied to nationalist ideologies. In the context of community activism, nationalist ideologies provide a framework with which to understand local inequities and a language to argue for a reconstruction of locally configured sociopolitical and economic relationships through the development of a critical consciousness of the racialized and classed experiences of the Puerto Rican diaspora.

Critical pedagogy and counterstorytelling in the Puerto Rican diaspora

Critical pedagogy challenges traditional views on education that portray teaching as a technical profession responsible for the neutral transmission of knowledge and skills. In contrast, critical pedagogy views teaching and learning as always political (McLaren, 2003). Critical pedagogy involves the political act of "merging the study of formal technique with social critique" (Shor, 2009, p. 300). The job of critical educators is to support their students in the process of challenging and transforming the social worlds they inhabit, particularly the elements of those worlds that create and reproduce inequality and oppression (Freire, 1970). In that sense, academic engagement goes beyond the intellectual examination of disciplinary knowledge to include the use of knowledge to responsibly act upon our worlds. A critical education, according to Duncan-Andrade and Morrell (2008), involves the design of learning activities that (a) are relevant to students' lives, (b) affirm and invite student knowledge, (c) challenge the culture of low expectations and promote excellence, (d) have the potential to impact the lives of students and their communities, and (e) encourage and support students' reflection on their learning.

When tied to a critical view of the diaspora experiences of the Puerto Rican communities living in the United States, critical pedagogy provides a framework for addressing the educational inequities that many Puerto Rican youths experience. A responsive education for Puerto Ricans, who historically have struggled with oppression, requires a pedagogy that understands students' histories within larger political, social, and economic systems that are characterized by disparate relationships between the United States and Puerto Rico (De Jesús & Rolón-Dow, 2007). Additionally, it needs educators who are committed to creating educational spaces for students to challenge deficit perspectives about their communities and engage in transformative action that addresses their experiences of exclusion and their status as second-class citizens whose language, culture, and history are often misrepresented or made invisible by mainstream discourses.

In this chapter, I show how Puerto Rico High was committed to caring (Antrop-González, 2006; Rolón-Dow, 2005) for Puerto Rican students by providing an educational environment that encouraged them to challenge their social worlds and empower them to engage in social change. I argue that the school's educational practices were shaped by its staff's understanding of the ways that the lives of students were located in transnational spaces shaped by colonialism and the unequal distribution of power and resources. Furthermore, I argue that schools have traditionally underserved Puerto Rican students precisely because they fail to address students' experiences as members of a diaspora. Thus, I suggest that a critical pedagogy for Puerto Rican students should be grounded on a complex understanding of how their lives are shaped by the political history of Puerto Rico and the ways in which that history frames the experiences of its diaspora.

Research context

This research project was conducted at Puerto Rico High, a Puerto Rican alternative high school located in the U.S. Midwest, in a community that reflected patterns of transnationalism. This community was influenced by the movement of people and resources between the United States and Puerto Rico, but more importantly, the community's understanding of its residents' experiences was heavily influenced by discourses about the history and political status of Puerto Rico. The transnational nature of community practices was evident in linguistic and other cultural practices such as the community's use of Spanglish and the hosting of cultural events that seamlessly incorporated music genres such as rap and hip-hop with others such as bomba and reggaeton.[3] It could also be found in the political commitments of local organizations, which included campaigns in support of the liberation of political prisoners who, while living in the United States, have fought for Puerto Rican independence; efforts to denounce police brutality and political practices by the governments of Puerto Rico and the United States alike; and a campaign in support of a student strike at the University of Puerto Rico. Finally, local organizations contributed to the promotion and preservation of Puerto Rican culture through projects that included local Puerto Rican parades and festivals, the creation of a museum of Puerto Rican arts and culture, and the development of educational programs that used Puerto Rican history and culture as a basis for the design of curricula and other learning activities. Thus, looking at schooling practices at a school that is responsive to this community may provide new ways to conceptualize and understand the educational experiences of the Puerto Rican diaspora.

Puerto Rico High was part of a network of alternative schools that served different communities across the city. At the time of the research, Puerto Rico High had approximately 165 students distributed across three main educational programs: a high school, a GED program, and a program for young parents that provided not only education for students, but also day care for their children. Ninety-nine percent of the student population identified as belonging to a community of color. Sixty-four percent of the students of color identified as Latina/o, while 35% were African American. According to data from the network of alternative schools, 83% of the student population came from low-income families.

Puerto Rico High was located in a neighborhood that historically struggled with social issues related to poverty, health, housing, and discrimination, among others. A simple online search showed the community's struggle with these issues. Recent news headlines referencing the local neighborhood included multiple shootings, hit-and-runs, and an arson attempt. Also, the neighborhood was known for the presence of gangs and for incidents of gang violence. However, despite the many challenges faced by neighborhood residents, and perhaps as a result of that struggle, community members and organizations resisted these social problems. In this neighborhood, community-based organizations worked tirelessly to provide important services and resources to community residents.

The school was an affiliate of the Center, an umbrella organization that organized the efforts of other social services organizations in the neighborhood. Puerto Rico High was founded as a response to the lack of quality educational programs in the neighborhood and it was successful in improving the academic achievement of the neighborhood's youth, as evidenced by the school's high graduation rate (80%, compared to the city's graduation rate of 55%). Puerto Rico High's history stood as evidence of the ways that, in the face of struggle, the Center and the broader community actively engaged in transformative action to improve the quality of life of neighborhood residents. With that history in mind, the high school was chosen as a research site because it was founded on a tradition of social justice.

Data collection and analysis

Data were collected during the academic year 2008–2009. Data used for analysis included field notes (Emerson, Fretz, & Shaw, 1995; Spradley, 1980) of classroom instruction and schoolwide activities and events, interviews with members of the school's instructional staff, school and classroom documents, and community texts (e.g., newsletters and magazines). I interviewed the school principal, the dean of student affairs, and three members of the instructional staff to gather information about their educational experiences, their views about Puerto Rico High's educational programs, their experiences with and beliefs about their students and colleagues, the guiding principles for the design of the school's curricula, and their perspectives on the relationship between Puerto Rico High and the larger community where it is located. Interviews were between 45 and 90 minutes long.

Raymond, the school principal, was a Puerto Rican man in his late twenties who had just assumed his position, after serving as an assistant principal and teacher at the school. Julia, the dean of student affairs, was a Puerto Rican woman in her late twenties; she was also assuming a new position at the school, after serving as a mentor and coordinator for the socio-emotional learning team. Samuel, the Puerto Rican studies teacher, became a full-time history and social studies teacher after being a volunteer at the Center and a youth leader at a local youth space, teaching history part-time at the school's program for young parents, and serving as a counselor at the high school. He was a Puerto Rican man, also in his mid- to late twenties. At the time of the research, he was completing an alternative teaching certification program. Danielle was a biracial woman (Puerto Rican and Caucasian) in her early thirties who was in her third year of teaching at Puerto Rico High. She taught social studies classes, including U.S. studies and African diaspora studies. Elsa, the English teacher, was a White female in her mid-twenties who, at the time of data collection, was in her first year of teaching. She was enrolled in an alternative certification program to get her K–12 literacy teaching certification.

Open and focused coding (Charmaz, 2000; Coffey & Atkinson, 1996; Strauss & Corbin, 1990) were used to analyze the data collected. The purpose of the analysis was to determine the level of alignment between the structures and functioning of the school and the goals of critical pedagogy. I also wanted to understand how the school's understanding of students' experiences as a diaspora community was evident in the ways teachers discussed students, the community, and pedagogy, and how this understanding shaped the design of instructional activities and community projects and events.

While conducting research in this community, I had the opportunity to participate in multiple events, projects, and initiatives led by the organizations studied, and to teach a class at the high school after completing my data collection. I also developed close relationships with teachers, staff, and community residents. I believe that my involvement with the community facilitated my access to multiple community spaces. My identity as a Puerto Rican woman who moved to the United States to attend graduate school also made it easier to develop such relationships, as I was seen as someone who shared some cultural traditions with community members, and someone who had access to important social resources. Being welcomed in those spaces also meant that I had a responsibility to contribute to the well-being of a community that opened its doors for me. That responsibility involved becoming an ally to the community and using my social resources—particularly those related to my position within academia—to contribute to the community's fight for social change. I believe that such engagement was important to disrupt and challenge privileged perspectives about research objectivity and about the relationship between the researcher and the researched. As a critical scholar, it was important for me to take on the responsibility, alongside community members, to insert my work into the activist tradition of the community.

Findings: A critical pedagogy for DiaspoRicans and the case of Puerto Rico High

In this section, I discuss how Puerto Rico High teachers addressed the needs of their students (a) through a recognition of the material and symbolic consequences of the political relationship between Puerto Rico and the United States in the lives of diaspora youths, and (b) by developing an educational program that merged an understanding of DiaspoRican experiences with the goals and practices of critical pedagogy. This framework resulted in an educational experience that sanctioned the cultural traditions and values of the Puerto Rican diaspora, challenged the oppressive circumstances that Puerto Rican diaspora communities face, and encouraged youths to critically examine their social circumstances and actively engage in social justice.

Puerto Rico's political dilemma and its influence on DiaspoRican youth

Many of the students at Puerto Rico High came to the school after dropping out or being pushed out of local public high schools. They often entered the school with a record of academic failure, disengagement, and behavioral issues. Many had endured difficult life events. However, rather than blaming them for their struggles with schooling, Puerto Rico High teachers understood that students' experiences were shaped by a flawed system. Elsa, the English teacher, explained how she saw the connection between the personal and systemic in her students' struggles:

> I think that a lot of teachers come in and are like, "What's wrong with these kids?" you know, and it's very personal. But for me, I was equipped at least with a little bit of knowledge and understanding that it's a big history behind why the students behave the way they do in class. (Elsa, Interview, 8/31/09)

The school principal had a similar perspective on students' lives. He explained:

> Those conditions, those situations that our students are going through, are a manifestation of not just the wrong individual experiences, but their experiences as a people…. And, you know, those conditions, again, they are social conditions, they are social problems. (Raymond, Interview, 4/7/09)

The history of the colonial status of Puerto Rico provided a framework for Puerto Rico High and other community organizations to understand the collective struggles faced by the youth in the neighborhood. Similar to Padilla (1987), the leadership of the the Center and Puerto Rico High believed that the colonial relationship between Puerto Rico and the United States has made the Puerto Rican diaspora an internal colony. That oppression is both material and symbolic, as it includes the material experiences of discrimination, violence, and poverty, as well as the symbolic violence of deficit-oriented narratives about Puerto Ricans. The reconstruction of such narratives was central to the Center and Puerto Rico High's engagement in social change. Their efforts focused on the reconstruction of Puerto Rican history, on the rewriting of local community struggles, and on developing an educational program that recognized such history and was responsive to the needs of students and their communities. For example, the Puerto Rican studies class taught by Samuel often discussed Puerto Rican nationalist figures, many of whom had historically been vilified both in the United States and in Puerto Rico. However, Puerto Rico High framed this history as one of resistance and struggle for political freedom and justice. Moreover, their vilification was seen as parallel to the belittling of the Puerto Rican people as a whole. In a conversation with the school principal, he discussed the legacy of one of these historical figures, and he explained how the reconstruction of this man's narrative was also a reconstruction of Puerto Rican identity. As he explained:

It's like one piece of a puzzle to reconstruct an identity. It's one piece of a puzzle to establish a historical memory...and they [students] realize all the attempts that have been made while this man was alive and while this man has been dead to completely tear apart who he was, and in that sense to tear apart who Puerto Ricans are.... We're flipping it on its head and saying, this person was significant enough in Puerto Rican history. (Raymond, Interview, 4/7/09)

Yet, this reconstruction was not merely a way of challenging limited narratives about Puerto Rican history, but also a way of using the new narratives to reconstruct the education of local youths. As DiaspoRicans, Puerto Rico High students participated in a society that did not recognize them as full citizens capable of important contributions. Raymond, the school principal, understood this very well, because as a young Puerto Rican male, he struggled with living in a system that has denied Puerto Ricans their place in the historical narrative of the United States. He explained:

I began to realize that I was not the only one in that situation and, in fact, it is an entire people who not only don't know where they come from, who they are, and where they're going, but it's a part of a system that denies people who they are, where they come from and, therefore, where they're going.... That is part of this Americanization. People say it's selling out, but what do people have to sell out if they don't know who they are, where they come from, and where they're going? It's keeping a person's soul empty in order for the body to do whatever it is that you want it to do. And that's part of the system of colonialism. (Raymond, Interview, 4/7/09)

Raymond understood his experiences as part of a systematic oppression that historically denied Puerto Rican people the right to embrace their cultural and historical heritage and to define their future trajectories. He understood this denial as the result of a system of colonialism that attempts to control minoritized communities because their oppression benefits those in power. Furthermore, Raymond discussed how these experiences of exclusion and invisibility were part of his life as a student in the United States, where his Puerto Ricanness was not recognized, valued, or affirmed:

I was able to have a couple of conversations with [my grandmother] and I learned a lot about where my family came from and all the hardships that my grandmother went through with my father, my aunt, my uncle, to do what she did, which was survive.... You know, and, I was like, "Man, that's, isn't that history?" you know, 'cause it wasn't just about her life and her experience, but Puerto Ricans in general, which I really didn't know what a Puerto Rican was! You know, other than a last name, other than an island, other than Spanish... and that was frustrating. I started to get more involved with conversations with my grandmother but also reading about history, reading about people's struggles in the U.S. and outside of the U.S.... I felt like I was moving in a positive direction, that I was becoming something that I wasn't before, that I was able to actually stand in my own two feet and that was something that felt really good, and I wanted other people to be able to have that, you know, for themselves. So, I guess that's a part of what inspired me to become an educator. (Raymond, Interview, 4/7/09)

Raymond not only located his experiences as a student within a colonial history of Puerto Rico that crosses geographic borders and shapes the lives of Puerto Ricans as they move between Puerto Rico and the United States, he also identified education as a space for liberation. More importantly, his understanding of his own experiences helped shape his views about his students and his expectations with regards to instruction in the school he leads. His educational approach required teachers and curricula that valued and affirmed Puerto Rican youths' experiences, identities, and cultural practices—which are often characterized by hybridity (Nieto, 2000)-that recognized students' experiences and knowledge as valuable resources for education, and understood students' communities as resourceful.

Puerto Rico High as a space for redefining the education of DiaspoRican youth

Puerto Rico High's educational programs located anticolonial discourses and practices at the center of a critical pedagogy mission that spoke directly to the experiences of DiaspoRican youths. Puerto Rico High's mission privileged the development of a critical consciousness that allowed the students to rethink themselves as members of a community that has historically been shaped by colonialism, to see their struggles as collective, and to understand their local experiences as part of historical processes, structures, and dynamics. The school's mission was "to provide a quality educational experience needed to empower students to engage in critical thinking and social transformation, from the classroom to the Puerto Rican community, based on the philosophical foundation of self-determination, a methodology of self-actualization and an ethics of self-reliance" (school's web site).[4] When I asked Raymond to comment on the concepts of self-determination, self-actualization, and self-reliance, he emphasized the importance of understanding such terms as statements of collective agency and not of individual action. He explained:

> [It's] not about individual self-determination...[it's] a people that have the right to determine their own future, and that's what we're referring to when we are talking about self-determination. For example, we have in this school this whole concept of social ecology.... The overarching concept of social ecology would be practiced through a process of urban agriculture in the context of community sustainability, ok? Puerto Ricans have the highest rates

of mortality when it comes to the issue of obesity, when it comes to the issue of diabetes, have some of the higher rates of asthma, these are serious health conditions that a people are experiencing in a community, that our students could have the capacity of building a model of sustainability that a community can benefit from and help to attack some of those issues of health.... So, when we talk about social transformation [it's] not one student being able to transform their family problems, [it's] about a student being able to recognize that their problems are not isolated, in fact, it's a whole people that have this problem—how do we go about solving these problems as a people? (Raymond, Interview, 4/7/09)

This collective view of community building and critical education aimed to encourage students to become critical and active agents of change. The mission was shaped by the history and discourse of the Puerto Rican independence movement. The anticolonial discourses from this political tradition gave Puerto Rico High and the Center a lens to look at the experiences of DiaspoRican youths. According to Raymond, Puerto Rico High provided a learning experience for students that was in stark contrast to their experiences in the local public schools where "they are mistreated ever since the moment that they walk into the door, when they walk through metal detectors, when they're frisked and they're wanded, when they go into the classroom and the teachers could care less as to whether or not they're learning anything." (Raymond, Interview, 4/7/09). Raymond went on to explain some of the reasons Puerto Rican high was created:

...to say that those practices are a reflection of racism that exists towards our young people and it's detrimental, and it's also a violation of our young people's human rights towards access to education, and a part of what our school has done since the 1970s is to say we're gonna create something different that meets the needs of our young people, that attempts to engage them in the process of learning even after their interest and curiosity in learning has been trampled on after 16, 17, 18 years of being in these public institutions that could care less about who they are, where they come from.... [The school] is a part of the practice that these other people have upheld, same people I named—Juan Antonio Corretjer, Albizu Campos, Lolita Lebrón, etc. So, without these people and without this practice, our school wouldn't exist. (Raymond, Interview, 4/7/09)

In that sense, anticolonial discourses provided a framework for designing an educational program that was also grounded in the central tenets of critical pedagogy. The structure of the school and its instructional practices reflected some of these ideas. The following vignette was constructed from field notes taken during my time at the school:

Students in the main building go up the stairs, where they can see multiple murals allusive to the nationalist movement of Puerto Rico. These students take classes at the Lares, Jayuya, Ponce, and Vieques classrooms. Here, the classrooms are named after Puerto Rican towns and cities, those that were important to the nationalist movement. If one happens to be in the main building on a Wednesday at 11:30am, after second period, one will witness a *batey*. *Batey* is a Taíno word that was used to name the village space dedicated to community gatherings. A *batey* at Puerto Rico High is a community meeting that takes place in the main lobby of the main building of the school where announcements are made and performances from students are seen. Following the announcements and performances, the community proceeds to sing the Puerto Rican anthem. Students and staff are asked to stand facing one of the many Puerto Rican flags displayed (in cloth or paint) in the lobby space, with their right hand on the left side of their chest or their left fist up in the air. The dean of student affairs stands on a chair and begins to sing. The song she is singing is not the official anthem of the Commonwealth of Puerto Rico. Instead, she sings "La Borinqueña Revolucionaria," written by Lola Rodríguez de Tió. This "revolutionary" anthem was written for and sung by the nationalist movement of Puerto Rico, and stands as a silenced song that is often interpreted as a threat to Puerto Rico's current commonwealth status and to the possibility of statehood. After students sing, they are dismissed to go back to class or lunch.

The vignette illustrates how the school organized itself to challenge traditional ideas about schooling, about minoritized youths, and about the history of Puerto Rico. The school challenged traditional schooling practices at the same time as it rehumanized the community through the reclaiming of its history as part of a Puerto Rican diaspora that historically had to negotiate its position as an internal colony. Students' educational experiences were located at the intersection between the political situation of Puerto Rico and the oppressive circumstances endured by the local community. This focus on anticolonialism, critical pedagogy, and transformative action allowed the school to become a liberatory educational institution. Ramos-Zayas (1998) argued that these nationalist identities may guide a successful plan for the education of Puerto Rican youths, especially those who live in communities that struggle with poverty, discrimination, and violence.

Samuel's Puerto Rican studies curriculum reflected the emphasis on disrupting colonialism. He explained his class as follows:

> The main theme or topic [of the class] is colonialism, and I picked that because I think it's a reality in terms of our history as a people and in terms of our present, current conditions. Whether you're in Puerto Rico or whether you're in the United States, colonialism is a recurring theme.... So, for me, it's defining it, but at the same time, talk about how Puerto Ricans have resisted it, and that we're not victims of colonialism, but we resist colonialism. (Samuel, Interview, 7/20/09)

Samuel used colonialism as a guiding concept for his class, as he saw colonialism manifested in the history of the Puerto Rican people, both locally and globally. He taught lessons about policies that negatively impacted Puerto Rican communities and continued to shape their lives. For example, Samuel taught a unit about policies of population control that the United States imposed on Puerto Rican women, which included using Puerto Rican women for clinical trials of the contraceptive pill, and a sterilization campaign that targeted Puerto Rican women. During the class, Samuel discussed the ethical implications of such policies as well as the discourses about Puerto Rican people that justified such policies. This included the portrayal of Puerto Ricans as a community that needed to be controlled and their positioning as second-class citizens whose rights were violated through the manipulation and misinformation of people with regards to these procedures.

Teaching also involved helping students understand the tradition of resistance of the Puerto Rican diaspora and their role in social change. As Samuel explained, Puerto Rico High was:

> part of the positive aspect of what the Puerto Rican community has been able to do since it migrated here, so we also celebrate that in the school, and we show [students] how their families have been part of that, and even how they, being in the school and the things that they do, how they're also part of it. (Samuel, Interview, 7/20/09)

To achieve this, Samuel developed a unit that asked students to investigate the histories of migration of their families. Students were required to interview family members about their migration to the United States, in order to better understand how their families' histories related to larger histories of migration, to document their struggles in the United States, and to explain their families' contributions to the history of resistance of the local community.

The teachers' views of students and their communities recognized the difficult living conditions that they often faced. Even though the struggle often became a difficult burden to bear, these teachers recognized the resourcefulness of the community and their students' ability to enact change. They did this by inviting, challenging, and redefining students' lives. Affirming students' lives involved recognizing the hybrid nature of their experiences, cultures, and identities. This was evident in the community's sanctioning of youths' use of language and their production of music and art. During community events, English, Spanish, and Spanglish were often used together by participants. Also, a mix of hip-hop, bachata, bomba, and reggaeton music—often heard in both English and Spanish—was common during festivals and other events. As Julia, the dean of student affairs, explained, hybridity was important because it represented a response to community members' experiences of exclusion in transnational spaces:

> But you speak Spanglish and that's a new, that's a new language we're making.... It's a new way to say, "You know what? You've never really said that we are American, and you never—and over there in Puerto Rico or wherever your home country is, you're never really that either, 'cause you're born and raised here."... So we have a right to assert that identity.... So, what are we? And we don't ask ourselves that, we define it, and I think language is a big part of that...that's who we are, and that doesn't mean that it's wrong, it means that it's creative and it's new and it's one of the ways that we use to engage one another, but also to define ourselves in a space that we're denied, both ways. (Julia, Interview, 3/3/08)

This experience of being denied, excluded, and silenced in multiple social contexts highlighted the need for educational spaces that sanctioned the hybrid linguistic and cultural practices of Puerto Rican students who inhabit political and symbolic borderlands (Anzaldúa, 1987). It also created the need for instructional practices that addressed the invisibility of the stories of students and their communities in disciplinary knowledge. For example, in her English Language Arts class, Elsa discussed the exclusion of the stories of people of color from traditional literary canons. She also created a writing unit where students wrote stories about meaningful events in their lives. Elsa wanted students to recognize and understand that their stories were not isolated from those of other people. Therefore, she provided a list of texts that were written by her students' schoolmates, and required students to identify texts that discussed issues similar to those addressed in their own narratives. Finally, she asked students to identify important social issues that their stories addressed. During class, she explained to students:

> Hey, this is my story. It has hurt me. It connects to bigger issues. I'm not the only one who experiences it. A lot of other people experience this kind of thing. We need to do something about it. That's your call to action. (Classroom video, 5/18/09)

In the class, Elsa used student writing for discussions about literary genres and devices, and also welcomed students' personal narratives as a way to connect literature to conversations about social issues. In her own words:

> First, it was their own stories...and bringing it into the classroom gives it that officialness, that this is something worthy of study, that this is something that we should not only be telling, but that is important that we tell. (Elsa, Interview, 8/31/09)

By bringing students' work and lives into the classroom, Elsa's goal was to help students see their experiences as personal, immediate, and real. She also wanted them to see their struggles reflected in the experiences of their own peers, so that they could understand that the problems they were facing were part of a collective history.

The educators of Puerto Rico High recognized their students' ability to enact change. They also believed that literacy was central to social change (Freire & Macedo, 1987). Local youths often used poetry as a form of activism. The school supported such engagements through the creation of a poetry club that performed at school and local competitions. Also, Puerto Rico High students, teachers, and alumni often performed their work during school events, marches, protests, and other community events, including the Wednesday *bateys* and a whole-school town hall meeting held every Friday. During my time in this community, I experienced many events where students, alumni, and teachers from Puerto Rico High, as well as other community poets, participated in poetry nights where youth and adult voices worked together to critique their social worlds and reclaim their identities, their strengths, and their place in society. Similar to Morrell's (2008) definition of writing as change, the poems alluded to the power of words in challenging social disparities and creating hope.

In her English class, Elsa discussed a spoken word piece that she had written and analyzed to illustrate her expectations for students' writing. Below are some excerpts from the poem Elsa read:

> Right, you give me that look
> that, "here we go again" look
> that wide-eyed, shaking the head look
> that "look at this mess" look
> Look, white man look
> you look to me as an ally
> searching my eyes for his silent pantomime
> his emotions are on his sleeve...
>
> I see myself within you
> but I would rather die than return that look
> I am not your ally, I am not a crook
> I do not feel that look
> I'm a spy for the other side and to return that gaze would be a lie
> Nice try
>
> (Classroom video, 5/13/09)

Elsa's poem discussed her ideas about whiteness and her struggle as a White woman fighting against racism. She described a personal experience she had with a White male teacher with negative attitudes toward a group of students of color. This man's actions toward students were read by Elsa as deriving from a deficit-oriented perspective on students' communities. She explains how this man saw in her a possible ally for the oppression of these young people. She refused to answer his call, and stood in solidarity with the communities she cared about, communities in which her own students participated. Elsa went on to explain that her piece addressed the issue of the invisibility of whiteness. She added that fighting racism required the participation of people from different racial backgrounds. She said:

> It's not just White people that need to deal with racism. People of color are sick of the inequality in the world. One great example can be found in Jordan's piece "Our struggle." (Classroom video, 5/13/09)

In her statement, she is referring to a poem by a Puerto Rico High student, which read:

> We are the people in thirst and the desert is the Gringos
> But we find water cause we are Taínos
> Strong, intelligent just like everybody else
> Just a different complexion and some without wealth
> I want to rewind this all because I don't think y'all catch my drift.
> I want the Gringos and Latinos to switch. Mind Body and Soul
> To get put down and hear everything we were told
> To feel the struggle and pain that tears us apart.

In this poem, Jordan spoke about the struggles of the Puerto Rican community—and other Latina/o communities—with poverty and discrimination. However, rather than portray these communities as victims, she emphasized the strength and resilience that these communities have shown in the face of oppression.

Similarly, Raymond's poetry also attested to the Puerto Rican diaspora's sense of hope and commitment to resisting colonialism and oppression. He wrote a poem in honor of a Puerto Rican political prisoner. In his poem, which he performed multiple times at the school and community events, he (re)constructed the history of the nationalist movement as one of heroism, and redefined the community as resourceful, resistant, and capable of changing their own social conditions. He wrote:

> It is us, *Nuestra Gente* (our people),
> That have been able to flip the script on our conditions.
> And symbolically hit home runs...
> Like the heroic figure of Roberto Clemente.[5]
> It is because of him and people simila'
> That within the struggle against conditions that limit-cha'
> That our, *Presencia Boricua* (*Boricua* presence), will never be deemed *Ausente* (absent).

The poem emphasized the role of the local community in social change. In the poem, change is described as emerging from an empowered Puerto Rican community that can use its own resources to enact change for themselves, and "[t]o meet our own needs and serve our own peeps...creating our own Institutions."

A DiaspoRican critical pedagogy allowed Puerto Rico High to create educational programs that addressed the needs of DiaspoRican students. These educational programs encouraged students to take a critical look at how social structures and dynamics shaped their experiences, and to actively engage in the reconstruction of discourses and systems of inequality. The success of Puerto Rico High's critical pedagogy framework was partly due to its focus on the particular experiences of the Puerto Rican diaspora. By taking a serious look at the role of colonialism in Puerto Rican history and its consequences for the Puerto Rican diaspora, Puerto Rico High created a model for educating Puerto Rican children that was culturally relevant (Ladson-Billings, 1995) and culturally sustaining (Paris, 2012).

Conclusion: Toward a DiaspoRican critical pedagogy

I have used Puerto Rico High as an example of how educational institutions may improve the education of Puerto Rican children by attending to their experiences as a diaspora. This focus on DiaspoRican experiences involves a commitment to recognizing and challenging the colonial history of the Puerto Rican people, and to designing educational programs that encourage students to redefine and reconstruct discursive practices and sociopolitical processes that perpetuate their oppression. Such critical engagement with the world has been advocated by critical pedagogy scholars for decades (Duncan-Andrade & Morrell, 2008; Freire, 1970; McLaren, 2003; Shor, 2009). Yet, I argue that a DiaspoRican critical pedagogy should account for Puerto Rican students' experiences as an internal colony of the United States and as members of a community that negotiates identities, relationships, and political commitments in transnational social spaces.

The teachers at Puerto Rico High explained the importance of recognizing the material and symbolic consequences of colonialism for Puerto Rican students. Their students had struggled with poverty, discrimination, violence, and educational inequality. The teachers viewed these experiences as partly the result of the ways that the unequal political relationship between Puerto Rico and the United States translated into a social system that relegates Puerto Rican people to second-class citizenship status.

Puerto Rico High remained committed to supporting the academic and social success of Puerto Rican students. They did this by affirming students' experiences, challenging their oppression, and supporting their development as critical and active citizens. This involved the development of an educational program that recognized that students lived in transnational social spaces shaped by movement across discursive and geographic spaces, by hybrid linguistic and cultural practices, by historical experiences of oppression, and by a tradition of resistance. Teachers used their classrooms and other community spaces as spaces for challenging disciplinary knowledge, for using literacy as a tool for resistance, for sustaining cultural practices, and for redefining the goals of education to emphasize the importance of critical consciousness and transformative action.

Puerto Rico High's reconceptualization of Puerto Rican history, of the experiences of the community it served, and of the youths that attended the school provided a framework for understanding how the Puerto Rican diaspora is constantly constructed and (re)constructed in social spaces where historical experiences, social identities, and political discourses cross geographical, political, and symbolic borders. It also invited educators to develop responsive and effective educational programs for Puerto Rican youths that (a) affirm their identities, values, and experiences, (b) examine the long-lasting effects of colonialism in the lives of the Puerto Rican diaspora, (c) provide spaces for young people to examine their positions in transnational social spaces and to disrupt the disparities that often result from the political, economic, and social relationships that emerge in such spaces, (d) recognize the Puerto Rican diaspora's tradition of resistance, which also occurs in transnational social fields, and (e) invite students to become active agents of change themselves.

Notes

1. I use the word *minoritized* to highlight the socially constructed nature of minority status, which responds to unequal power relationships and social dynamics, rather than mere demographic figures.
2. All names of places and people are pseudonyms.
3. Bomba is an Afro-Caribbean musical style traditional in Puerto Rico that involves interactions between drummers, dancers, and singers. Reggaeton is an urban musical style that originated from Latin and Caribbean music including Jamaican dance hall, Latin hip-hop, salsa, and electronic music, among others.
4. The URL of the school web site is not cited, to protect the identity of the school and its teachers and students.
5. Roberto Clemente was a Puerto Rican major league baseball player who died in an aviation accident as he was traveling to help earthquake victims in Nicaragua.

References

Antrop-González, R. (2003). "This school is my sanctuary": The Dr. Pedro Albizu Campos Alternative High School (JSRI Working Paper no. 57). East Lansing: Julian Samora Research Institute, Michigan State University.

Antrop-González, R. (2006). Toward the school as sanctuary concept in multicultural education: Implications for small high school reform. Curriculum Inquiry, 36(3), 273–301.

Antrop-González, R., & De Jesús, A. (2006). Toward a theory of critical care in urban small school reform: Examining structures and pedagogies of caring in two Latino community-based schools. International Journal of Qualitative Studies in Education, 19(4), 409–433.

Anzaldúa, G. E. (1987). Borderlands: La frontera: The new mestiza. San Francisco: Aunt Lute Books.

Charmaz, K. (2000) Grounded theory: Objectivist and constructivist methods. In N. K. Denzin & Y. S. Lincoln (Eds.), Handbook of qualitative research (pp. 509–535). London: Sage.

Coffey, A., & Atkinson, P. (1996). Making sense of qualitative data: Complementary research strategies. Thousand Oaks, CA: Sage.

De Jesús, A., & Rolón-Dow, R. (2007). The education of the Puerto Rican diaspora: Challenges, dilemmas, and possibilities: Introduction. CENTRO Journal, 9(2), 4–11.

Dobles, R., & Segarra, J. A. (1998). Introduction. Harvard Educational Review, 68(2), vii–xv.

Duany, J. (2002). Mobile livelihoods: The sociocultural practices of circular migrants between Puerto Rico and the United States. International Migration Review, 36(2), 355–388.

Duany, J. (2003). Nation, migration, identity: The case of Puerto Ricans. Latino Studies, 1, 424–444.

Duany, J. (2007). Nation and migration: Rethinking Puerto Rican identity in a transnational context. In F. Negrón-Muntaner (Ed.), None of the above: Puerto Ricans in the global era (pp. 51–63). New York: Palgrave Macmillan.

Duncan-Andrade, J. M. R., & Morrell, E. (2008). The art of critical pedagogy: Possibilities for moving from theory to practice in urban schools. New York: Peter Lang.

Emerson, R. M., Fretz, R. I., & Shaw, L. L. (1995). Writing ethnographic fieldnotes. Chicago: University of Chicago Press.

Freire, P. (1970). Pedagogy of the oppressed. New York: Continuum.

Freire, P., & Macedo, D. (1987). Literacy: Reading the word and the world. Westport, CT: Bergin & Garvey.

Johnson, L. R., & Rosario-Ramos, E. M. (2012). The role of educational institutions in the development of critical literacy and transformative action. Theory into Practice, 51(1), 49–56.

Irizarry, J. G., & Antrop-González, R. (2007). RicanStructing the discourse and promoting school success: Extending a theory of culturally responsive pedagogy for diasporicans. CENTRO Journal, 9(2), 37–59.

Ladson-Billings, G. (1995). Toward a theory of culturally relevant pedagogy. *American Educational Research Journal, 32*(3), 465–491.

Levitt, P., & Schiller, N. G. (2004). Conceptualizing simultaneity: A transnational social field perspective of society. *International Migration Review, 38*(3), 1002–1039.

Marquez, B., & Jennings, J. (2000). Representation by other means: Mexican American and Puerto Rican social movements. *Political Science and Politics, 33*(3), 541–545.

McLaren, P. (2003). Critical pedagogy: A look at the major concepts. In A. Darder, M. Baltodano, & R. Torres (Eds.), *The critical pedagogy reader* (pp. 69–96). New York: Routledge.

Morrell, E. (2008). *Critical literacy and urban youth: Pedagogies of access, dissent, and liberation.* New York: Routledge.

Negrón de Montilla, A. (1975). *Americanization in Puerto Rico and the public school system, 1900–1930.* Río Piedras: Editorial Universitaria.

Nieto, S. (1998). Fact and fiction: Stories of Puerto Ricans in U.S. schools. *Harvard Educational Review, 68*(2), 133–163.

Nieto, S. (Ed.). (2000). *Puerto Rican students in U.S. schools.* Mahwah, NJ: Lawrence Erlbaum.

Padilla, F. (1987). *Puerto Rican Chicago.* Notre Dame, IN: University of Notre Dame Press.

Paris, D. (2012). Culturally sustaining pedagogy: A needed change in stance, terminology, and practice. *Educational Researcher, 41*(3), 93–97.

Ramos-Zayas, A. Y. (1998). Nationalist ideologies, neighborhood-based activism, and educational spaces in Puerto Rican Chicago. *Harvard Educational Review, 68*(2), 164–192.

Ramos-Zayas, A. Y. (2003). *National performances: The politics of class, race, and space in Puerto Rican Chicago.* Chicago: University of Chicago Press.

Rinaldo, R. (2002). Space of resistance: The Puerto Rican Cultural Center and Humboldt Park. *Cultural Critique, 50,* 135–174.

Rolón-Dow, R. (2005). Critical care: A color(full) analysis of care narrative in the schooling experiences on Puerto Rican girls. *American Educational Research Journal, 42*(1), 77–111.

Schiller, N. G. (2005). Transnational social fields and imperialism: Bringing a theory of power to transnational studies. *Anthropological Theory, 5*(4), 439–461.

Shor, I. (2009). What is critical literacy? In A. Darder, M. Baltodano, & R. Torres (Eds.), *The critical pedagogy reader* (2nd ed.) (pp. 282–304). New York: Routledge.

Solís-Jordán, J. (1994). *Public school reform in Puerto Rico.* Westport, CT: Greenwood Press.

Spradley, J. P. (1980). *Participant observation.* Fort Worth, TX: Harcourt Brace Jovanovich College.

Strauss, A., & Corbin, J. (1990). *Basics of qualitative research: Grounded theory procedures and techniques.* Newbury Park, CA: Sage.

Villenas, S. A. (2007). Diaspora and the anthropology of Latino education: Challenges, affinities, and intersections. *Anthropology & Education Quarterly, 38*(4), 419–425.

Whalen, C. T. (2005). Colonialism, citizenship, and the making of the Puerto Rican diaspora: An introduction. In C. T. Whalen & V. Vázquez-Hernández (Eds.), *The Puerto Rican diaspora: Historical perspectives.* Philadelphia: Temple University Press.

From "La Borinqueña" to "The Star-Spangled Banner": An emic perspective on getting educated in the diaspora

EILEEN M. GONZALEZ

The first line of the famous national Puerto Rican anthem by Lola Rodriguez de Tio, *"La Borinqueña"*—*"La tierra de Borinquen, donde he nacido yo"* ("The land of *Borinquen*, where I was born")—sent chills down my spine as I heard it sung each morning in the school that I attended in Bayamón, Puerto Rico. My heart filled with pride as I let that line, the rest of the lyrics, and the melody fill my heart, run through my veins, and emanate through a smile, as I joined my childhood Puerto Rican classmates in singing the song. This affirmation of my identity through song was the perfect way to begin each day. It helped me feel cared for, and gave me a sense of belonging to a larger community. The transition between home and school was seamless for me, as I was encouraged to achieve academically, and I felt connected to a long line of Puerto Rican intellectuals who were part of my history. In short, I was proud to be Puerto Rican, and academic pursuits seemed as "Puerto Rican" as the *coqui*, the native tree frog that lives only on the Island.

My sense of self and views of schooling were challenged and shaken to the core shortly after my ninth birthday, when my mother informed me that we were moving to *Los Estados Unidos*. The shift from singing "La Borinqueña" to the "Star-Spangled Banner" was more than an exchange of one song or ritual for another. In my estimation, it also signaled the repositioning of my Puerto Rican identity from something to be embraced and supported in my Island school to a characteristic I needed to suppress or shed to become more fully "American." Drawing from my (im)migration narrative and subsequent schooling experiences, I utilize this chapter to describe this shift, framing my experiences within a diaspora framework. It is my hope that this chapter resonates with the experiences of other DiaspoRicans and serves as an informative narrative for those who educate our youth.

Una aventura: Identifying and negotiating new words and worlds

Arriving in the United States was somewhat bittersweet. Part of my heart was sad because I was leaving the world I knew, and the other part was excited to begin a new life in a new land. This new beginning would take place in Central Florida, home to a growing Puerto Rican community. I experienced the gamut of feelings that come with making a move to a new, unfamiliar place, ranging from excitement and joy to fear and trepidation. My mother went to work as a bilingual teacher, my older sister entered high school, my younger sister entered kindergarten, and my twin sister and I entered the 4th grade. *La aventura* (the adventure) began.

I tried to be brave, to put on a good face for my *mami*, as I traveled to school on that first day of 4th grade. I was a confident student in Puerto Rico, but suddenly felt insecure and unsure of myself in this new context. As I walked into school, I was struck by the cacophony of English voices, each louder and more assertive than the next. I was immediately stumped when the one thing that I knew how to do was no longer available to me as a tool; my language, my voice, my words...all silenced. In addition to being inaudible, as my Spanish tongue was paralyzed by fear, I also wished to be invisible in that moment. I closed my eyes and wished myself back into the comfortable confines of the Escuela Elemental Rafael Hernandez in Bayamon. To my dismay, when I opened them, nothing had changed. As my inquisitive mind moved to appraise my new surroundings, I became aware that none of the other students looked like me. My *trigueña* (literally, wheat-colored) complexion and dark hair, phenotypical traits commonly found across the Island, seemed to stand out in this sea of White and blonde.

As I walked into the classroom I felt fear overtaking my body. I didn't know what to do, what to ask, where to sit and anxiety built up when I realized I had to figure this out by myself. I looked around and decided to mimic what others were doing. I sat down at a desk that seemed larger than normal; maybe it just seemed that way, as the weight of these new experiences seemed to make my already small frame seem smaller. I was unable to move; yet, my emotions were running faster than the speed of light.

In the midst of these emotions, I heard incomprehensible words over the loudspeaker that seemed to be meaningful speech for everyone else. All of the other students stood up and faced the flag that was at the front of the room. I remember hearing the unfamiliar Pledge of Allegiance, and being unable to follow along with my new classmates. Longing for "La Borinqueña," I closed my eyes once again and tried to imagine myself back in my old school in order to feel a glimpse of comfort. The emotions were overwhelming, and I could no longer hold them in. I felt tears filling my eyes. For the first time in my life, I felt like a foreigner. Despite my status as a U.S. citizen, I felt like an alien left to fend for myself in this unfamiliar context, without any assurances from teachers or accommodations to ease my transition into this new world.

As the weeks passed, I felt even more alienated from schooling and my peers, and I was transformed from a social being with tons of friends who loved to engage in conversation to a withdrawn, painfully shy. and quiet student. There was nothing about my new school that embraced who I was, where I came from, and what I aspired to become. Presented with two distinct cultures and sets of cultural norms, I was forced to choose between being Puerto Rican or American. I felt like there were no opportunities for the expression of a hyphenated or bicultural identity.

A prisoner in my own skin

Many times, life outside of home became overwhelming. I felt like a prisoner in my own skin, because I no longer felt like I was part of the world of schooling, a world I had understood and embraced just a few months back in a different setting. How I missed my *isla*, my *Borinquen*. I remember coming home one day and telling my mother that I wanted to forget my Spanish and I wanted to be *Americana*. This idea seemed like an easy route to take in order to end the struggle of surviving in the new world without ever feeling welcomed. When my mother heard this she took a deep breath and told me that we would talk over dinner as a family. My mother's words to my sisters and me were assertive: "Yo vine a este pais para que ustedes tuvieran mas oportunidades. Ustedes no tienen que escoger. Todas en esta familia somos Puertorriqueñas viviendo en los Estados Uunidos y por estar aqui no somos menos Puertorriqueñas" ("I came to this country so that all of you could have more opportunities. You don't have to choose. All of us in this family are Puerto Ricans living in the United States, and being here does not make us any less Puerto Rican"). She told us to be proud of who we were. Our home became our *Borinquen*. My mother was *La Borinqueña*. Her affirming words each morning and afternoon became the heart and soul of discovering that we could overcome the struggles of living as a Puerto Rican in the United States, and that we could even make it an opportunity. She would often say,

"Siempre recuerden que el saber dos idiomas es mejor que solo uno" ("Always remember that it's better to know two languages instead of one"). She would follow this with, "Somos y seremos orgullosas Puertorriqueñas hoy, mañana y siempre" ("We are and will be proud Puerto Ricans, today, tomorrow, and always"). These words of affirmation relating to the importance of my identity gave me strength to begin each day, and provided a safe haven when I arrived back home. I needed this comfort, as my school experiences often left me feeling like an isolated outsider.

Because I was unable to speak English, I was placed in a bilingual program. This meant that I spent most of my school day in a classroom with other students who did not speak English. I spent brief moments in the morning in a homeroom with other English-speaking students, and shortly after, I went to a portable classroom where I was instructed in Spanish. Those 20 minutes spent in homeroom were usually pure torture for me. During this time the teacher took attendance and the students interacted with each other and got ready for the school day. Anxiety built every morning as I got ready for school, and intensified as I walked into school. I felt alone, afraid, sad, and often, humiliated. I heard students observing my every move, and often they giggled. I assumed that they were talking about me, and that made me want to cry. Perhaps they were simply observing my body language, as I truly felt a sense of nervousness every time I walked into the classroom and was exposed to that environment. It was as if I was invading their *casa* (house), and my *casa* was very far away. Oftentimes the teacher was unaware of what was happening in the classroom. It was a busy time for everyone; however, for me, the time seemed to pass in slow motion. During these first 20 minutes of the school day, I felt that I wanted to run to the world that I knew. I needed to feel some comfort, I needed to tell someone how I was feeling, but I was trapped with no way out.

Living and learning in the diaspora

Feelings of happiness and comfort came about the minute that the bell rang and I went to my portable classroom, removed physically, linguistically, and culturally from the larger school community that did not seem to care about my existence. The silence no longer had to exist as I walked in that classroom, because it was a bit like my old school in Puerto Rico. I felt welcomed and I felt free. I was able to speak and I was understood. There were several other Latino students in this classroom, and we spent most of the day together. We had intensive English as a Second Language classes daily in order to learn English as quickly as possible. The goal of this program was to transition all of us out into monolingual English classrooms as soon as possible, without necessarily taking into account the importance of maintaining linguistic and cultural identities. Although our main content courses were taught in Spanish, that lasted only a short while. Teaching content and academic skills in my primary language while I acquired English was helpful. However, it always felt like a race to reach the next level of English in order to be exited from the bilingual program. My bilingualism and biliteracy were not nurtured in that context, as assimilation and English dominance seemed to be the main goals. The goal of the school was to put assimilation ahead of education.

When the school day was over, life was different. I entered my home, and my sisters and I often talked about our experiences in school. When my mother heard us she chimed in, "Se que este cambio es dificil, Saldremos adelante" ("I know this change is difficult, we will come out ahead"). She also reminded us that we were going to be smarter: "En unos meses, ustedes podran hablar dos idiomas y en el futuro, tendran mas oportunidades que todos los que solo saben hablar Ingles" ("In a few months, you will all know how to speak two languages, and in the future you will have more opportunities than all of the students that only speak English"). Our *Borinquen* gave us a sense of peace; she reminded us that the struggles were not in vain.

Although I felt comfortable with my teachers and my Latino peers, I often felt that I spent much of my time observing my English-speaking peers. I wanted to know what their world was like. I wanted to experience school, classes, and friendships without feeling like an outsider and being stigmatized for being one of the Latino kids. Due to the separation of the portable classroom from the school building, I often felt isolated from the school experience of my English-speaking peers. I tried to figure out who they were and how I could fit in. I wanted to be part of their world, yet my lack of English proficiency inhibited me from doing so. For the first time in my life, I did not want to be Latina. I did not want to speak two languages. I did not want all of those opportunities that my mother talked about. I simply wanted to fit in.

I continued to work hard and practice speaking English with my sisters and my ESL teacher. I did not dare attempt to speak to my monolingual peers for fear of them laughing at me. After one school year in the bilingual program, I was given permission to attend math classes and science class with my monolingual peers. I had acquired enough of the English language to be able to attend these classes and hopefully succeed. I was thrilled when my teachers disclosed this information. I would be part of the groups and would start to fit in. As I began attending the new classes, I encountered the unexpected: I realized that I was still invisible. I was physically present, but to my teachers and classmates, it did not matter. I remember thinking to myself, "I worked so hard to get here and I am still not noticed." This was difficult, but I continued to draw strength from my family and my mother's admonitions to continue working hard in school.

By the time I was in middle school, I was fluent in the English language and thriving academically. Math was my strong subject, and I took advantage of that. I was placed in higher-level math classes, and I was often chosen as the math tutor for my peers. They had no choice but to befriend me. They needed me. During lunch and specials, I had many more friends than I did during the upper elementary years. I was able to communicate, and I was experiencing their world. However, I often wondered, if they didn't need my help in subject areas, would they still want to be my friends? Acceptance was of prime importance as an adolescent. Academics allowed me to experience the feeling of being accepted, yet I often wondered whether, despite the friendships we had, my peers would always see me as an outsider or an intruder.

For years I felt segregated in school settings, and as I entered high school the experience seemed to be no different. Navigating high school was somewhat challenging. I attended a very diverse high school in Connecticut, in another established Puerto Rican community. The patterns of segregation were evident here more than any other place. There were racial groups: the "Whites," the "Blacks" and the "Latinos." There were social groups: the "popular" group, the "nerds," the "hippies." Students were also segregated based on perceptions of their academic capabilities: the "high ability" group, often known as "college track," and the "lower ability" group, often known as the "non-college track."

The challenge for me was that I didn't fit into one single category, and I felt that my life was compartmentalized. I was a Latina attending higher-level academic classes, and I wanted to part of different school committees that often categorized me under the "popular" group. Latinos were underrepresented in the "high ability" group, so to be part of this group, I had to again accept some level of cultural/ethnic isolation. I was determined to be a leader and learn to manage my isolation while also successfully navigating these different contexts. At home, I had the strong support necessary to validate my cultural and linguistic identities of being a Puerto Rican. I was encouraged to embrace my cultural, linguistic, and ethnic identities and to show others the value and strength in these identities.

The journey was not easy. At times I felt trapped. The Latinos called me "White girl" and my feelings were hurt. Simultaneously, the "White folks" viewed me as a Latina outsider. Through leadership roles in school committees and the help of teachers and other advocates for multiculturalism, after 4 years I was able to make the best of these multiple worlds I navigated, and to successfully complete high school.

In college, I was sad to see the low numbers of Latinos who were able to enter higher education, and even sadder to see that the stratification of groups still existed, and was more noticeable than ever. I was fortunate enough to meet one Latino student who became my best friend. We navigated the college experience together. My greatest disappointment in college was when I experienced discrimination from my education professors. I navigated through the school of education, and although I learned about content areas and theories of education, I never had a course on teaching and learning in different cultural contexts and teaching and learning of diverse learners. I often thought, "How are they preparing teachers to help students like myself?" When I approached the department head about my concern, she told me, "We are making efforts to make those changes, but there are no courses offered for now." I had another professor tell me that due to my bilingualism and lack of experience in the elementary grades in the U.S. schools, I would have to take two steps for every one step that my monolingual peers took. As devastating as those words were, that was the beginning of my professional journey. I was determined to be an advocate for students whose identities are not well represented in the curricula that schools use, and whose teachers are not aware of the importance of embracing cultural differences.

Upon graduating from college I pursued a career in education. For several years I worked as an ESOL teacher, and later as a dual language teacher in Connecticut. Simultaneously, I began my work at the master's level in bilingual/bicultural education. Navigating doctoral study as the only Latina in an institution of higher education has been, at times, isolating. Although I have met wonderfully supportive colleagues and faculty, often I still yearn for the support that can be found only in higher education communities where there are more Latinos present.

I returned to graduate school feeling increasingly frustrated because of new initiatives designed to meet the requirements of the No Child Left Behind Act and the implications of the legislation for Latino students. Emanating from these personal experiences, I decided to pursue research related to the experiences of Latinos in K–12 schools. My personal struggles as a student inform the lenses with which I approach my projects. My goal is to embark on a career as a college professor, teaching courses and conducting research related to the education of Latino students, particularly those who are learning English as an additional language. I see my role as a professional as inextricably linked with establishing and supporting the development of pathways into higher education for Latinos and other underrepresented students.

Making meaning of diaspora

Rendered visible in my personal narrative of my experiences living and learning in the Puerto Rican diaspora are three themes or aspects of diaspora—
displacement, creating community, and developing critical consciousness—that
have shaped my experiences, educational opportunities, and career choices.
Often, personal narratives are seen solely as individual stories that illuminate
personal struggles and triumphs, and in some ways, this narrative follows
that trend. However, in my estimation, my story is not unique. The afore-
mentioned threads that are interwoven through it speak to the experiences
of others within the Puerto Rican diaspora, and aspects of it connect to the
experiences of other diasporic communities. Locating my experiences within
a larger framework, I hope that my story can inform the work of educators
working with DiaspoRican youth, a group who, as noted throughout this
book, has been underserved by schools.

My point of departure for making meaning of my experiences begins with
my family's displacement from the island of Puerto Rico. Migration or immigration is often viewed as a choice. Often invisible are the policies and practices
that inform decisions to leave one's homeland. Like many other families, my
family moved to the United States for economic opportunities. What began as
a temporary move—we thought we would move back to Puerto Rico within
a couple of years—has lasted more than three decades. Being away from my
homeland was difficult, and we had to develop a sense of belonging in a new
place, one that was not always welcoming of Puerto Ricans. This displacement
shaped not only my experiences but also the meaning I assign to them. The
displacement of Puerto Ricans is unique in that they come to the United
States as citizens but nevertheless are treated as outsiders. My citizenship status was insufficient for shielding me from the racism and xenophobia I experienced in school. It was not until I made connections with Puerto Ricans and
other Latinos here in the States that I began to feel comfortable.

The second aspect of diaspora that shaped my experiences is the connection to established Puerto Rican communities in the United States, first in
Florida and then in Connecticut. Fortunately for me, not only did I have my
mother and sisters to provide support for me as I navigated life and learning
in the diaspora, I was also immersed in communities filled with Puerto Ricans
dealing with the same issues we were. Schools ignored or maligned my culture, but the community embraced my Puerto Rican spirit. I simultaneously
felt isolated in school and included in my community. Without that communal support, I do not think I would have experienced the academic and
personal success that I have. These communities have long-standing histories

of struggle for equal education and access to opportunities. My narrative is embedded in this larger struggle for educational equity.

Finally, emerging simultaneously with my understanding of diaspora is my critical consciousness around the experiences of DiaspoRicans. As a student I experienced educational neglect, but I was able to succeed in spite of the obstacles as opposed to because of the institutional structures that should have been put in place to support students like me. When I became a teacher, I realized that my experiences were not isolated. The educational system as it currently exists does not promote the academic success of DiaspoRican students. I decided to pursue graduate study to increase the likelihood that I can get into a position to initiate systematic change. Understanding oppression and how to combat it is central. However, improving the educational experiences for Puerto Rican students in U.S. schools requires that critical consciousness be informed by a diaspora framework. Despite, or maybe because of my experiences, I still believe that schools should be havens for all students, and should honor the cultural and linguistic resources students bring with them to school. This narrative is the beginning of my journey to integrate these two bodies of knowledge. It is my hope that educators will be encouraged to follow my lead.

"The heartbeat": Education within and outside diaspora

Kristen Negron with Jason G. Irizarry

Being Puerto Rican is very important to me. When I was young I learned Spanish as well as English because both were spoken in my home. My parents identify closely with their ethnic heritage and have passed on that pride to my brother and me. One thing that really helped me was that my family was able to go to Puerto Rico almost every year while I was growing up. These trips to see our family helped us stay connected and renewed our sense of pride in our cultural identities as Puerto Ricans. Since we lived in Hartford, Connecticut, it was also easy to stay attached to this identity because the majority of the people in my community are also Puerto Rican. In fact, the city of Hartford has the second largest concentration of Puerto Ricans of any city, by percentage of the population, outside of Puerto Rico. I never had to defend my Puerto Rican heritage until I left Hartford to attend a magnet school in a nearby community. I knew that stereotypes about Puerto Ricans existed, but I never really had to confront them directly, given that most of my neighbors and friends were Puerto Rican. However, as I ventured out of my community to attend a magnet school with kids from different towns and cities, I came face to face with these negative perceptions. However, because of the pride of being Puerto Rican instilled in me by my parents, I would not let others' negative views of my culture diminish my perception of it. The city of Hartford, my home, is often referred to as "the Heartbeat." In many ways this is an appropriate metaphor, as the Puerto Rican community there has been a lifeline for me, instilling me with pride, hope, and a commitment to social justice and educational equity.

In this chapter, I describe my educational journey as a Puerto Rican in search of educational opportunities that will allow me to achieve my goal of working to promote higher education in my community. Central to this story is the role that living in Hartford among Puerto Ricans who experienced educational neglect and consistently fought for opportunity played in shaping how I think about the possibilities education holds for Puerto Ricans in the diaspora.

Education in the heartbeat

In contrast to the stereotype of Puerto Ricans as apathetic about education, my parents held high expectations for my brother and me, and provided as much support as they could for us to be academically successful. Neither of my parents attended college, but both completed high school, my mother in Hartford and my father on the Island. Despite their high aspirations and belief in our abilities, the Hartford curriculum, at least during my time in the system, was not what I would call challenging. It was also not diverse. We were not taught anything that would not appear on the yearly standardized tests we were forced to take. The school that I attended was all about what educational researcher Louie Rodriguez has dubbed "test prep pedagogy." My schooling in grades 1 through 4 mainly consisted of completing worksheets and writing prompts aimed at improving our test scores; they did little to quench my intellectual thirst. For example, for 3 years, in 3rd through 5th grades, we were assigned to write an essay each week on topics such as, If you were to become an animal for a day, what would it be, and why? This is not exactly what I would call challenging, but there were a number of skills that had to be demonstrated in the five-paragraph essay in order to do well on the state exam and also pass my classes. I became a master of these skills and learned to write essays quickly and efficiently, hitting all the right notes to get me the highest possible grades on my essays. For the longest time, this was the reason that I despised writing. It took all the fun out of it and made the process into a simple formula designed to only take up 45 minutes of your time. Most of my elementary education consisted of reading, writing, and math prompts that were disconnected from my experiences as a Puerto Rican child. It was not until 5th grade that I had something that resembled a science class. One of the major experiments for that year was taking our pulse while at rest and then doing 10 jumping jacks in quick succession and retaking our pulse. Not exactly "rocket science" or an experience that would get one excited about the possibilities of science.

While I found Hartford schools lacking academic rigor and devoid of approaches to teaching and learning that could be described as multicultural, there were social benefits to attending school in the Heartbeat. Most of my friends were Puerto Rican, and most of us were growing up bicultural and/or bilingual. We all shared a sense of camaraderie because most of us had similar life experiences stemming from being Puerto Rican in the diaspora. There was a sense of community and shared struggle that always made me feel comfortable in school, even when I knew that we were being shortchanged by the system. Even though I never saw my culture or cultural frames of reference included in the curriculum, and despite the discrimination we faced from culturally insensitive teachers, I took solace in the fact that I wasn't enduring this experience alone. My identity as a Puerto Rican and part of this community at least partly buffered me from the internalized oppression of an inferiority complex that can arise from educational marginalization and neglect.

In addition to not seeing myself reflected in the curriculum, I was also struck by the lack of Puerto Rican and other Latino teachers. Most of the adults working as teachers, administrators, and other professional staff were White, even though the community and the student population of the school were comprised largely of people of color. I never had a teacher of color for my core subjects. The only African American teacher that I remember having was my art teacher, who had us do paper maché projects for about 3 years because the school did not have an adequate budget for art supplies. We never saw ourselves reflected in the teaching staff, which sent a message to us that Latinos were not teachers. The only Latinos that I did see on the staff were teachers' assistants and the people who worked in the child care organization that I attended. The point that I am trying to make is that none of the people who really had any control over my academic life shared my ethnicity. Because of this, it seemed as though they really did not understand the population they were serving. Most teachers did not understand their students and never really seemed to make an effort to do so. Their focus was always on the information we needed to retain in order to pass a test, and never shifted to demonstrate any level of care for any of the issues we were dealing with—good or bad. My disdain for standardized tests stems from my experiences and regret for the many years of my schooling that focused on passing a test rather than learning things of substance.

Leaving the heartbeat in search of educational opportunities

When my brother Milton was in 5th grade his math teacher saw that he needed to be in a more challenging academic environment. She suggested to my parents that he be entered into a lottery to see if he could earn a spot in a new magnet school that had opened the previous year in response to a court order that attempted to relieve the "racial isolation" that students in Hartford experience as a result of "White flight" to the suburbs. My parents filled out the application, and one day they received a letter saying that he had been accepted. At the time the school had a rule that if a student had any younger siblings, they would automatically be enrolled once they started their 6th grade year. My parents were extremely happy about this because they wanted more for both of us, and they knew that this was the best option. The following year I started at the magnet school, the Metropolitan Learning Center for Global and International Studies (MLC).

I vividly remember my first day on the school bus, watching Hartford pass in my rear view as we journeyed to my new school, located in an industrial park among other businesses. I simultaneously felt uneasy about leaving my familiar, nurturing surroundings and exhilarated at the chance to experience a different type of education, one that challenged me, fostered a love of learning, and prepared me for life. My first day at MLC was the biggest culture shock I had ever experienced up to that point. I entered the brand new, state-of-the-art building and immediately felt like there was a different level of investment, even if only monetary, in my education. Walking into the building and seeing lockers with no graffiti, clustered classrooms that held only 20 students, compared to 30 in Hartford, and a smart board in every classroom—it was overwhelming. The school's student population was made up of students from five different districts: Enfield, East Windsor, Windsor, Windsor Locks, Hartford, and Bloomfield, where the school was actually located.

Once class actually began, so did my real education. This was the first time that I shared a classroom with White students, as many chose the magnet school over their local suburban schools. Though my incoming class was still "majority-minority," there still was a period of adjusting to having White students in my classes and learning alongside them. I had five core classes a day, each with a different teacher, and I felt that I was finally learning something worthwhile. Science was no longer a simple game, but involved real experiments with beakers and Bunsen burners. We had an actual lab with sinks and a chemical shower in the event that something went wrong. (It was never really necessary, but nice to know that it was there.) I had to learn how to not only do a lab well, but also write a lab report, something that I had never before experienced. Most of the concepts that were talked about that year were completely foreign to me, but I absorbed all I could with the excitement of a child on Christmas morning. Social studies went from an abstract concept that I had heard about on television to something tangible that I interacted with everyday. I learned about the history of Connecticut, something I had never even considered studying.

I went from a school with limited supplies to one where each student received a laptop to use during the year. This resource helped students complete their assignments while also becoming more technologically savvy, knowledge we would need in the real world. Prior to my brother and I attending the school, we never had a computer in my home. None of my friends in Hartford did. It was a year of adjustment, learning to type up a paper efficiently, rather than handing in a couple of sheets of lined paper I had ripped out of a notebook right before class. We learned how to deliver effective presentations using PowerPoint and other technological tools.

While I would not trade the experiences that I had at Metropolitan Learning Center for the world, it was not all a bed of roses. Since I was no longer surrounded by those who shared common life experiences, I had to make some adjustments. In Hartford, surrounded by other Puerto Ricans, I never really felt like I was a "minority." This was definitely not true in my new school. I was one of seven Latinos in my class of 120 students. Because I grew up in Hartford surrounded by Puerto Ricans, I had a slight accent, as did most of the Hartford Puerto Ricans in my class, regardless of whether we were born here or on the Island. I was a bit self-conscious of my accent and felt pressured to disguise it. I did not want people to make fun of me because of the way I spoke or how I pronounced some of my words, so I tended to over-enunciate. Eventually, I lost my "Hartford/Puerto Rican" accent, something that upsets me a bit to this day. I also had to learn and understand what it meant to be Puerto Rican in this new context. I wanted to combat the stereotypes that I was facing about being Puerto Rican and from Hartford, and I also wanted to create new, real images of my culture and my hometown. I do not know how successful I was in this endeavor, but I like to think that I changed a few minds, just like my mind was changed more than a few times throughout my years at the school.

Since MLC had a global and international studies focus, there were plenty of opportunities for local field trips, as well as for international travel. I was lucky enough to go to Washington, D.C., Spain, London, Paris, and Rome while I was in high school. I was lucky enough to have parents that could afford to send me on these trips. Additionally, emulating their work ethic, I also found a part-time job, or jobs, depending on the year, to help pay for my trips. I loved going on these trips because they expanded my world. I had the opportunity to see places I would probably have never even dreamed of had I stayed in the Hartford school system, and for that, I will forever be grateful for the time I spent at MLC.

While I appreciate the opportunities that I received as a result of my brother winning a lottery for admission, I am also keenly aware that the overwhelming majority of my friends in Hartford were systematically denied access to the type of education I received at MLC. Why couldn't a school like this exist in my community? Why weren't all kids in the state, regardless of their racial, ethnic, or economic backgrounds, afforded the opportunities to attend a good school? Perhaps most pressing for me was the question: Why did I have to leave my community to have a chance at academic and professional success?

My life in multiple diasporas

Because I had access to a college-prep curriculum, unlike many Puerto Ricans in my community, I had the privilege of applying to and getting accepted at several colleges. I enrolled at the University of Connecticut in fall 2008, and that experience was a complete and total shock for me. The student population is overwhelmingly White, and there are few Latinos, particularly Puerto Ricans from urban communities. I felt lost for the first few days of school, as I longed to hear the familiar sounds of my community. Although there had been few Puerto Ricans enrolled in my high school, each night I returned to my community and was able to interact daily with people who cared for me. Living away from home, at a predominantly White institution of higher education, represented for me another layer of diaspora. First, living as a Puerto Rican in the States represents one dimension of the diaspora experience. Being a member of a Puerto Rican community with a rich history was a blessing in many ways. Puerto Ricans had worked to create spaces across the city that reflected the contributions of Puerto Ricans to the cultural fabric of Hartford. Several schools bear the names of noteworthy Puerto Ricans; we have even had multiple Puerto Rican mayors. Despite some of the problems that plague the city, the Heartbeat was just that for me—a lifeline representing a connection to my Puerto Rican cultural roots.

Having to leave my community and travel to high school to have a chance at a quality education, or at least access to coursework and experiences that are largely unavailable to young people in Hartford, represents another dimension of diaspora for me. I challenge the notion that educational opportunities should be based on the luck of a lottery or having to leave your community, but I appreciate the education I received. I had to leave my community and feel the stress of knowing that I was one of the "lucky" ones—that I had opportunities that other Puerto Ricans in the diaspora could not access. In some ways, attending school outside of my community was a source of tension with my friends. I saw myself as grounded and proud of my Puerto Rican identity. Some of my friends saw me as "less Puerto Rican" because I left the community for secondary education. That displacement and temporary resettlement resembles the experiences of many Puerto Ricans dispersed from the Island.

Attending a predominantly White institution of higher education, being further physically disconnected from my community without sufficient support to navigate that space, represents another dimension of diaspora. I was bombarded daily with other students' negative perceptions of Hartford and the people who live there. Often naively, and without malice, students would make comments about my community that stereotyped my family and the people with whom I identified most closely. This discrimination is common to Puerto Ricans in the United States.

My passionate feelings regarding the Heartbeat and my desire to improve the conditions of my community have shaped my career choice and the experiences that I have sought out in college. The summer before my junior year, I applied and was accepted as a tutor/counselor for the Upward Bound program at UConn, and that experience solidified for me what I wanted to do with the rest of my life. After working with students, including Puerto Ricans, from urban communities, I decided I wanted to become a guidance counselor at a high school in Hartford, and work to create access to higher education for youth from my city.

During my senior year I was able to personally and professionally reconnect with my community as I participated in the Urban Semester, a study-abroad type of program that aims to immerse students in urban communities. I interned at a nonprofit organization within the community and developed a more complete sense of the services offered (and still needed) in my community. Again, I value my experiences at UConn, and leaving my community allowed me to become more well-rounded. However, my goal is to come full circle, and return to Hartford with the new skills that I have developed to give support to youth whom the state and government have been hesitant to support. These skills, coupled with an insider's view of the impact of diaspora, will position me to make a valuable contribution to the Heartbeat.

Contributors

Enrique Figueroa is an independent scholar who resides in Brooklyn, New York. A former Executive Director of a non-profit youth development organization, his research interests include Puerto Rican education and the shifting demographic of New York City.

Nilda Flores-González is Associate Professor in Sociology and Latin American and Latino Studies at the University of Illinois at Chicago. Her work focuses on race, identity, youth, and Latinos.

María E. Fránquiz is Dean of the College of Education at the University of Utah in Salt Lake City. Her research focuses on Latin@ biliterary development and bilingual teacher education.

Eileen M. González is Assistant Professor in the School of Education at the University of Saint Joseph. Her research explores initiatives aimed at improving the academic achievement of Latino/a English Language Learners.

Jason G. Irizarry is Director of the Center for Urban Education and Associate Professor in the College of Education at the University of Massachusetts-Amherst. His research focuses on urban teacher recruitment, preparation, and retention with an emphasis on increasing the number of teachers of color, culturally responsive pedagogy, youth participatory action research, and Latino students in U.S. schools.

Shabazz Napier is a senior at the University of Connecticut. A point guard on the men's basketball team, he was named the American Athletic Conference Player of the Year for 2013–2014.

Kristen Negron is a graduate student in the School Counseling Program at the University of Connecticut. She aspires to become a high school guidance counselor in Hartford, Connecticut, upon graduation.

Sandra Quiñones is Assistant Professor of Literacy Education in the School of Education at Duquesne University. Her qualitative scholarship focuses on Latina/o education, with an emphasis on bilingual-bicultural elementary teachers' experiences and perspectives of *ser bien educado* and being well educated.

Michael Rodríguez-Muñiz is an advanced doctoral candidate in the Department of Sociology at Brown University. His work focuses on Latino/a politics and the sociology of knowledge and race.

Rosalie Rolón-Dow is Associate Professor in the College of Education and Human Development at the University of Delaware. Her research focuses on the intersections of sociocultural identities and educational equity and opportunity and on the anthropology of Latino/a education.

Jonathan Rosa is Assistant Professor in the Department of Anthropology at the University of Massachusetts Amherst. His work focuses on language, race, and U.S. Latinas/os.

Enid M. Rosario-Ramos is Assistant Professor in the School of Education at the University of Michigan in Ann Arbor. Her work focuses on youth civic engagement and adolescent literacy.

Index

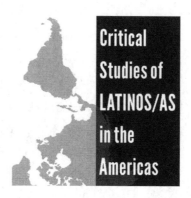

**Critical
Studies of
LATINOS/AS
in the
Americas**

Yolanda Medina and Ángeles Donoso Macaya
GENERAL EDITORS

Critical Studies of Latinos/as in the Americas is a provocative interdisciplinary series that offers a critical space for reflection and questioning what it
means to be Latino/a living in the Americas in twenty-first century social,
cultural, economic, and political arenas. The series looks forward to extending the dialogue to include the North and South Western hemispheric relations that are prevalent in the field of global studies.

Topics that explore and advance research and scholarship on contemporary topics and issues related with processes of racialization, economic exploitation, health, education, transnationalism, immigration, gendered and
sexual identities, and disabilities that are not commonly highlighted in the
current Latino/a Studies literature as well as the multitude of socio, cultural,
economic, and political progress among the Latinos/as in the Americas are
welcome.

To receive more information about CSLA, please contact:

Yolanda Medina (ymedina@bmcc.cuny.edu) &
Ángeles Donoso Macaya (mdonosomacaya@bmcc.cuny.edu)

To order other books in this series, please contact our Customer
Service Department at:

(800) 770-LANG (within the U.S.)
(212) 647-7706 (outside the U.S.)
(212) 647-7707 FAX

Or browse online by series at:

WWW.PETERLANG.COM